"I've known Bernard from high school, and since then, he's been a family friend. He's a steady guy and someone who I can rely on. I've got him on my speed dial."

—Fidael Yusof
Market Researcher

"Bernard is passionate about life. He does not care what others think of him. The fact that he is an ultra-marathon finisher (100km) is living proof that he is a man of strong determination and resilience. He possesses strong leadership, a stay-positive mindset, and he inspires others with the work he has done. He deserves to be respected simply by who he is, not just because he has succeeded in life. In Bernard, I see a spiritually wealthy man."

—Edison Sew
Senior Project Manager

LIMITLESS SUCCESS

with

BERNARD YEO

Also Featuring
Other Top Authors

© 2020 Success Publishing

Success Publishing, LLC
2810 Trinity Mills, #209-221
Carrollton, Texas USA 75006
questions@mattmorris.com

All rights reserved. No part of this book may be reproduced, stored in a retrieval system, or transmitted in any form or by any means - electronic or mechanical, photocopy, recording, or any other - except for brief quotations in printed reviews, without the prior permission of the publisher. Although the author(s) and publisher have made every effort to ensure the accuracy and completeness of information contained in this book, we assume no responsibility for errors, inaccuracies, omissions, or any inconsistency herein.

Table of Contents

Chapter 1
THE ONE SECRET TO LONG LASTING FITNESS
By Bernard Yeo 10

Chapter 2
THE POWER OF MANIFESTATION
By Matt Morris 14

Chapter 3
THE PERSON YOU COULD HAVE BEEN
By Steve Moreland 17

Chapter 4
WHAT MAKES SOME PEOPLE MORE SUCCESSFUL THAN OTHERS?
By Maxwell Adekoje 22

Chapter 5
DREAM IT. DO IT!
By AbdurRazaq Abdul-Aziz 27

Chapter 6
FEAR AND SELF-DOUBT TO FEELING GOOD IN MY OWN BODY
By Adda Hafborg 33

Chapter 7
MY SUCCESS IS ACHIEVED BY CREATING STRONG RELATIONSHIPS
By Andre' Serraile 37

Chapter 8
REDEFINING MY DEFINITION OF SUCCESS
By Arlene Binoya-Strugar, Psy.D. 43

Chapter 9
WHY A 30-YEAR FINANCE PROFESSIONAL CHOSE NETWORK MARKETING AS HIS VEHICLE TO FINANCIAL FREEDOM
By Bill Ryan 47

Chapter 10
THE DANCE LIFE
By Blake Elder 52

CHAPTER 11
POSITIVE ENERGY BEHIND CLOSED DOORS
By Calvin Bennett 59

CHAPTER 12
HOW BIG IS A SILVER PLATTER WITH TRAGEDIES?
By Carol Eberle Peterson 62

CHAPTER 13
5 STEPS TO BECOMING A GOOD ENTREPRENEUR
By Jasmina Cernilogar Mihajlovic 65

CHAPTER 14
UPLIFT YOUR POTENTIAL
By Christine Powell 68

CHAPTER 15
POSITIVE THINKING
By Douglas Dendy 72

CHAPTER 16
SUCCESS IS BEING ABLE TO LIVE A LIFE OF PRIORITIES NOT
OBLIGATIONS
By Dr. Jim Storhok 76

CHAPTER 17
IN AN INSTANT
By Eric Maddox 81

CHAPTER 18
RESCUED INTO MANHOOD
By Frank Mbanusi 84

CHAPTER 19
LIVING AN INSPIRED, PURPOSEFUL, AND AMAZING LIFE
By Jeremy Hoort 88

CHAPTER 20
TRIUMPH THROUGH A BUMPY ROAD
By James Mbele 92

CHAPTER 21
HOW I WENT THROUGH THE LOWEST OF LOWS TO BECOME
SUCCESSFUL
By Jamie Lester 96

CHAPTER 22
THE SECRET SAUCE TO NEVER QUITTING
By Jayde Martinez Santana 100

CHAPTER 23
HELPING PEOPLE AND CHANGING THEIR LIVES FOREVER
By Jim Cusick 104

CHAPTER 24
SMALL TOWN GUY, BIG TIME WHY
By Joshua Holland 108

CHAPTER 25
WE ALREADY HAVE ALL WE NEED
By Juan Enamorado 112

CHAPTER 26
MY DEFINITION OF SUCCESS
By Kadri Kristelle Karu 116

CHAPTER 27
IT IS YOUR TIME
By Kammy Chibueze 121

CHAPTER 28
THE FIRST TIME I FAILED IN MY LIFE WAS THE DAY I WAS BORN
By Kate Jones 125

CHAPTER 29
DIRECTION AND PURPOSE
By Kenneth Hill 129

CHAPTER 30
REINVENTING YOURSELF EVEN IF IT WASN'T YOUR PLAN
By Laarni San Juan 132

CHAPTER 31
SCARED OF BUTTERFLIES?
By Larysa Bednarchyk 136

CHAPTER 32
WINNING THROUGH THE WRINKLES IN LIFE
By LaShonda McMorris 140

CHAPTER 33
GOD IN MY STORMS OF LIFE
By Lilian Tsitsi Musa 145

Chapter 34
PRAY HARD WORK HARD: A ROUTE FOR ACHIEVING SUCCESS AND HAPPINESS IN LIFE
By Luis Guerra 149

Chapter 35
YOU MIGHT SCREAM, YOU MIGHT CRY, BUT GIVING UP IS NOT AN OPTION
By Magga Sigga 153

Chapter 36
I AM NOTHING. YET, I HAVE EVERYTHING
By Maiko Johanson 157

Chapter 37
LACK OF FINANCIAL LITERACY IN INNER CITIES
By Marquis Staton 161

Chapter 38
THE 5 PRINCIPLES OF NETWORKING
By Nicholas Arbutina 165

Chapter 39
BELIEVE YOU CAN
By Peter Muzik 169

Chapter 40
ROADBLOCKS IN LIFE COME FROM OUR MINDSET
By Robert Bucko 174

Chapter 41
THE STREAM
By Sabrina Henne 179

Chapter 42
SUCCESS STARTS AND ENDS WITH SELF-LOVE
By Sean Reid 183

Chapter 43
CHANGE YOUR FOCUS *FROM WHAT IS NOT IN YOUR CONTROL TO WHAT IS IN YOUR CONTROL*
By Shameel Fazaldin 186

Chapter 44
PUSHING THROUGH
By SherRie M. Blango 191

CHAPTER 45
RULE YOUR MIND, ROCK YOUR BEST LIFE
By Steph Shinabery 196

CHAPTER 46
EVERY DAY ALL IN!
By Tabetha Tuck 200

CHAPTER 47
KEY TO SUCCESS IS FOCUS
By Jason Reid 204

Chapter 1

THE ONE SECRET TO LONG LASTING FITNESS

By Bernard Yeo

Stand at a busy intersection and observe the people passing by. What do you notice? A significant number of people are overweight. In today's world, the internet and social media provide information about health and fitness in an instant, yet the number of overweight people is increasing.

If you struggle with being overweight or lack motivation for exercise, I might be able to help.

Being in a comfort zone makes us feel safe and certain in routine activities and habits, so we may feel that stepping out of this zone could bring unexpected risk and stress. For instance, if you've never been the exercising kind, you'll need the motivation to get started and stay on course, right?

Most of us know someone who had the sudden motivation to lose weight, whether it was to impress a girl or get in shape for the summer or a planned holiday. But once the girl moves on to be with someone else or when the event is over, the motivation disappears, and the weight gain returns.

You see, these motivations are external influences. It's not necessarily a bad thing. It is effective for jumpstarting a fitness program. I used to think all it required was enough motivation to act and succeed in getting healthy and fit. I soon learned it also takes determination and willpower to stay motivated, which is why so many people give up after a while.

So, how do some people make keeping the weight off look so easy? How do they stay so motivated for so long? What is the differentiating factor?

There is another element more powerful than motivation. And it is not another kind of motivation. I often wondered why I could stay motivated long enough to be successful at certain things while some of my friends couldn't. Then, I came across research by Dr. Maxwell Maltz, a cosmetic surgeon. He noticed that after correcting imperfections on his patients' appearances, some still felt they were ugly, and this led to his discovery of self-image. In his book, Psycho-Cybernetics, he said, "A human being always acts and feels and performs in accordance with what he imagines to be true about himself and his environment." So, it wasn't what his patients saw when they looked in the mirror. It didn't matter because they considered themselves ugly.

Self-image determines the actions and decisions a person makes every day. For example, someone might have a goal to lose weight, but he continuously sabotages his efforts by overeating sugary foods. Why is that? His self-image is that of an overweight person and so his subconscious mind will consistently act in accordance with his self-image.

Effective weight management starts with motivation, but it won't sustain you. You need to program your subconscious mind and develop a good self-image to be successful in the long term.

Looking back on my life as an example, I started smoking in my early thirties. It probably started with friends over at my house. They wanted to smoke, and I wanted to be social. Soon I was taking smoke breaks with my work colleagues as well. But, after a few months, I didn't feel good about smoking. I felt that it wasn't me. Unbeknown to me at the time, it was probably Dr. Maltz's influence from the power of self-image. Perhaps my self-image of being a non-smoker came from my father. He smoked ever since I knew him and then he passed away from cancer when he was only fifty-one years old. Prior to discovering he had cancer, his engineering company still had hundreds of thousands of dollars owing to the banks for machinery leasing, loans, and recurring costs in operating a factory. My mother, my brothers, and I had to pick up from where he left off as it was our only source of income. It was terrifying because we didn't know anything about operating a business. Losing him was the hardest episode of my life and it was a shame that he couldn't teach us any business skills in time.

Not to brag, but I found it wasn't difficult for me to quit smoking as I had no withdrawal symptoms or nicotine cravings. So, despite the many people around me who smoke, I couldn't be influenced for long. While people normally fail to quit smoking, you can say that I *failed* in smoking!

Another significant event in my life was when I wanted to lose weight in December 2010. I was already in my late thirties and I had not exercised for years. While I was deciding on what to do, I found out that my cousin, Thomas, had just finished a full marathon. Ever since I was a teenager, I admired people who ran a full 42.196 km. I couldn't even run 5 km without stopping a few times. So, my cousin's success inspired me to get into running.

My idea of succeeding was to totally immerse myself in running. First, I set a goal to run a marathon in six months. Then, I bought a book on the beginner's guide to running a marathon. I started to train according to the plan in the book with almost no deviation. I watched proper running techniques on YouTube, I signed up for shorter races leading up to the big event, and I became aware of my food choices. I imagined myself running like Ancient Greek messengers delivering letters in times of war.

On marathon day, it was a tough and hot race. I had cramps in muscles I never knew existed. But I completed the race in five hours and one minute.

Over the next few years, I would run more marathons and even a 100 km ultramarathon. In 2018, I decided to shift from running to lifting weights.

In my marathon example, I was initially motivated to run a marathon in six months. I was motivated by my cousin's success. But, I also totally immersed myself in the sport, so much so that being a long-distance runner formed part of my self-image, which made me get out there to train, regardless if it was too hot or raining.

Now, we circle back to my original promise to you - to help you be successful in your fitness journey. I recommend you get started by motivating yourself and developing the self-image for long-lasting change. How long should you keep yourself motivated – until you achieved your goal and transformed your self-image.

Start your fitness journey with a reason. For me, it was my wife and children. I never want them to experience what I went through with my father's death. Write a letter to yourself (don't type on a computer) and tell yourself why you want to be fit. The letter can be any length, but the longer it is, the better. I want you to make a *promise* to yourself that you will achieve your goal. I say promise because breaking promises is more emotional than just missing a goal. I have taken out letters to myself written months ago and whenever I read them, I get emotionally charged.

Another powerful technique is to announce your goals on social media like Facebook. Letting all your friends know and holding yourself accountable can be incredibly powerful. You will get a lot of motivation and encouragement from your friends. Similarly, with your letter, on Facebook, you are promising your friends.

Build your self-image. Dr. Maltz said to change our self-image, we must use our imagination. By imagining a new healthier version of ourselves, our actions will be redirected to make it come true.

It can be hard to imagine because we are preoccupied with distracting thoughts, so meditation can be effective through implementing more of our senses to achieve our goals. So, here's what I want you to do: Take your self-image vision from the back of your mind and put it in front of your eyes by writing it out on paper. Again, there's something real about the act of writing things down. You employ the sense of sight, touch and hearing your written words in your mind. Create a vision of what you want to be. Put it on your desk or refrigerator and look at it everyday.

When You Don't Feel Motivated

Here's the other side to achieving your goals. There will be days where you don't feel motivated to do anything. You won't feel like going to the gym or for a run. I've faced laziness and procrastination too. There are some people who suggest dressing in a gym or running attire is motivating to get going. If you find an effective technique, then use it.

Here's what worked for me. When I was a runner, I told myself I'll only run for five minutes. If after 5 minutes I don't feel like running anymore, I'll stop. But, after five minutes if I feel like I want to continue, then I will run for another five minutes. Then I evaluate again if I want to continue or stop. I have run extra distances because of this mind hack. And, if your exercise is at the gym, tell yourself to go but only commit to do the warmup sets of your favorite muscle group, then decide if you want to continue the workout or not. You haven't failed if you stop after five minutes. Think of it as a sloppy day and let it go.

Another way to beat motivation (or lack thereof) is to integrate fitness into your life. Consider using resistance bands while watching television, set exercise time using calendar appointments, or have friends pick you up at scheduled times to go to the gym. Stick to these ideas and I promise you, you'll see the change in your self-image.

I want to close this chapter with the story about the scorpion and the frog. You may have heard of it, but I have a different view. The insert below is from Wikipedia:

"A scorpion asks a frog to carry it across a river. The frog hesitates, afraid of being stung by the scorpion, but the scorpion argues that if it did that, they would both drown. The frog considers this argument sensible and agrees to transport the scorpion. The scorpion climbs onto the frog's back and the frog begins to swim, but midway across the river, the scorpion stings the frog, dooming them both. The dying frog asks the scorpion why it stung, to which the scorpion replies, "I couldn't help it. It's in my nature."

Just like it is the scorpion's nature to sting, you must establish a healthy self-image with fitness in your nature. If you do, you will never have to struggle with weight issues again.

Biography

Bernard Yeo is known for his love for personal development and dedication to personal fitness. Having run marathons for several years and switching to weight training, he has redirected his passion for coaching others on how to fight the battle of the bulge and gain fitness. With years of virtual traveling overseas and YouTube on his belt, he now makes actual adventurous and challenging trips with his ex-classmates every year. Bernard lives with his wife and two sons in Kuala Lumpur, Malaysia.

Contact Information

Facebook: https://www.facebook.com/BernardYeo
Instagram: https://www.instagram.com/justdoit.mindset/

Chapter 2

THE POWER OF MANIFESTATION

By Matt Morris

It had been about three days since my last bath. Not that you could even call it a bath. Every two or three days, I would find a gas station bathroom that would lock from the inside. I'd take off all my clothes, splash water up from the sink, soap up, and then splash water to rinse off. I remember always praying that no one would be waiting outside because the floor would be soaking wet.

I had completely run out of money. I had also run out of credit. I was approximately $30,000 in debt and couldn't even make the minimum payments on my credit cards. I had been forced to live out of my car because I couldn't afford rent or even $20 a night to stay in a sleazy motel. I was selling above ground swimming pools in southern Louisiana during the two hottest months of the year and didn't get paid commissions until the pool got installed six to eight weeks later. So, for two months, my Honda Civic was my home sweet home.

Sitting all alone in my car that night, I was overly aware that my life had hit rock bottom. Not only was I lonely, broke and living out of my car, but I had just showered naked in the rain in the church parking lot in which I was parked. To be specific, I had showered under the gutter runoff from the roof of the church.

The burning question in my mind that night was, "How?" How in the world had I gotten myself into this situation? I knew I wasn't there because of a lack of effort or even a lack of intelligence. (I wasn't lazy, and I actually considered myself to be a pretty smart guy.)

After experiencing both utter failure and extreme success in my life, I have become acutely aware of what exactly manifested that situation. I'm also aware of what has now allowed me to become a self-made millionaire, travel around the world to over 50 countries, become a best-selling author and speaker attracting audiences of thousands every year.

You might think what caused those results were the *actions* leading up to them because, as we know, every action does produce a result. Most people focus only on the "how to's" but never seem to achieve their full potential because the decision to take proper or improper actions is a byproduct of your original intention. If the intention is not set properly, one will almost always make the wrong decisions on what actions to take which, in turn, lead to an undesired result.

What lies at the heart of manifesting your full potential is your intention.

What is intention? The dictionary defines it as the end or objective intended or purpose. While that sounds incredibly simple, utilizing the power of intention needs a bit more clarification of how you truly manifest that purpose for yourself.

An intention is your inner belief of what is already present but has simply not manifested in physical form yet. A true intention comes with the commitment and honest belief that anything else is an absolute impossibility. You see, when you're committed to a result, it's already done. Without it already being done in your mind, it cannot be considered a true intention but simply a fleeting wish.

When it comes to achieving your result, the simplest and widely accepted model for you to follow is what we call *cause and effect*. Think of your result as your effect. Your job is to identify and create the cause that will produce your effect.

Most people naturally assume that the cause is the physical actions or the steps you need to take to get your desired effect. What I'm proposing to you here, however, is that the series of action steps is not the real cause. The actions are really part of the effect.

So, the question is then, what's the cause?

The real cause is the intention you made to create that effect in the first place. The moment you say to yourself, "let it be so," is the real cause. Without the decision or your intention, the effect will never manifest. Your intention is ultimately what causes everything in your life to manifest.

If you want to achieve a goal, the most crucial part is to *decide* to manifest it. It doesn't matter if you feel it's out of your capabilities to achieve it. It doesn't matter if you can't see *how* you're going to achieve it. The *how* is insignificant because the universe will usually never manifest the *how* until *after* you've made the decision.

If you look at the origin of the word "decide," it is actually "to cut off." Your "decision" then should be framed in your mind as cutting off any other option other than your desired result. If failure is an option in your mind, your true intention is actually failure.

So step 1 is to *decide* not to wonder if you can do it and not to think of all the reasons that are holding you back. If you want to start your own business, then decide to make it so first. If you want to get married, decide to attract a mate. Whatever it is you want out of life, make a decision and a commitment *first*, and *then* work out the *how*.

If you have doubts in your head, you will find doubts in the world. You see, my belief is that the universe can sense a lack of commitment to a goal. It's like those people who say they are going to *try* to do something and *see how it goes*. When you come from a place of uncertainty or if you're wishy-washy about your goal, then the universe is not going to help you achieve it.

When you have total certainty in declaring your intention, you attract people like a magnet. When you are energized, motivated and have declared your goal to be so, that resonates in your being, and the universe aligns itself to work with you to manifest your intention.

You must also realize that your subconscious mind is infinitely more powerful than your conscious mind and that your subconscious mind controls your outcome 100%. When you are uncertain consciously about your goal, your subconscious does everything in its power to hold you back. You see, your subconscious acts like a computer. It accepts 100% of the data your conscious mind gives it. When your conscious mind feeds it negativity, it produces negative results for you. When your conscious mind feeds it excitement, positivity, and certainty, it produces all the energy and creativity it possibly can to ensure that you accomplish your intended result.

If you want to achieve any goal, your first step is to declare it and then to clear out all words like "hopefully," "can't," "maybe" and the killer - "try." When someone tells me they're going to "try" to do something, I know that they're *not* going to do it.

Such words are all signs of a lack of commitment, that you don't believe in yourself and that you're using your own power against yourself.

You see, we all have the same amount of power – it's just deciding if we want to use our power negatively or positively. When you use your power negatively, you're saying, "let me be powerless." If you think weakness, you manifest weakness. If you project certainty, you manifest certainty.

"Energy flows where attention goes."

You get whatever you think about most often. Whatever you think about expands. Therefore, we must constantly focus on what we want!

Remember, "we" create our destiny by the committed focus of our intention.

Biography

Author of the International Bestselling *The Unemployed Millionaire*, Matt Morris began as a serial entrepreneur at 18. Since then, he has generated over $1.5 billion through his sales organizations totaling over one million customers worldwide. As a self-made millionaire and one of the top Internet and Network Marketing experts, he's been featured on international radio, television and spoken from platforms to audiences in over 25 countries around the world. And now, as the founder of Success Publishing, he co-authors with leading experts from every walk of life.

Contact Information

http://www.MattMorris.com | http://successpublishing.com/

CHAPTER 3

THE PERSON YOU COULD HAVE BEEN

By Steve Moreland

We Texans pride ourselves on a few things. Toughness is Rule #1, and it means "no tears allowed." Our indoctrination begins the moment we arrive.

The other rules follow. Do only BIG things, especially if others say it can't be done. Rub some dirt on wherever you're bleeding; scars prove your worth. And do Right, even if the Lord God, herself, threatens you to do otherwise.

Brutal. Spartan, some would say. But definitely the kind of folks you'd want covering your back in a fight. Its belief carved deep in our soul that there is simply NO FREE LUNCH. And did I mention, we love to fight? Yep, and we don't know what that thing called a "truce" is all about.

At age twelve, I started "earning my worth." My phone rang off the wall with grass-cutting jobs in the Texas infernos called summer because my dad drilled me to deliver results beyond expectations. No excuses. Just disciplined results!

Went right to work after graduating with academic scholarships – working for three Fortune 500 companies and going to college at night. At twenty-five, I started my own brokerage firm in Dallas. By thirty, I'd made it to millionaire status, flew in private jets to do deals in European castles, hid money in numbered Swiss bank accounts, and spoke on international stages raising millions for venture capital deals.

I was Vice president of offshore operations for a boutique hedge fund based in Turks and Caicos, CEO of 58-office tax and trust firm based in Salt Lake City, and co-principal for a start-up SaaS company out of Irvine, California. Part of every month, I lived at my office in the banking district of Nassau, Bahamas, where I acted as the vice president of new business development for a middle eastern banking syndicate.

Occasionally, I woke up at a place my then-wife and children called home. And it was here that I slowed down enough to rub some of that Texas dirt on my hand, tremors that began from only sleeping on overseas flights and stumbling forward so fast everything had become a blur.

It wasn't the success, the money, the black VISA card, or the fans (though they were awesome!). It was something more insidious. Something more potent than mamby-pamby pixy dust from motivational gurus with their crybaby stories.

My dad had decreed standing orders. "You can rest when you're dead!" And this came from his creed that a man only earns a medal on his gravestone if he dies in combat. I'd been trained to fear only one thing. "Hell is meeting the person you could have been!"

And when Fate's blood-stained hurricane found me, I was ready. Ready to blindly march into Hades itself. And, like the Greek myth of Sisyphus, I remember thinking to myself, "Maybe God is not good." I recall feeling agony, real soul-crushing pain that made me wish I could just die and get it over. Wallowing in my self-pity after losing everything, I'd succumb to that state of a *victim* of Fate. And that dirt didn't fix the wounds I'd caused my family for the undeserved trials and tribulations my foolishness had caused.

Though I was brought up with my dad's relentless Marine Corp code of conduct and my mom's Christian beliefs, I doubted those beliefs. And, like the Bible's character Job, I blamed God for not protecting us from this horror. I beggingly prayed for an instant and easy fix. I just wanted that magical snap of a finger and everything to be like it used to be. But that never happens, does it?

Strength isn't forged in the cauldron of luxury and comfort. And medals don't get pinned to your uniform for holding hands and singing "Kum Ba Yah." It took time to face my demons and do the most excruciating thing I'd ever done. Take responsibility for my stupidity. Realizing that I couldn't change the past or erase what my mistakes had cost my family, I had to decide – blame others and wallow in self-pity or use hell to become better!

In school, we're first taught the lesson that prepares us for the test. But, in life, we face the Test first; later, we learn the Lesson.

The grade is what we become through it all. It's pass or fail, heaven or hell. Yes, hell is when you meet that person you could have been. But heaven is so much harder. It means rising again and again within the blood-stained hurricane of Fate. Only this repeated discipline distinguishes the few from the many, the extraordinary from the ordinary, the worthy from the worthless.

That person you could have been is only Hell if he or she stands better than you chose to become! **Hell, then, is meeting the *better* person you could have been.**

My penance for failing that critical life Test is to better our world. If Fate's blood-stained hurricane has not found your life yet, she's just hiding over the horizon, waiting until you're at your most vulnerable. If you're willing to listen to someone that knows about life's ash heap, I share the Lessons learned *after* my failed Test. They're about how thinking differently empowered me to thrive where most cannot survive. No fluffy bullshit. No rah-rah! Just what worked.

May the following battle-tested advice return you from your seemingly impossible hurricane *"tested – and found not wanting."*

Have you ever been really curious about something? Obsessed even?

Since I was a kid, I wanted to unravel this thing called thinking. I thought to myself, if I could only understand how the few we call successful actually think, I might be able to make the world a little bit better. Because, for the most part, they are not any different than us, right? But with one exception, they see things differently in their minds.

Personal development "coaches" blather about managing our thinking. It is THE key, agreed. But it's not enough to know *what* to do. We've got to know *how* to do it. It's the subtle and often hidden difference between learning science without the art of knowing how it applies to real-world situations. Most "well-meaning" coaches deserve an "A" for science but an "F" in art. Never earning a medal from within Fate's blood-stained hurricane means their theories can only get you one place – a chance to meet the person you could have been.

Here's an example of a coach with earned rank, Dr. Viktor Frankl – author of *Man's Search For Meaning*. Frankl didn't just survive six years of Nazi concentration camps, he changed the world forever with his discovery of how we create meaning through our thinking. Better thinking creates better doing, and better doing creates a better being.

Frankl forced me to think. I mean, really think. All of a sudden, what Professor Eli Goldratt wrote in *The Goal* became crystal. "If we continue to do what we have done, which is what everybody else is doing, we will continue to get the same *unsatisfactory* result." Isn't that what we do so very often - more of what everyone else has done, expecting a different outcome?

We are what we've done, right? So, aren't our actions - what we *do* - what creates who we *become*? In short, "doing creates being." So, who we are today – our being, is a product of our past doings? Becoming someone better can only happen by doing differently. And this different had to start in the thoughts deep within.

Because I wanted a different future, one that honored the sacred by making the world better, I could no longer afford to think like everyone else. Maybe you're brighter than me and already know this. But for me, this realization was like Eureka! And instantly, I felt something deep inside.

If my prior thinking caused my current doings (my actions and habits that are known as my reality), **then why couldn't I change my future by changing the way I was thinking now?**

Socrates (Greek philosopher 470 B.C.) taught a Secret passed through to his student Plato to his student Aristotle (Greek philosopher 384 B.C.). Aristotle planted this secret into the mind of a 13-year-old prince. This secret method of thinking changed history.

At 16 years of age, the prince led his cavalry at the Battle of Chaeronea, decimating a supposedly unbeatable army. At 20 years of age, he became the king of Greece, marched his army towards Persia, solved the riddle of the Gordian Knot, destroying all who opposed. At 24, he destroyed the supposedly unconquerable city of Tyre.

At 25, he became Pharaoh of Egypt only to return to the desert near modern-day Babylon to lead his 50,000-man army against a force of 500,000 led by the Persian emperor Darius. Charging into the front line on his legendary black stallion Bucephalus, he achieved the impossible and became emperor of the known world.

By age 30, he had conquered the largest empire in history and is still studied in war colleges today for his battlefield genius, ethical governance, and unrivaled valor.

The Secret thought? "Be what you wish to seem."

The Result? One *impossible* difficulty after another - conquered!

His Name? Alexander

How is he remembered? Alexander the Great!

Hell is meeting the person you could have been, right?

So these Lessons learned after the Test lead to better actions, which lead to becoming a better being. That means that tests uncover our weaknesses so that we can learn greater lessons. What and who we became through the Tests and Lessons reflects our grade.

If we're honest, we'll admit that we often create our own storms. And then we blame others when they must be endured. But if we use the agony, we find something called grit. Grit is commitment bathed in love to become better than we were the day before. It's a relentless dedication to rise to become better, stronger, and smarter. It's a refusal to quit, even when we feel we can't get up again.

The question is, will we? Will we persist after the problems that were caused by our poor thinking – and the actions that followed? Or will we just quit due to the fear of failing, never suffering the scars that come from learning our lessons? Yeah, no easy answers. If it were easy, everyone would be the best possible version of themselves.

Those that fight to be better are never pretty. They're bloody from one battle after another. They don't know how to give up. And their scars reflect rank, how many times they returned to the chaos of the hurricane instead of hiding and waiting for the rescue that never arrives.

The Secret of "Be what you wish to seem" comes down to *"acting as if"* you've already achieved your ultimate end. What kept me marching through my blood-stained hurricane was my Gravestone, the ultimate end of what I could still become, if I changed my thinking.

Follow me. Every gravestone can fit about ten words on it. These words express how we lived, as witnessed by those that saw the real version of us, not the fake one we wear to impress others.

So, how did I *not* end up in Hell, meeting the person I could have been?

It boiled down to the little videos I saw in my mind's eye. I daily relived my greatest nightmare, experiencing it deep in my soul – again and again. The nightmare that my children chiseled on my Gravestone, "A quitter with excuses, like most." I actually saw the ceremony and those that I loved standing in silence. These words are why I refused to take the easy way out and quit.

I kept marching by visualizing, daydreaming about what I did not want to be remembered for. Sounds morbid, I know. But this propelled me to find a way to rise once more and keep moving forward, even when I felt the Lord, had abandoned me. I decided that my children would never be ashamed of their father, which caused every action to become a reason to be more, by living to do more, for others.

And on occasion, I'd dream of a moment when my children might forgive me for my poor thinking. On that good day, I'd see a different gravestone, having become that person that deserved words like "A Better World Exists Because He Determined To Think Better."

So, try my proven exercise on for size. Ask yourself the following:
1. What would your family and closest friends write on your ultimate end? (Why not ask them, if you have any guts?)
2. What do you *not* want them to chisel on your Gravestone?
3. What do you hope they will chisel on your Gravestone?

It's really simple. **How you choose to be remembered is who you will become!**

By routinely practicing this exercise, you'll be crystal clear about how to thrive within Fate's hurricane.
- You will know what actions that you cannot *do*
    - That which will cause you to become ***who*** you do not wish to be remembered as;
    - That which will cause you to do ***what*** you do not wish to be remembered for.

- You also know exactly what actions you must *do*
    - That which will cause you to become ***who*** you wish to be remembered as;
    - That will cause you to do ***what*** you wish to be remembered for.

It may be cliché, but our very thinking sparks our every action. These doings, added together over time, construct our being - *what* and *who* we become.

A short expression chiseled in stone broadcasts to a future world our *being* because of our *doings*. Did we dishonor the sacred, settling for what everybody else is doing and continuing to get their same unsatisfactory results?

Or did we ***think*** better, in order to ***do*** better, so that we could ***be*** better?

This is the Secret. My gift to you, as Aristotle long ago shared with Alexander, "be what you wish to seem." We become what we choose to be. It's all about our thinking.

Now you know that Hell is NOT meeting the person you could have been.

Hell is meeting the *better* person you could have been.

Biography

Steve Moreland is a native Texan known for dedicated practice and success. His Rubicon system teaches people how to perform the common under uncommon conditions. Motivated by the Latin creed FORTES FORTUNA ADIUVAT "Fortune favors the brave," his mission is to deliberately cause affirmative outcomes that would not have occurred otherwise.

Contact Information

Rubicon Website: gonerubicon.com/
Rubicon Facebook Page: https://www.facebook.com/RubiconPerforms/
Instagram: livebravely_dieworthy
Facebook: https://www.facebook.com/steven.moreland.5205
LinkedIn: https://www.linkedin.com/in/steve-moreland-088730118/

Chapter 4

WHAT MAKES SOME PEOPLE MORE SUCCESSFUL THAN OTHERS?

By Maxwell Adekoje

Why do some people do exceptionally well, and others don't? Every human being is built for success and wants to be successful, but only a few become successful. The percentage of successful people seems to be about 10 percent, about the same range, year after year.

What is success? How can you join this constant and unchanging 10% of the population? Understanding success is the first step to attaining success. These principles took me from $20, when I first came to the US, to becoming a proud owner and CEO of an MLM marketing company.

Success is a thought process that gives birth to a discovered purpose. The most significant gap between successful and unsuccessful people is the way they think, which reflects on their attitude, beliefs, and mindset. If the way we think is paramount to our success, why do we still have the same wrong mindset? Let me share a little story I once heard from a friend.

In 1990, a known musician built a house with N20 Million; the same year, Jim Ovia started Zenith Bank with the same amount. Zenith bank in Nigeria is one of the most reputable banks in Africa.

Today, you and I don't have a room in the musician's house, but I have an account in Jim's bank, and you probably do, too.

The house was built in Lagos, Nigeria, and remains there to this date.

Jim's bank started in a corner and now has over 500 branches in Nigeria and many international branches.

Millions upon millions transact business in Jim's bank daily.

The house is becoming dilapidated. In 2015, he SPENT more money to renovate the house and bought a Nissan Pathfinder with N10 million, an additional liability, while in the same 2015, Jim's bank MADE a profit of N105.7 billion.

Zenith bank employs hundreds of thousands of people and feeds families.

This is the difference between a successful mindset and an unsuccessful mindset. If you buy a car for N20 million today, in 20 years' time, you will be ashamed to drive it. On the other hand, if you invest that same amount in a lucrative business or an asset, it may be worth billions of nairas in 20 years. (Jim Ovia is now worth 980 million dollars, with the official dollar rate of N350. That means he is worth N313 BILLION NAIRA, all because of an investment of N20 million. Every penny in your hand is like a seed; you can decide to eat it or sow it. When you plant it, it will bear many more seeds in the future. Now, you can see why successful people think differently.

Success demands that you develop a certain type of thinking and perception about the way you see things. It doesn't matter how many degrees or talents you have; it's your thinking and attitude that keeps you small.

Attitude plays a vital ingredient in your success; it's a product of belief. You can't have an attitude beyond your belief. Your attitude comes from your platform of belief. If you associate with only poor individuals, you will think like them.

If you hang around the restaurant long enough, you will get something to eat. We become our environment unknowingly. Stay in an environment that will aid your growth.

People with a great attitude are coachable with a teachable and welcoming atmosphere. Take responsibility for your attitude; it belongs to you.

How can you alter your attitude? Here are three simple steps:
1. Fill your mind with good thinking; you can't fill your mind with bad stuff and expect to alter your mind. Be selective and guard your mind with armor.
2. Marinate and digest the good thinking you put in. Dr. Maxwell Maltz, a plastic surgeon turned psychologist, wrote: "It usually requires a minimum of about 21 days to effect any perceptible change in a mental image. Following plastic surgery, it takes about 21 days for the average patient to get used to his new face. When an arm or leg is amputated, the "phantom limb" persists for about 21 days. People must live in a new house for about three weeks before it begins to "seem like a home."
3. Practice good things, so they get into your mind and become a part of you.

It's the thinking of a person that makes them see circumstances differently. After years of dealing with problems, I started realizing that a problem is a human definition of an opportunity to grow. If you call it a problem, it immediately takes a negative notation. If you see it as an opportunity, it becomes positive. A problem really only becomes a problem when you see it as a problem. If you want to become a person of impact, you must fill your mind correctly.

After reading the book, "Think & Grow Rich," repeatedly, I realize that human beings can alter their life by changing their attitude. Wow!

The most valuable instrument for success is the 15.24 cm between your ears. No one can live beyond the limit of their thinking; it must be altered. You're simply a presentation of your thoughts. Because of the way my mind was programmed as a child, I had to reprogram my thought process.

First, I had to discover my purpose in life, feed my mind with new beliefs. I'm possible. Marinate on the new thinking and back it up with execution.

Information does not bring transformation; conversion does.

If you don't like who you are, change it to who you think you should be. Your thinking is more powerful than any promise.

Everyone came to this earth fully loaded with purpose; discover it. You're important to the world with a purpose to do something significant. Most of our perceptions are other people's concept about us. You didn't know you were weak until someone told you. Your life is shaped and cultured by what you hear or see.

The little difference in people is their attitude; the larger version is if it is positive or negative.

A seed can be held in your wallet for 40 years and never become a tree even though the seed has a tree in it. Most people go through life carrying their greatness in their wallet rather than planting it.

Trees aren't found in the soil; they are hidden in the seed if you can get it out of your wallet and plant it.

We are like a tree serving the world our juice; plant yourself on fertile ground. Watch out for the weeds. People heading nowhere are ready to pollute your seed. Break away from people to become more. You must outgrow some people. I call it isolation. Know when to go! "Isolation to growth" is best illustrated by the story of a lobster. How do lobsters grow? A lobster is a soft animal that lives inside a rigid shell that never expands. So, how do they grow? By isolation.

A lobster isolates from predators and casts off the old shell and produces a new one; then, after a while, they repeat the process.

The lesson of the story: the lobster feels uncomfortable, then grows. Most people will never grow until they walk away from people who are continually polluting their life, solidifying the wrong beliefs in them.

Always walk away and remember to repeat this process of renewing your mind.

I can't end the chapter without talking about some key traits of success - confidence and focus.

Confidence

Confidence is a product of your belief. The way you think about yourself is the way you unknowingly behave. It's interesting how an elephant with so much power behaves like a gazelle in the presence of a lion.

Mindset is everything; thinking is the belief system exposed. I had to alter my thinking, and my attraction instantly took a turn around.

Focus

Without focus, you will never finish. I find the Lindenberg's story to be one of the best illustrations of how focus can lead and keep you on the path of success.

Lindbergh, Charles Augustus (1902-1974), an American aviator, made the first solo nonstop flight across the Atlantic Ocean on May 20-21, 1927. Other pilots had crossed the Atlantic before him, but Lindbergh was the first person to do it alone nonstop.

From New York to Paris (nonstop) in 33 hours, 30 minutes, he made a statement to the press. He said, "At a point, I considered going back, but when I examined the fuel gauge, I realized the remaining fuel could only take me across, not back, so I maintained."

Lindbergh's feat gained him immediate international fame. The press named him "Lucky Lindy" and the "Lone Eagle."

Nothing destroys focus like options.

Nothing frustrates the success of a plan like the mindfulness of plan B.

If there is an imploring alternative to your dream, then trust me, you will soon leave the idea.

Follow your dream as if there were no choices; your life depends on it. Narrow in your focus; deal with distractions.

Keep your eyes on the eight ball. It may be tough, but it's attainable if you don't abandon it for other options.

Stay focused, burn the boats

When they arrived, he ordered his men to burn the ships. I wonder the thoughts in their minds as Cortés promptly thrust his sword. Successful people think differently; they start with the end in mind; unsuccessful people start with the beginning and never see the end.

Here's the lesson: Retreat is easy when you have the option; always see the end first.

Let that marinate in your mind for a minute.

We all cling to something that acts as our escape plan or our exit strategy. It's our safety net; "the just in case factor" is the biggest dream killer..."

Our thought tells us, "This is my safety exit, just in case *things go out of hand*." You immediately lack momentum and register a failure that was waiting to happen.

We delay action until we no longer have fear. Aside from that, our actions are narrow attempts never intended to succeed.

What are your ships? Why are you afraid to let go? Let that ruminate in your mind and write them down? What ship do you need to burn NOW? Trust me, success is in the "now" and not in the tomorrow.

The longer you ponder to act, the more likely you will never do it. What makes it hard to burn your boats is mostly the fear of the unknown called the comfort zone.

John C Maxwell, my mentor, talks about success. For success to happen, your comfort zone must be disturbed.

Nothing makes sense like burning the boats to feel good afterward.

Most of the things we call obstacles are placed there by ourselves, and we ask, "Oh why?" No one packaged it for you; it was your decision not to do the things that create change like burning the boats.

What Cortés did was to cancel the retreat option and create a NEW mindset to succeed or die, which takes us to another resounding trait of success - CHARACTER.

Character is bigger than death; that's the only reason why this story will never die. Cortés doesn't need a tombstone to be remembered.

Roosevelt described character as the decisive factor in the life of an individual that brings honor. Character speaks without words. Your character gives weight to your words; your life becomes your words. Successful leaders never get their reward in the beginning.

"Life chooses what we go through, but we decide how we sail through it." - Maxwell Adekoje

Live every day like today is your last time to impact lives.

You have greatness in you, and you have more than enough to become a person of value. The world badly needs you. Find your purpose and live a life of fulfillment.

Biography

Maxwell's life is a story about hard work, endurance, and inspiration.

Originally born in Nigeria, Max first traveled to the United States at a young age, with just $20 in his pocket, seeking the American dream. Like so many who began their working life and career in a new land, the first venture in Max's career in the US was not particularly a great success. Ultimately, there were several failed attempts, but each one along the way served to grow his ambition and sense of belief in the promise of the US and what it could offer to him as a businessman and professional.

First working at a car wash, a restaurant, and numerous other entry-level jobs, Max would regularly sleep three hours daily for years at a time. He was still paying tons of bills, working long hours, and was ultimately unhappy. Despite these challenges, Max never gave up on America and the promise it offered to a young man with a dream and a readiness to realize it with hard work.

Despite this, Max encountered a moment of truth driving home from work one day. So tired in his car, he fell asleep at the wheel, crashed and nearly killed himself. It was at this moment that he knew he needed to change gears in order to change his situation and pursue a life that would deliver him the rewards he deserved.

He wanted to pursue a real American dream, the one that led him to America in the first place and not the one of him washing cars as when he first arrived.

This was when he began exploring ways to grow his own business and grow his net worth. It was around this time he found out about multilevel marketing. Having resolved to chase down a new life for himself, soon after this new career path crystalized, Max was achieving great success in his new field.

Today, he is a top sponsor with numerous awards accredited to his name. He is also the CEO of his own MLM company. Recognized as an international training coach and speaker, Max is proud to be a member of the John C Maxwell Team. While Max is delighted by his success today, he remains hungry for more and goes to work each day with the intention of doing better than ever.

Contact Information

Phone 757-235 6978
Email tmc@mytaprootmc.com

CHAPTER 5

DREAM IT. DO IT!

By AbdurRazaq Abdul-Aziz

My father was my first mentor. Growing up, he provided guidance that became the cornerstone of my accomplishments. He ensured that my siblings, and I had an excellent education by enrolling us in the best primary and secondary schools in Jos, Plateau State.

As a child, I remember my father owned an electrical store, and he set up a popcorn shop for my mother. I recall during the holidays while in primary school; he would take me to the store. I enjoyed playing with the big black phone on his desk and looking at his stock cards and ledgers.

My siblings and I also helped out in my mother's popcorn business, and this continued into secondary school. At a very young age, my father showed and taught me entrepreneurship even though I didn't quite understand it then and sometimes; I even resisted it because I felt he was too hard on me. In the late seventies, nearing the end of my secondary school education, my father closed his electrical shop and ventured into a professional cleaning business.

After completing secondary school, I went on to do my A levels before going to university. As an undergraduate studying accounting at the University of Jos, my father made sure I was involved in his cleaning venture. My first paid job was as an employee in his company known as Duraclean Specialists Nigeria Limited.

I was attending university and working at the same time. After graduation, I went to Lagos State to observe the mandatory one year National Youth Service Corps (N.Y.S.C.) required of all eligible graduates in Nigeria, and I served at the Shell Petroleum Development Company (SPDC). After completing my service, I was employed by SPDC on a contract agreement renewable every quarter. After two quarters, and before the next renewal, I quit to go back home to work with my father. He was delighted with my decision and made me the General Manager of Duraclean Specialists Nigeria Limited, where I was in charge of the daily business operations. I thought I would be more efficient if I acquired a business education. Subsequently, I enrolled for a Masters of Business (MBA) course at the University of Jos, which I completed successfully.

After acquiring my MBA, I felt ready to expand our family business. I suggested to my father that we open a branch in Abuja, the new capital of Nigeria. Although he was skeptical at first, it was then that he taught me one of the most important lessons of business. He pulled out a pen, some blank sheets of paper and said we need to formulate a plan. Together we itemized all the resources required to open a new branch in Abuja. At the end of the exercise, the final cost was more than ₦10,000,000.00. He looked at me and said, "Young man, we don't have such an amount at this time. Let's keep this in view for the future." I was disappointed but not deterred. Determined to go to Abuja, I had to find a way to cut the budget and began thinking of ways to do so. I studied the plan and pinpointed the highest costs. Three stood out:

1. Office Rent
2. Accommodation Rent
3. Utility Vehicle

So, I asked my father, "Dad, if I provide a solution for these three components of our plan, will you supply the rest and allow me to go to Abuja and open the new branch?" "Yes," he said. "Perfect!" I responded. I approached one of his closest friends who I knew had an office in Abuja. I requested a small space in his office until I was able to rent my own office. He obliged.

Next, I contacted a Musa Narkoji, a good friend who was working in Abuja and asked him if I could stay with him until I could afford my own accommodation. He agreed.

Finally, I spoke to my father about the utility vehicle and explained to him that we didn't need a new one as we could revamp one of the vehicles we had. He consented. In September 1999, I arrived in Abuja to open the new branch of Duraclean Specialists Nigeria Limited. I had big dreams and was excited about the expansion of our company. I hit the ground running and began to implement the marketing skills I learned in business school.

Seven months in, and despite all my efforts, we did not make a single sale. I was depleting my working capital; it was so bad that I almost threw in the towel and even contemplated shutting down the entire operation. However, I remembered my father's wise counsel, "Never start what you cannot finish." Besides, I could not go back home and tell him I failed. I had also met an amazing girl. We started a serious relationship and were discussing marriage.

Failure was not an option at all, so I soldiered on with a strong will to succeed. A few weeks later, we made our first sale, which led to several more sales, and eventually, we landed a substantial contract with a government agency. We broke even, and our new branch flourished as we acquired more clients. Government agencies were some of our biggest clients; however, there was one problem. Although government contracts were lucrative (and still are), I felt they had two significant downsides: red tape and exploitation. These were major concerns for me. I am unmotivated by undue lengthy processes and uncomfortable with compromising ethical norms. Despite this situation, our business continued to grow steadily. In the meantime, my fiancé, Korede, and I got married.

One day in October 2007, I went to the dentist for a root canal procedure. Ouch! I don't know about you, but I dread visiting the dentist.

After the procedure, as if to soothe my pain, my dentist, Dr. Gloria Agboghoroma asked a simple question, "AbdurRazaq, do you like to travel?" "Yes," I responded.

"Fantastic! I want to invite you to a briefing regarding a travel plan," she continued.

I accepted her invitation. She gave me the details of the meeting, and I left.

I would not have thought much about her invitation but something she said as I was leaving piqued my curiosity. She said, "Go with your checkbook" (back then payment cards were not widely-used). I remember receiving a similar invitation before from a friend who also mentioned a checkbook.

Hmm, what could this seminar be about, I wondered and decided to attend. I showed up for the meeting on the appointed day with my checkbook. However, I decided to leave it in my car for safekeeping, if you know what I mean.

The venue of the meeting was the Sheraton Hotel Abuja situated in the city center. The reception was cordial, and the ambiance of the meeting room was superb. I was impressed. The presentation commenced on the hour, and the presenter was eloquent from start to finish. Guess what? I dashed off to my car at the end of the presentation and got my checkbook.

I subscribed to the highest travel package that she offered. I loved the product, but most importantly, I was intrigued by the business opportunity. I was hooked the moment she quoted J. Paul Getty during her presentation. "I would rather earn 1% of 100 people's efforts than 100% of my own efforts." Suddenly, I realized the power of leverage. I remembered joining two companies with similar business models while at university, but at the time, I did not realize they were network marketing companies and did not know about the powerful concept of word-of-mouth marketing.

I could not explore my network marketing business immediately because Korede and I were expecting our third child. Our daughter was born on November 28, 2007. After the celebration of our new baby, I began preparations to ramp up my business. Sadly, on December 19, 2007, I was knocked down by a motor vehicle.

When I opened my eyes, I felt pain, excruciating pain all over my body, especially my right leg, which was suspended by a contraption. Where am I, I wondered. I heard voices, and very slowly, I turned my head but was forced to stop because of the racking pain in my head.

I heard the sound of soft voices and muffled crying. Korede's face came into view as she moved closer to me. "What happened?" I asked her. Quietly, my wife told me that a few days ago, after parking my car, I got out and was knocked down by a speeding motor vehicle. She explained that I was rushed to the hospital and had been unconscious for the past four days. She said everyone was worried. I told her I couldn't remember the incident.

I suffered temporary amnesia, as well as a broken leg, collar bone, and had severe bruises. My worst fear was not being able to walk again. However, in spite of the distressing situation, I prayed to God and envisioned myself walking again. After regaining full consciousness, I was scheduled for surgery within two weeks, which was carried out successfully. I remained in the hospital under care and observation. For over two months, I was bedridden and unable to do anything without assistance. Eventually, I was discharged from the hospital, and to this day, I can vividly remember being carried and lifted into the car and the same process being repeated when we arrived home. It was a bittersweet experience. I was happy to be back home but sad that I was incapacitated.

The road to recovery was not easy. Even at home, I was in bed most of the time and needed assistance to do everything. Over time, my broken leg healed, and I began physiotherapy, first at home and later at the hospital. Imagine learning how to walk all over again. My therapy sessions began with handrails, and gradually I moved to walking with double crutches, then one crutch and finally a cane. These successions occurred over several agonizing months.

In August 2008, while hobbling on one crutch, I received a text message. It was an invitation to attend the celebration of the first anniversary of a company. I was perplexed and thought the text message was sent to me in error. In any case, I showed Korede the message, and she told me it was from the network marketing company I joined two months before the accident. I said, "I don't know what you are talking about. I didn't join any network marketing company."

Korede got up from the bed and walked out of our bedroom and returned holding some papers.

She raised her hand and said, "Here are the membership documents you signed."

I had forgotten about my network marketing company because of the temporary amnesia I had suffered after my accident. Korede collected my phone and looked at the message again.

She said, "The celebration will take place on Saturday. Today is Tuesday. We have three days to get you looking like Prince Charming! This is what you need to get your spirits up!" Truthfully, the physiotherapy sessions, coupled with the debilitating pain, had taken its toll on me. Also, I suffered depression as a result of being confined to the house for many months. Korede resisted my reluctance to attend, and on that Saturday, my darling wife ensured we attended the event.

The anniversary celebration was held at Sheraton Hotel Abuja, the same hotel where I attended the company's business presentation the previous year. My wife and I sat at a table with four other guests. The highlight of the occasion was when the anchorwoman began to call out names of individuals who subsequently proceeded to the front of the hall to receive cheques.

One after another, people went up to the stage and received their cheques while the audience applauded. I was fascinated and asked the gentleman next to me what these people had done to be rewarded in this manner. He answered by saying, "Are you not a member of this company?" I didn't respond and continued to enjoy the show.

Later, the presenter announced it was time to recognize the top three earners. She called the third and second person, and both of them ran up to the stage amidst thundering applause and upbeat music to receive their cheque.

Suddenly, everyone stopped clapping, the music stopped, and all the lights on the stage were dimmed except one spotlight. The announcer was about to reveal the number one earner.

Fireworks lit up the stage and the song "Stand Up (For The Champions)" by Right Said Fred erupted! The atmosphere was electrifying. Instinctively, I grabbed the hand of the man next to me again and shouted, "What did he do?"

There was only one picture in my mind, me on stage with the fireworks and all the energy and excitement I felt that night.

After the fanfare, the man whose arm I grabbed told me that all the people who received cheques that night had simply worked their business by sharing the product of the company with others. For doing so, the company rewarded them with income accordingly.

I told myself that if they did it, I can do it too. I promised myself that one day, I would be the guy on stage with the fireworks. By the time my wife and I left, I was energized and full of life again. As soon as we arrived home, I got to work by making a list of potential customers and business partners. The following morning, I started making phone calls and invited prospects to my company's hotel business briefing. I was on fire! My Network Marketing career took off with a bang. I earned my first cheque of nearly ₦20,000.00 in my first month of activity. My organization steadily grew, and so did my earnings. Exactly six months later in February 2009, guess who the guy was on stage with the fireworks. Yes, yours truly! I became the top earner in the company.

Network Marketing is like the old movie title, "The Good, the Bad, and the Ugly." Because of what I initially heard about the industry, I had a negative perception about the industry. However, I'm glad that I was open-minded enough to listen to a formal presentation. I discovered that Network Marketing provides an opportunity for financial and time freedom. After joining my first company, I succeeded in a short period. I have been involved with Network Marketing for over ten years, and it has been an enriching experience, especially the last six in my current company.

In December 2013, I stumbled upon a business opportunity I felt was best suited for women, so I encouraged my wife to get involved and assisted her in establishing the business. However, two months later, my perception changed after attending a boot camp training by the company, on behalf of my wife. The trainer had come from Canada, the home country of the company. Over the course of three days, he showed me the vast potential of the company. I took over the business from my wife and immediately set a target to hit the top ranks in the company in twelve months or less. There was only one way I could achieve this: find people who were hungry for success like me, work together, and build a formidable team. And that's precisely what we did. We began to build an organization, one person at a time. We quickly developed a global team of more than 5000 distributors in less than two years.

The journey has been remarkable, and I owe my success to every partner in our team. Five months after I decided to work the business, I earned a monthly income of $10000 and became the fastest person to do so in the history of the company. Two months later, I earned $25000, the fastest (7 months) in the company as well. I was awarded the 2014 Corporate Recognition Award at our Annual Convention held in Toronto, Canada. Over 12 months, I earned more than $100,000.00 and was inducted into the Six Figure Club in my company, and by extension, the industry of Network Marketing. In February 2015, precisely within the 12 months that I predicted, I achieved the third-highest rank in the company and qualified for an all-expenses-paid exotic vacation in Mexico. Six months later, I became the fastest person ever to reach the second-highest rank in the company in 18 months (actually 16 months because my wife had the business for two months). With this new position, I qualified for a higher stake in the global annual revenue of the company, a pre-paid luxury car, and a Royal Caribbean Cruise on the magnificent Majesty of the Seas cruise ship.

I have won multiple awards, including the prestigious President's Cup, which is the highest award in our company. Additionally, I had the distinguished honor of being selected as a member of our company's elite Leadership Council Group (LCG), an advisory body to the management of our company.

Outside our company, I have the privilege of making a remarkable impact on the industry of Network Marketing worldwide. Not only have I been interviewed on Business for Home, but this prominent online Network Marketing resource recognized and selected me as a "Recommended Distributor" out of millions of distributors globally. I have been featured on MLM Nation, The Fearless Networker and most recently, Reignite Network. A few years before joining my company, my wife and I had bought a semi-completed building in Abuja, Nigeria. Earnings from my Network Marketing business assisted us to complete our home. Currently, we live a great lifestyle in Abuja with our three amazing daughters.

All these achievements were possible because Network Marketing provides a level playing field for everyone, regardless of who you are or where you came from. All you need to do is find a good company, have a burning desire for success, learn the required skills, and apply yourself. This business is all about serving people; therefore, your greatest asset is your team. The late Zig Ziglar put it best: "Help enough people get what they want, and you will have all you want." Our team started with eight individuals. Presently, we have more than 6000 partners in over 25 countries including Nigeria, United States of America, Japan, Ghana, United Kingdom, Saudi Arabia, France, South Africa, and Italy, just to name a few.

Our team has produced several top leaders in our company. The future is bright, and the journey continues.

I look forward to serving more people in this noble profession.

Let's go DO IT!

Biography

AbdurRazaq Abdul-Aziz is more than a successful entrepreneur. Every day, he helps people change their destiny by starting their own business. As a top earner and leader in the industry of Network Marketing, he has won several awards and incentives due to his training, coaching, and mentoring of thousands of distributors in more than 40 countries.

His remarkable impact has been recognized by the industry-renowned magazine Business for Home. He has also been featured on MLM Nation and The Fearless Networker, along with some of the best leaders in Direct Sales.

He lives a great lifestyle in Abuja with his wife and their three amazing daughters.

Contact Information

Facebook https://www.facebook.com/abdurrazaq.abdulaziz
LinkedIn https://www.linkedin.com/in/abdurrazaq-abdul-aziz-782b8828/
YouTube
https://www.youtube.com/channel/UCGgJnAWpwbwWKmLwpcxVvDA?view_as=subscriber
Twitter @AbdurRazaq
Instagram https://www.instagram.com/a.abdurrazaq/?hl=en

CHAPTER 6

FEAR AND SELF-DOUBT TO FEELING GOOD IN MY OWN BODY

By Adda Hafborg

"The more we hide our feelings, the more they show. The more we deny our feelings, the more they grow." - Unknown

Here is a gift from me to you. My story can hopefully help someone in the journey from fear and self-doubt to feeling good in their own body and mind. I lived a good, safe life in Iceland with my hubby, my teenage daughter and our three dogs in a beautiful modern house with two cars. Both of us had good jobs.

But, I have always known that I am not an ordinary woman who is satisfied with living life without action and adventure. I didn't want to listen to my inner self for many years, because from the outside, everything looked good and I felt okay. But, something was missing in my life.

Deep down in my heart, I desired more freedom to travel the world, learn about other countries and get to know more people and their cultures. One cold day in November 2011, our friends came over, and they wanted us to work with them on network marketing.

For three years, people all around me had tried to recruit me into this "thing," but I had tried network marketing twice in the past, and I was never going to do it again. The strange thing is that whenever I say to myself "never again," the opposite seems to happen. I am very polite, so I said "yes" when they showed us the presentation, but after that, I said a BIG "NO, THANK YOU." When they were leaving, one of our friends said these golden words to me "Adda, it is ok to change your mind." That night, I could not sleep; my mind was on fire.

"This is good; this is something for me, I can do this." After three days, I called one of our friends and asked, "Can you guys sign me in, please?" After one year of all kinds of struggles and victories, I decided to go all in, and I quit my corporate job. People around me were skeptical and asked, "Are you really going to quit a very good job for this pyramid thing?" I said 'yes' with pride, but deep inside, I was scared. "What if this is not going to work for me?" My fear and self-doubt started to kick in, but with positive self-talk and reading books about personal development, I kept on going. My hubby and I made a contract with each other before quitting my job. If my salary in our network marketing company did not at least double in six months, I would look for another job. I was unstoppable. I did not want to look for another job. I loved the people and the freedom in network marketing.

I had made my decision... My eyes glowed with positive energy. "Let's do this," I said. My mind was full of faith; I believed in myself, the company and my team. The growth started to be unbelievably fantastic. For two and a half years, we had great MOMENTUM, and we started to build businesses in other countries as well.

The internet is a great tool to build businesses worldwide. My team was growing fast. I started to travel the world to support my team, and I loved it. I am so grateful for all the great friendships I have built with fantastic people all over the world because of network marketing. I have friends in Iceland, Holland, Michigan, Minnesota, Denmark, Norway, Sweden, Finland, Spain, Germany, Latvia, Estonia and many more.

Then during the summer of 2015, life happened to me. I had self-doubt to the point that I was making my decisions based on what other people were saying about me behind my back, not what I knew was the truth about myself. I was constantly struggling with confidence and always second-guessing myself. What I've learned from my experiences is that I need to feed my mind with positivity every single day. I need to surround myself with positive people who think of solutions like me.

All of us have good and bad days in our lives. I truly believe that if I let go of other people's opinions and listen to my own positive voice every single day, I can find a positive daily balance. I've found out a few things that help a lot with my self-doubt and confidence; these may help you too:

1. Stop comparing my accomplishments to that of my friends and colleagues. I find that I doubt myself the most when I'm comparing what I'm doing with what other people are doing. When I compare my accomplishments to a colleague, I start feeling inadequate. My colleague's accomplishments are not a litmus test for my success. One key thing to remember when we find ourselves in this mental pattern is that everyone is on his or her own journey. I find that I am most successful in my personal and professional life when I am following what works for me and what makes me feel good, even if it is different from what the people I look up to are doing.

2. Forget about what everyone is thinking about me.
When we care about what everyone else is thinking about us, we inhibit ourselves. We often would rather do nothing and not get judged than do something and risk being criticized. Worrying about what other people think of us will continue to hold us back from doing some great things.

3. Accept that my fears and doubts are within me, and I need to give them room, and not try to escape them.
Whatever thoughts and feelings come up inside of me, I'll be ok with them. Stop resisting what I feel and think. Avoidance is not the answer. Even though fear and doubt are painful, they are not the problem; my reaction to them is. Problems arise when we try to get rid of, hide or control our self-doubt and fear. When we start accepting how we feel and think in any given moment, we start noticing that feelings and thoughts are like the clouds in the sky; they are just passing by.
Whenever I feel the urge not to take action, I remind myself to act on what I truly desire: making meaningful connections and enjoying life to the fullest.

4. I believe pure gratitude from our hearts is a powerful help in every situation in our lives.

In a study by McCraty and colleagues (1998), 45 adults were taught to "cultivate appreciation and other positive emotions." The results of this study showed that there was a mean 23% reduction in the stress hormone cortisol after the intervention period.

Moreover, during the use of the techniques, 80% of the participants exhibited an increased coherence in heart rate variability patterns, indicating reduced stress. In other words, these findings suggest that people with an "attitude of gratitude" experience lower levels of stress.

In another study by Seligman, Steen, and Peterson (2005), participants were given one week to write and then deliver a letter of thanks in person to someone who had been especially kind to them, but who had never been properly thanked.

The gratitude visit involves three basic steps:

First, think of someone who has done something important and wonderful for you, yet who you feel you have not properly thanked.

Next, reflect on the benefits you received from this person, and write a letter, expressing your gratitude for all they have done for you.

Finally, arrange to deliver the letter personally, and spend some time with this person talking about what you wrote.

The results showed that participants who engaged in the letter-writing exercise reported more happiness for one month after the intervention compared to a control group. Expressing gratitude not only helps us to appreciate what we received in life; it also helps us to feel that we've given something back to those who helped us.

5. Read positive books every day.

One of the best ways to boost my confidence is to listen to or read some of my favorite self-development books.

My favorite sources are:
- The Magic Of Thinking Big by David J. Schwartz
- The Greatest Networker In The World by John M. Fogg
- The Seasons Of Life by Jim Rohn
- Think And Grow Rich by Napoleon Hill

I put the audiobooks on my iPhone and listen to them whenever I'm walking, driving or chilling at the beach. I also spend quiet time on my balcony with a book.

6. Write in a gratitude journal at the beginning of each day.

It is so easy to focus on what we don't have rather than what we do have. Giving those feelings energy will only create more situations which I don't like to have in my life.

Instead of focusing on what I am lacking, I like to focus on what I have and what I have accomplished. Feelings of gratitude put us in a positive frame of mind. When we're feeling positive, we're feeling good. And when we're feeling good, good things happen.

7. When my decisions were made back then, I had many negative thoughts, my self-doubt took over, and I often gave up even before I started.

Mel Robbins' tips. "The 5-second rule," has changed my life. When I count 5-4-3-2-1 go... I just do the things I planned to do, and it feels good.

Okay, back to my story. All our five children had started their own lives; my husband and I were in our big house (with our dogs). That Fall of 2015, my hubby and I got divorced, and I moved out. I felt miserable. Few people knew that because I was always smiling, but in my eyes and in my heart, there was no joy. I kept on doing my network marketing business, but it was not easy. In one year, I lost about half of my team members. I was depressed and felt sorry for myself. "Poor, miserable me."

But one day, when the smell of the spring passed through my window, I decided that "Ok, Adda, now is the time for you to find your 'big girl shoes' and stop this negative nonsense." I remembered that somewhere in my notes, I had three great questions from the Dale Carnegie training that I had once used before at a difficult moment in my life.

Here are the three questions. It is very important to write down the answers honestly.

1. What is the worst thing that can happen?
2. What is the possible thing to do about it?
3. What am I going to do about it?

These questions helped me to focus on what I really want in life and to follow my dreams with a positive attitude. In July 2016, I decided to move to Spain. One of my best friends invited me to rent a room in her apartment near Torrevieja and see if I would like to build my own home in Spain one day.

It's been over two years now, and I am building up a fantastic life with my fiancé in a beautiful little town in southern Spain. I can go to Iceland to be with my grandchildren and my family, and they also come to Spain. The world is not so big after all. My network marketing business is growing again, and I am not scared of the future anymore.

It is up to me to accept my fear and self-doubt and put up a positive exception to every situation so that I can be the best version of myself on a daily basis. I believe that what we feed our brain daily is the foundation of our future. Hope you all are having a great day today, just like every other day.

Biography

Adda Hafborg is an Entrepreneur, Mentor, and Influencer. She has built her leaders' organization in 13 different countries. Her strength is her positive long-term vision. She influences others to reach their goals and find balance in life while she leads by example.

Contact Information

Facebook https://www.facebook.com/arny.halfdansdottir#!/arny.halfdansdottir
YouTube https://www.youtube.com/channel/UCeR16SV7vlekxEnbBMplwfw
Instagram https://www.instagram.com/addahafborg/

CHAPTER 7

MY SUCCESS IS ACHIEVED BY CREATING STRONG RELATIONSHIPS

By Andre' Serraile

My parents were both born in Louisiana in the 1930s; this was a time when people had to be strong to survive. My father's mother, my grandmother, was a maid and she made about $40 a month and his father, my grandfather, was a chef. Sadly, things didn't work out, and my grandparents split up. My grandfather moved to New Orleans. He died before I was born. Now my father was being raised by a single parent. Back then there was no welfare, as I understood at that point in history. If a person couldn't find work back then, well, you can guess the alternatives. Living during the Great Depression was tough.

My mother was the oldest of a large family of 14. My grandfather on my mother's side died early too. My grandmother remarried and had two more children; this is the reason for the large family. Now, my father had help being raised by my great uncle, who had started an insurance company in the small town where he lived. My father was thus learning about business from an early age. My great uncle, my grandmother's brother, showed him how to be a man. His son, my father's cousin, became like a brother to him and my father made him my godfather. My father would run a paper route, giving him even more early experience in business. However, that was not enough to help his mother out, so, he quit high school to join the Navy. He served in the Korean War, 1950-1955, working in the searing heat of the boiler room. He sent money home to my grandmother and even paid off the mortgage on the house.

Nevertheless, my father eventually came back home and met my mother. They were married. Sadly, soon after my grandfather passed on.

Therefore, even before I was born, both my actual grandfathers on both sides had died, along with my grandmother on my father's side. As a result, my mother's step-father was the only grandfather I knew, and I had only one grandmother alive, who was on my mother's side. It didn't matter though; he set a great example as a carpenter that worked very hard. He also was in the Army. I believe he served in WWII. I was brought up to believe that no matter what, blood begets blood and family was family. For example, even though my mother had step-brothers, they were her brothers. And I was taught that my mother's step-brothers were my uncles. No exceptions.

Now, my parents moved to Tyler, Texas. My mother was considering becoming a nurse. My father tried to secure work, but he soon attempted to reenlist in the Navy, but they said they don't take men with dependents. So, he walked out that office and into the Air Force office, rejoining the service as an airman. He went to serve in West Germany, before its reunification. He sent for my mother and my brother and I were born there. Now, I was too young to remember anything, so I didn't learn any German. Soon, however, we came back to the US, and while riding in a car back to Louisiana, I had my first birthday. So I guess that is why I love traveling so much. Later, when we were living in California, my sister was born. Fortunately, my parents had a game plan to give us all a better life. My mother wanted to go to college. The plan was set in motion after my father took a tour of duty in Vietnam from 1964-1967. He was an aircraft mechanic that serviced F111 fighter-bombers after flight missions. My mother started college at Grambling State University during this period. My brother, sister, and I stayed at my grandparents. My father would send money to pay for college and some to my grandmother to keep me and my siblings fed.

I was about two years old when my father left, so I couldn't remember what he looked like. When he came home from Vietnam, I was five, and my mother had to reintroduce me to my father, saying, "André, this your Daddy." I just told myself, okay then, this is my father. Now, I say all this to show that a goal can be achieved if you don't make excuses; my parents are a great example, and young children are flexible because they don't know any better. My mother and father made their sacrifices to create a better lifestyle for their family. So, that event shaped my thinking that sacrifices are usually made to achieve a greater goal.

Next, my father received orders for Nellis Air Force Base in Las Vegas, Nevada. At that time, the population of Las Vegas was only 64,405. My mother graduated from college and became a teacher. She secured a contract the Clark County School District and started teaching at a high school. My parents liked Las Vegas, so they said, "This is home." Well, when I started to attend school, my father took me fishing on the weekends. On Sundays, my parents took us to church. He brought me up to love listening to music and watching sports at this early age. By the time I was in the fourth grade, I had been given a violin, and I was taking lessons at school. Well, integration was introduced, so I took a bus to another school. I told my new band director that I was learning violin and he said: "I don't teach violin." I told my father, and he said, "Try out this cornet," and I told my new band director I was going to learn this instrument instead. He said, "Good. I can teach you how to play it."

At this time, I was exploring the desert lots around the town, and I would collect nuts and bolts and other things and put them into jars because I believed they could be useful for something. I had also been a cub scout. Then I heard that people were saying that I would be a businessman because I saw an opportunity in everything. I started playing flag football. The team won second place in the league. When I started junior high school, I tried out for the basketball team and the track team and got cut. I had an interest in tennis, and I was asked to play on the golf team. Well, I shot a 103! However, I was improving on my cornet, and I was excited about my progress. So, this became my real focus. Soon, I was playing and marching in parades.

When I got to high school as a freshman, I played in the marching and concert bands. I joined a band that played for a special choir group the choir director had formed. We performed various styles of music including pop, country, rock, and soul. As a sophomore, I became the lead trumpet player for all the bands. I even made superior marks for city solo ensemble and attended Nevada State solo ensemble. I had also got selected for Clark County Honor Bands and was selected to perform in the Nevada State Honor Band.

My mentor was Mr. Tom Porrello. He was a phenomenal lead trumpet player and played across the country. He played for many entertainers, like jazz drummer icon, Buddy Rich, and the celebrated singer, Frank Sinatra. He gave me some good advice. He suggested not to major in music. Learn something different in college, so, you can get work and not just be a struggling musician. It's feast or famine in that business. If I had developed my talent, I could go back and attend music school later. Well, that's what he suggested, but I learned music on my own from real musicians in Las Vegas. Now, earlier I had an interest in becoming a lawyer or a pilot, or maybe both. But I guess music was my main concern back then. As mentioned, during this time and even while in junior high school, I had developed an interest in business. I had also learned how to type, and I would type term papers and thesis for students and doctoral candidates at Northern Arizona University, where my mother was getting her master's. I would charge 25 cents a page. I made $125 one summer.

I participated actively in high school and had been involved in many organizations, like the National Honor Society, the Senior and Junior Cabinets, and Boy State. College came into the picture, but I was undecided about which one to attend. Well, my mother suggested I also go to Grambling State University and that the band department was good too. My father told me, starting from when I was about 15, that I should be ready to make a decision about what direction to take because at 18 years of age, I would not be living in his house. I would joke around about it, but I knew he was serious. If not college, it would be the military or, if I found a job, he would let me stay for a few months more to save up money for an apartment. Frankly, I was more than ready to leave for college because I was ready to get some background knowledge to start a business. One week after my high school graduation, that summer after, I left for Grambling State University, and I thought it would be nice to learn the campus layout and get a head start taking some courses. So this way I would be able to hit the ground running for the Fall Semester.

Also, during the summer I could attend band camp. I had received a band scholarship. I applied for other scholarships too. These scholarships covered my first two years of my college education. I had also received an Army ROTC scholarship. The Army paid for the last two years of my college education with books included. I had learned a lesson in the process of getting the Army scholarship. I really wanted the pilot scholarship for Air Force ROTC, but the officer in charge told me that it would be a slim chance of getting it. So, I went complaining to the Army when I should have waited to see my financial statement. I came back for the fall and found out that I did receive the pilot scholarship. I was very upset. I had learned a big lesson to be patient and never let anyone put doubts in my mind.

I had two educators that influenced me in leadership skills. One was the band director for the famous GSU Tiger Marching Band, Prof. Conrad Hutchinson Jr. and the head football coach, the legendary Eddie Robinson of the Grambling State University Football Team. Prof. Hutchinson Jr. was a strict disciplinarian in regard to musical performing and following the schedule. He did not like you being late for anything. I had the opportunity to travel to perform at Yankee Stadium in New York City and Tokyo, Japan. Also, I appeared in the famous Coca-Cola commercial.

Unmistakably, meeting Coach Eddie Robinson was an honor and a privilege. Yet the coach was a very humble man, albeit driven for excellence in his coaching role for the GSU Football Team. His greatest accomplishment was to be named, "The Most Winningest Coach in College Football" with 408 wins. All his wins were at Grambling State University. He taught me a lot about leadership skills by example. By the way, his wife, Doris, his son Eddie Jr., daughter, Rose, and his grandchildren had accepted myself and my sister, who also graduated from GSU, as family. I used to visit Coach Eddie at his home regularly.

Ultimately, I was commissioned as a US army officer in the Armor Division. I left for Fort Knox, Kentucky for basic officer training. I had not received my diploma yet. I had to take the necessary courses and sent the credit hours back to Grambling, and they sent my diploma to me while I was training. Through this, I have learned it does matter how you achieve your goal, as long as you accomplish it. After training, I was informed that it was my choice not to accept activity duty, so I decided to enter the civilian world because I wanted to get some work experience that I could someday use in my entrepreneurial endeavors.

To this end, I moved to Los Angeles, California for a job in a silicone factory. I was working in the quality control department. Well, because of an event that occurred at this job, I left to consider other options. However, I didn't quit. It was a leave of absence. During that period, my mother called me and said my father was sick and he requested that I come home to help her. So, I had a meeting with my boss, and he said I could come back, but I told him thanks, but I need to be at home to help my father. I felt that commuting back and forth from Las Vegas, Nevada to help my father would be taxing on me mentally.

Nevertheless, it proved to be a spiritual experience with my father. One day, we had a discussion about Jesus. He told me that without Jesus, you could not enter heaven and I that should continue to attend church. I had always attended as often as I could, but I had made a commitment to make it an important activity in my life. As he always told me, your word is your bond and if you say you are going to commit, follow through. If you can't, tell them that you can't commit, call that person and cancel. I felt so blessed to have a father like mine. He taught me the value of honest work, and he took me fishing, and that taught me about patience. He also told me that he and my mother had achieved a lot, yet he told me not to wait for the inheritance. He challenged me to strive for greater success. During that time, I had worked as a management trainee at a rental car agency for about a year, but it didn't work out. The next year, I worked as a supervisor for the detention center, downtown. I had also attended a casino dealer school and passed, yet I didn't look for work at the casinos. Unfortunately, things didn't work out at the detention center, so I started and completed the process of becoming a substitute teacher. Well, it was that time, during the summer, in July, my father passed away.

As I moved on from the death of my father, that fall, I started work as a substitute teacher. I stayed busy because I was not picky about what grade or subject area I taught. Consequently, during my first high school reunion, I met a fellow band member and told him that I was a substitute teacher. He said that he was a casino dealer. I had mentioned that I had attended dealer school but never started dealing. He admonished me that I could be good at it and I should start working as a casino dealer. Therefore, I started work as a craps dealer and, after I was able to, I also took substitute teaching assignments too. I had considered going back and getting my student teacher credentials and teaching full time. I had been accepted onto a program at Louisiana Tech University in Ruston, LA. I decided to decline because I believed that I would gain some fantastic people skills working in the casino. Years later, I had thought that, if I can get an IT degree, I can get into computer programming and eventually start a computer consulting business. However, after a while, I realized that I was not that committed to such a role. If I had started looking for an IT job the moment I had graduated, I might have transitioned into that field. However, I waited two years to start looking. I was too confident that I could find an IT position. I had received temporary work with shipping software for UPS, but I stopped the training because the hours were hard to keep because of my current job. So, I did have a path to IT, but, for whatever reason, I had reservations about my career direction.

As a result, I had learned from that event, and I had to reconsider my career path. Moreover, I had transferred to a role in a new hotel and casino. After a few years working there, I wanted to look for an opportunity where I could provide a service where there were no limitations, and which created a cash flow. I had looked into the real estate investment business, but I found out that I had to know what I was doing. It may not be important to some, but I knew you could get into trouble quickly if you don't know about the laws concerning real estate. To my surprise, I consulted a realtor about the laws, and I was advised to attend real estate school. I had researched and found out that if I put in the work, I can do well as a realtor and I can become an investor too. Also, I had read that it doesn't take a large capital outlay and brokerages provided office space and other resources and training.

Now, I had set a year to start a real estate school. After this, I had looked at a photo of myself taken at a Super Bowl party. I had noticed that I was overweight. I worked out, but, after research, I had found that going into my 50s, I couldn't eat like I did when I was in my 20s or 30s. I found a new diet and workout, and I went from 183 pounds to 154 pounds. I was so excited that I enjoyed telling others about my weight loss. Now, after my weight loss success, I was even more enthusiastic to start real estate school.

I had visited a couple of brokerages before I started. So I had decided to become a realtor. Therefore, I attended a real estate course online, and I took the real estate exam and failed. I found some resources and studied harder, and I then passed. Later, I was offered the opportunity to become a realtor at Berkshire Hathaway HomeServices Nevada Properties.

In conclusion, I am actively and continually striving to achieve as an entrepreneur. So, I would not say I am just a realtor, but also someone aspiring to provide value to others. I have elevated my sights above the status quo of what most accept. Desire, determination, discipline, and decisiveness are what I strive to maintain. I have learned that I live in a country where anyone can succeed, contrary to what some may say, that living in the United States has limitations. Here is a conversation I had with a military officer from Lebanon. He told me never to take my country for granted. He said that he could not believe that he sees people on the streets of the United States begging for money. He explained that the country he is from uses a caste system. If you were born to a family where your father is a medical doctor, you too could be a doctor. If you were born to a father who was a laborer, you are assigned a position as a laborer. You are not allowed to become a doctor. So, I beg to differ, if anyone here in the US has no chance to become successful. I challenge you to take advantage of the opportunities that are available to learn and develop your abilities and create your wealth, be it monetary, in relationships, or spiritually.

Biography

What makes Andre' Serraile an authority is that he has learned that his success is achieved by creating strong relationships and not striving to create an abundance of wealth. As he applies this principle to build and strengthen his relationships with his clients, he continues to study his craft and invest in improving himself.

Contact Information

Facebook: https://www.facebook.com/andre.serraile
LinkedIn: https://www.linkedin.com/in/andre-serraile-8b25141b/
YouTube: https://www.youtube.com/channel/UCTJkzCXJdB0TeGSJ_I1I5xg
Twitter: https://twitter.com/JazzyDre
Instagram: https://www.instagram.com/andresixpackabs.com_/
Website: https://www.andreserraile.com
Blog: https://andreserraile.wordpress.com/

Chapter 8

REDEFINING MY DEFINITION OF SUCCESS

By Arlene Binoya-Strugar, Psy.D.

Success can be defined in a variety of ways. I define it by the ability to evolve and grow mentally and emotionally, an arduous journey I went through beginning in my early childhood. My journey forced me to reevaluate the way I operate in relationships (specifically attachment), internalizing pain, reimagining my self-worth, and ultimately redefining my definition of success.

My original idea of success caused me to chase a goal that wouldn't make me happy. My idea of success can be attributed to how I was raised and the relationship I had with my parents. Separation of parents can have an emotional and behavioral impact on children. Children can become insecure. Aided with love and encouragement from my parents despite their separation, and from other caregivers, over time, led me to develop a healthy self-image and confidence. I have learned and evolved the way I attach to people in relationships, which has allowed me to embrace a path of healing. It's not a perfect method, and by no means, a "one size fits all" process, but what I am about to share with you has afforded me knowledge and courage to know myself better and become the best version of myself.

Attachment

The foundation for our self-image, how we view and value relationships, and how we cope with stressful situations in our life can be attributed to relationships in our early childhood. Attachment is one of these factors and is the primary function in a relationship.

Psychologist Mary Ainsworth says, "Attachment is a deep and enduring emotional bond that connects one person to another across time and space." Attachment and dependableness are a child's basic needs, so they ask these questions: Are you there for me? Am I worthy of your love and attention? Will you be there for me when I need you? The way these questions are answered develops the child's attachment style, views on relationships, emotional maturity, and decision making, which ultimately formulates a person's definition of success.

Ainsworth lists four attachment styles:
1. The secure attachment style. This attachment style has a positive view of self and positive view of others.
2. The insecure avoidant style has a positive view of self and negative view of others.
3. The insecure ambivalent type has a negative view of self and positive view of others.
4. The fourth attachment style, the disorganized attachment style has a negative view of self and negative view of others.

According to Clinton and Sibcy, "People with secure attachment styles believe that they are worthy of love, trust others and expect them to reciprocate love back to them. On the contrary, people with insecure attachment styles push people away and close themselves off emotionally to others in fear of abandonment. They're controlled by the pain in their lives and often question their self-worth."

Emotional scars are injuries, and even though they're not visible, they still take time to heal. When left unattended, like injuries, they become worse, infected, more painful, damage our lives in ways we may not even be aware of.

According to Clinton and Sibcy, "Healthy communication is a great immunizer. A healthy, open communication allows us to heal from attachment and emotional injuries by talking openly and honestly about our feelings. Internalizing and reflecting on our pain helps us distance the event from emotion and process facts. It allows us to use finite words to describe our failures, allowing us to move on and reframe the meaning of our lingering pain into a process of healing. We can reframe our feelings, or simply just let out and verbally release them. We can process a healthier way of coping with our pain, which leads us to the last process of healing - forgiveness."

Clinton and Sibcy further state "Whether it is forgiving ourselves or someone else, acceptance is the closing of the wound. Like on the body, even though remnants of the injury are still there and leave a mark, we are able to move on with our lives. Healing from attachment and emotional wounds is not about forgetting, it's about accepting, learning and moving on. It allows us to trust again and frees us from pain."

Cultural Identity and Self-Identity

Our culture shapes social norms, values, morals, and traditions which are inseparable from us. People are shaped by their culture and culture is shaped by them. I view my success on how my society preforms collectively. Harmony and interdependence are characteristics I value more. My success is determined by the success of the group to which I belong. It is a group effort, and each member is given the same value and recognition. A very eastern view, yes, but I was able to merge it with a very individualistic idea of success as well.

On the contrary, self-reliance and independence are greatly valued in an individualistic culture. Western cultures prioritize the success of the individual, despite the effort of the group. Both have their pros and cons, but while still heavily having a collective view of success, I am able to incorporate individualistic aspects of success which help me overcome aspects of my leadership style and mindset that could be interpreted as limiting.

Behavioral Change: Brain, Mind, Body

Daniel Amen, a renowned neuropsychiatrist, says "When your brain works right, you work right. When your brain is in trouble, you have troubles in life." Amen has conducted thousands of single-photon emission computed tomography (SPECT) brain scans and has discovered formulas that are harmful and helpful to our brains.

The Amen Clinic has listed many things that can hurt our brain:
- Brain injuries
- Drugs and alcohol

- Obesity
- Sleep apnea
- Smoking/caffeine
- Diabetes
- Hypertension
- Toxins
- Low Vitamin D, thyroid, testosterone, blood sugar
- Poor diets/sugar
- Stress/depression
- Lack of exercise
- Poor decisions
- Unhealthy peer groups
- Not knowing your own brain.

Brain habits that can help heal our brain are:
- Good decisions
- Conscientiousness
- Positive peer groups
- Protecting the brain
- Clean environment
- Physical health/exercise/healthy diet
- Healthy weight
- Eight hours of sleep a night
- New learning
- Killing automatic negative thoughts
- Omega 3s
- Gratitude
- Stress management.

Although I've listed the good and bad things for your brain, it's not that simple. Changing habits and behaviors is hard work, and it's even harder to break habits we aren't even aware of. Many of us associate failures with the lack of willpower, not enough motivation, weakness of character, or personality flaws to make changes in our lives; however, it's not because we don't know the negative effects of our bad habits, but because we don't know how to change.

James and Janice Prochaska constructed six stages to guide us to change our bad habits.
1. Precontemplation - I am not ready; not intending to take action in the next six months
2. Contemplation - I am getting ready; intending to take action in the next six months
3. Preparation - I am ready; ready to take action in the next 30 days
4. Action - I have made the behavior change but for less than six months

5. Maintenance - I am doing the new healthy behavior for more than six months
6. Termination - I am confident with the change, not tempted to relapse

By implanting all of these schools of thoughts, I have been able to change my outlook on life and relationships, heal from old emotional wounds, and reframe my mindset to succeed. I now understand my ways of thinking in groups and as an individual. My leadership style is connected to how I see myself in relation to other members of the group and how I value them. Overall, I am able to see the synergistic relationships between our habits, and how it affects our health (brain, mind, and body) and the quality of our lives.

Biography

From her humble beginnings, Arlene Binoya-Strugar, Psy.D. never quit. As a social scientist, she not only has a deeper understanding of human behavior but also has applied these teachings into her life. She used her personal experiences, educational and cultural background to increase her emotional and social intelligence in leading groups and to understand human aspirations. She is a social scientist with a passion for understanding human pain and experiences to improve human lives and existence.

Contact Information

Facebook: https://www.facebook.com/braingysticsintegrative
LinkedIn: https://www.linkedin.com/in/arlene-strugar-psy-d-a635602/
Website: www.braingystics.com

Chapter 9

WHY A 30-YEAR FINANCE PROFESSIONAL CHOSE NETWORK MARKETING AS HIS VEHICLE TO FINANCIAL FREEDOM

By Bill Ryan

I grew up on a farm and learned that success comes from three important attributes – Entrepreneurship, Focus, and Hard work.

My parents had a massive influence on my life, especially my Dad, who always told me to use my brain rather than my back to make a living. While he loved farming, he encouraged me to study hard, so I didn't end up becoming a farmer.

Farming life is mainly dependent on the weather, so it can be a struggle enduring many tough years of droughts, hailstorms, and floods. Typically, it is only every six or seven years when all the hard work pays off.

As a young boy, I had other ideas and dreamed of pursuing a career as a professional sportsman. I loved playing cricket, tennis, and rugby league. When I was 20, I left home and relocated to Sydney to have a crack at making the grade in rugby league. Although I wasn't the most naturally talented player, I was one of the most driven, competitive, and determined players who loved being part of a winning team.

I enjoyed some success, but the reality was that I wasn't good enough to play at the elite level.

At 23, I decided to retire from rugby league to focus on my banking career. And, when I say focus, I mean REALLY focus. I knew I had some catching up to do as I didn't go to university and my income at the bank was nothing to brag about.

I was engaged to be married and purchased a 2-bedroom apartment with my fiancé, who has now been my wife for more than 27 years. We had plans of starting a family within a few years, so I knew I had to quickly work my way up the levels to support the plans we had made. My wife and I both took on second jobs to reach our goals sooner.

Shortly after we married, I was introduced to the world of personal development. I started listening to cassette tapes, read books, and attended seminars on success and wealth creation. I began to apply what I was learning. This newfound knowledge, combined with an entrepreneurial spirit, focus, and a solid work ethic, was the perfect recipe for success. I discovered a few unique skills I never knew I had. And, there was one skill that stood out above all the others, and that was my natural ability to sell. I set my sights on mastering this skill as I believed this was the secret to creating the financial freedom I had dreamt of.

Then one day, I had an interview for a promotion into the Business Banking department, where a senior manager said to me, "Bill, you have reached a fork in the road of your banking career, and you need to make a decision. If you want to be promoted further, you will need to go to university part-time for 5-6 years to obtain a degree in finance. If you don't get a degree, then, unfortunately, you will be restricted to sales roles within the bank."

I still remember the way he spoke about sales. It was very apparent that this senior manager believed sales was the lesser of the two choices. Around that time, I was learning from sales legends like Zig Ziglar, Brian Tracy, Tom Hopkins, and Anthony Robbins. They all said the highest paid profession in the world was sales. So, I guess there is no surprise about which path I chose.

In the following years, I successfully applied for roles within the bank that had a high sales focus with the potential to earn sales bonuses and commissions. I worked in telemarketing, branch management, and eventually landed a role as a Business Development Manager. It was in this role that I was first exposed to a real sales position where, if you missed your targets, you were out of a job! If you exceeded your target, you were generously rewarded with commissions and bonuses. Since I grew up learning to be entrepreneurial, focussed, and hard-working, this payment structure was exactly what I was looking for and I started to excel.

Zig Ziglar famously quoted, "If you help enough people get what they want, you will get what you want." I went to work helping as many people as I could to get what they wanted, and the reward was significant.

My next big discovery was the Power of Leverage.

- I searched for ways to leverage my mind to start to think even BIGGER.
- I searched for ways to leverage my time to help serve even more people.
- I searched for resources I could leverage to inspire people to take action faster.
- I searched for ways to leverage assets to grow my wealth and the wealth of my clients.

I had never been more excited in my life as I discovered and applied these principles.

With great excitement, I knew I needed to start my own business to earn unlimited commission and further utilize the Power of Leverage.

I designed a business plan, left the bank, and began my mortgage broking business.

My income went through the roof, and by the end of the first year, I was earning more per week than my monthly salary at the bank.

Within three years, I developed a team of fifty-five mortgage brokers and a team of administration staff. Business was booming.

I was now earning more per month than what I earned at the bank annually.

My next discovery was realizing successful people always have more than one income stream. So, I started to invest in real estate, shares, and managed funds. I also invested heavily in my education and personal development.

A famous quote from Benjamin Franklin, "For the best return on your money, pour your purse into your mind."

I poured even more money into my mind by listening to CDs, reading books, and attending seminars in Australia and the USA. Within the next couple of years, I spent well in excess of one hundred thousand dollars learning how to trade stocks and options, and this investment quickly paid off.

My trading success inspired me to teach others how to do trade as well.

Utilizing the Power of Leverage, I developed courses teaching people how to trade U.S. stocks and options and spent the next few years teaching all over Australia and occasionally in New Zealand, right up until the unprecedented market crash in 2008. Not surprisingly, following the market crash, the popularity of these courses literally disappeared overnight.

It was at that time when investors flocked to other asset classes. In Australia, the property market was starting to gain momentum.

There is an old saying, "When one door closes, another one opens." Many people had been negatively impacted by the stock market crash, and it became clear the opportunities were now in real estate.

I had trained myself to look for opportunity in every adversity. I, therefore, completed the required studies to obtain my Real Estate Licence and began selling investment properties to create another income stream in addition to the mortgage broking business.

To further expand, I completed my qualifications in financial planning and founded a financial planning business to help people grow and protect their wealth.

I had developed revenue streams from three different businesses; mortgage broking, real estate, and financial planning. I also developed a passive income through property investment, shares, and options writing.

I was working day and night, and business was booming!

However, there was a downside to all of this; while I was making great money, I was neglecting my health and gained over 30 kilograms in a few short years.

Then one day, I took a long hard look in the mirror. At the age of 45, I was disgusted, disappointed, and shocked at how I had let myself go physically. Like my Dad when he was 45, I had a big stomach, and I no longer looked the fit and healthy man I once was. My energy levels were low, and my sleep patterns were terrible.

The sad thing is that my Dad, passed away at the young age of 55 from a massive heart attack, and I knew if I didn't change direction, I would end up exactly where he headed.

I always felt so ripped-off that my Dad was taken away from me when I was just a boy. I did not want my four beautiful children to lose their father, especially since my health was something I could control.

I searched for ways to lose the 30 kilograms. Unfortunately, I failed one weight-loss program after another. I tried reducing calories, eating healthy, and exercising regularly, but nothing seemed to work for more than just a few weeks. I started to doubt myself for the first time because up until that point, I always believed I could achieve anything I set my mind to.

Was I resigned to a life of obesity? Was I going to die prematurely just like my Dad? What sort of example was I setting for my kids? I was beyond frustrated!

That was until I was introduced to a nutritional system that involved intermittent fasting, nutritional cleansing, and supplementation. Within 75 days, I shed the 30 kilograms and my energy levels returned. For the first time in over a decade, I could sleep through the night. I was jumping out of my skin.

I started to share this exciting nutritional system with others who were frustrated with their health. They also transformed their bodies, and within a few short months, I helped over one hundred people regain their health and wellness.

It was at that time when I was invited to a seminar to learn more about the products. The presenter also had an incredible physical transformation. She shared the exciting business opportunity behind this incredible nutritional system. My ears pricked up when she told the audience how this had also transformed her financial life by earning millions of dollars over the last few years. She explained, to build this business successfully, there were only three things you needed to be:
1. Entrepreneurial
2. Focussed, and
3. Hard-working

My enthusiasm was uncontainable. She continued to explain this business was not a traditional business; this business was called Network Marketing.

This business model provided the ULTIMATE leverage allowing people to leverage their TIME, leverage their INCOME, leverage their MIND, and leverage SOCIAL MEDIA.

Some of the many benefits included:
- Location independent
- Flexible schedule
- No artificial caps on income
- No employees
- Low barrier to entry
- Low Risk / High Reward
- Level playing field for all
- Tax benefits
- Compound effect
- Mentorship

This business offered the opportunity to create yet another income stream. It had a compensation plan that included RESIDUAL income, which could further complement the ACTIVE income I had created with my businesses and the PASSIVE income I created through my investments.

She explained this company was taking advantage of the fastest growing trends around the world, including online shopping, weight-loss, energy and performance systems, and healthy ageing programs.

My wife and I were extremely excited knowing we could build this business together as a couple. We could create a legacy income that could be passed on to our children and our children's children.

We immediately got to work, and within the next three years, we were making a six-figure income part-time and knew we had finally found our vehicle to financial freedom.

Today, when people ask why a 30-year finance professional would want to sell his businesses to pursue Network Marketing, I share my experience with different business models and opportunities and explain why I believe this is the most incredible opportunity available for ordinary people to achieve extraordinary things.

This business can be anything you want it to be without the stress that comes with a traditional business or a job that simply doesn't provide the desired lifestyle.

We are now more excited than we have ever been because we know we are in the right business at exactly the right time.

This is truly the business of the 21st Century.

Biography

Bill Ryan is known to be three things - ENTREPRENEURIAL, FOCUSSED, and HARDWORKING. In his role as a finance professional for more than 30 years, he studied, applied, and taught his SUCCESS principles and lived by Zig Ziglar's famous message "If you help enough people get what they want, you will get what you want." To this end, he has dedicated his life to mastering the art of SALES, providing solutions to people's problems, and helping them achieve the outcomes they seek.

Contact Information:

Facebook: https://www.facebook.com/B1ll.ryan
Instagram: https://www.instagram.com/billr1907/
Website: http://www.billryan.com.au

Chapter 10
THE DANCE LIFE

By Blake Elder

My name is Blake Elder. I was born in Cleburne, Texas, in 1963. I was raised in a family of four by my parents, Bobby and Joyce, and my brother, Wade. We lived on a 110-acre farm just Southeast of Cleburne, Texas, in a little community called San Flats. Growing up, my Dad was always ambitious as he was able to thrive as a superintendent, school teacher, and a coach. With my dad working full time, my mom stayed home with us until I started 1st grade.

My family was very active in the sport of rodeo. My parents competed in many arenas performing various events including Bareback and Bull Riding, Steer Wrestling and Barrel Racing. My Mother even rode Bulls. They were so involved that they also announced, judged, and kept time for competitions. Following my parents lead, my brother and I participated in rodeo as we grew older.

Throughout my childhood, my family moved a couple of times. When I was five years old, my family moved to Blum, Texas, which is where I obtained my grade school education. Later, when I was 10, we moved to a place just west of Weatherford, Texas, called Brock. We stayed in Brock through the rest of my education and my family still lives there today.

I was a member of several clubs, including Future Farmers of America, Beta, Varsity Basketball, and the Rodeo team. After high school, I attended Weatherford Junior college for two years to get my foundation classes out of the way. At the time, I wasn't sure what I wanted to major in; I knew I wanted to do something to help people or in the teaching field, but I also wanted to make money and not struggle. I knew teachers did not have a high income, but with my basics out of the way, unbeknownst to me at the time, I was laying the groundwork and practicing for my future career by going out and dancing.

After graduating with my Associates Degree from Weatherford Jr. college, I transferred to Tarleton State University in Stephenville, Texas. At university, I was able to help start a fraternity, Delta Chi, and work at a local photo shop. In 1987, I graduated from Tarleton with a Bachelor of Science in Physical Education. This degree has allowed me to teach and coach basketball.

Throughout college, I held numerous jobs. My college career began with owning a photography business, where I took wedding portraits, graduation pictures, and Christmas photos. Two of my unique work experiences came later as I got a job at the Campus Corner doing party pictures for all the clubs, Sororities, and Fraternities on campus. It's not often that you get paid to attend campus parties. My second favorite was working at the local movie theatre as a projectionist. That job came with the perk of free movies.

While attending Tarleton, I danced in and won several dance competitions. I had a lot of fun and great partners who helped expand my love for dance. These college dance experiences helped me learn a lot about people and dance.

After graduation, I moved to Fort Worth, Texas, and got a job at a local dance studio. A year of working there, I realized I didn't enjoy working for someone else. I talked to the owners of a local C&W nightclub about renting space to teach lessons.

The owners of the C&W club agreed to let me rent space which led to me opening my own dance studio; therefore, in 1987 I opened my dance studio named "The Blake Elder Dance Center." Opening my own studio allowed me to take my work from part-time to full-time. While building my name and clientele, I juggled working at my dance studio and various clubs such as at West Side Stories, Cheyenne Cattle Company, and the Horseman club.

During that time, I got a call from a friend who taught at The University of Texas at Arlington. I got a job teaching there in 1995 and taught for 15 years. I taught 10 to 12 dance classes with 150 students and coached 4 to 6 basketball classes with 50 to 80 students each week every semester, which was a lot of work for little pay, but I loved it. For any of the students who wanted to learn more than the basic patterns I taught at the University, they would come to my studio for privates or group classes, which was a great marketing tool for my dance business.

In 2010, the Affordable Care Act became law, and it resulted in laying off several part-time teachers from the University, including me. The law put new restrictions on the University, which led to budget cuts. Unfortunately, I only got a 4-day notice.

This lay off led me to get serious about my studio, dance business, and network marketing. I was involved with a network marketing business called Stream Energy as well as several home-based startups. No matter how successful, I learned something from all of them.

I found out in the dance world that I had to focus on budgeting and planning. There are three months out of the year that business drops and revenue decreases. Due to low revenue during those three months, I knew I had to do something besides dance during those times. That's why network marketing looked so attractive to me; I didn't want to have a second job. I wanted to build something in which I was able to do the work once but got paid repeatedly.

Dance Life is the title I chose for my chapter because I have been dancing, competing, and teaching for over 35 years. Therefore, I lived and breathed dance for more than three decades.

With that being said, I've been self-employed for 30 years. I've been blessed to have taught group classes in over 20 Clubs including Cowboys Arlington, and now at Cowboys Red River in Dallas, Texas, I taught 15 years at the University of Texas in Arlington and helped put together and write the rules for the World's Richest Amateur Dance Competition. My friend called me and said Marlboro & Country Club Dance Enterprises wants to run a national dance competition. My friend was the national event coordinator, and he asked me to put together the rules, for the dances, and judges. I agreed, and we hosted dance contests in over 70 clubs the first year, and over 100 clubs the next three years. The National Finals were held at Cowboys in Arlington, Texas and Marlboro paid up to $10,000 for the 1st place in that dance competition.

Being in the dance scene has given me great opportunities to achieve success and help my students achieve success. My Dance Partners and I won 15 to 20 local club competitions in the late '80s, '90s and early 2000s, I have competed on the Country and Western and Swing Circuit for 15+ years. I've placed in many Jack & Jill contests and took 2nd in the showcase. Many of the students I taught ended up taking top honors, and some went on to teach professionally. This was all fun but a lot of hard work to consistently travel; therefore, it was time to stay local and not travel to compete. Instead, I focused on teaching others the joy of dancing and coaching others who want to compete.

I made a significant adjustment in life when I decided to change what I did. I stopped competing and focused on teaching at more clubs and coaching others at my studio.

Through this change in life, it opened so many opportunities for me to grow professionally and personally. I have taught well over 50,000 people to dance and have judged hundreds of dance competitions. I was the event coordinator for the World's Richest Amateur Dance Competition at the time, The Marlboro Country Dance Showdown. For four years, I ran a weekly Jack & Jill contest every Tuesday night at the Cheyenne Cattle Company. I was asked to manage several clubs throughout my career but declined the offer due to wanting to stick to the entertainment side of the business – not the bar side.

Bringing me back to my rodeo days growing up, I have been a member for 17 years and on the Board of Directors for the RCA Rodeo Cowboys Alumni. This association gives college scholarships to kids that perform rodeo in high school and make it to nationals. We do two big fundraising events each spring at Billy Bob's Texas or nearby restaurants. Each winter during the National Finals Rodeo (NFR) we hold an event at the Orleans Hotel and Casino in Las Vegas. In 2019, I was honored to be elected President of the RCA, Rodeo Cowboy Alumni.

Despite being busy and involved in the community, I help take care of my active elderly mother who still lives alone in her home. She requires a helping hand 2 to 3 days a week to do household chores. I've had to learn how to manage time efficiently to keep her prioritized. That being said, it is good to keep in mind the definition of insanity. That insanity is "doing the same thing over and over again and expecting a different result." I found out in life that practice does not make perfect, rather we need to ensure we are performing correct repetition to achieve the desired result.

Dance Life 5
Myth: Practice Makes Perfect

Truth: Correct Repetition Makes Perfect
Repetition reinforces good habits while striving for perfection.
Perfect *Practice Makes Perfect!*
Correct *Repetition Makes Perfect!*
If you do not perform a habit correctly, then you reinforce that bad habit repeatedly. This applies to all facets of life: personal relationships, business relationships, coworkers, and subordinates.

Throughout many years of experience, I have had the opportunity to run a dance studio, teach at clubs, teach at the University, and manage several network marketing companies. During this array of experiences, one idea seems to always hold true about finding clients, customers, or business partners:

Those Who Do, Will
Those Who Don't, Won't

If a person wants something badly enough, then they do what needs to happen to achieve that goal or complete that task. Often, if someone wants something to happen but do not have the means, then they will call in reinforcements by hiring an employee or asking a friend for help. When someone asks a friend to be part of a business with them, there are many pitfalls to be cautious of. First, the friend may not be very helpful at the business due to lack of knowledge or interest in the business. Another pitfall to be cautious of is adequate training. If you hire a friend as an employee, it is imperative to adequately train them and encourage them in the work they are doing. This will help motivate the person and help the person feel they make a difference at the company.

When you bring someone into your business, you will need to take the employee by the hand and show them the processes of the business. This will help the new employee know their duties and responsibilities while gaining small successes. By helping the employee succeed, the employee's confidence increases.

If you get hired for a position at a traditional job, then the company that hired you will put you through training so that you can perform your job duties well. Sales, or network marketing, functions in the same way. Although you're in business for yourself, you are not doing business alone. Throughout the process, you will run into hearing the word "no." Being successful means looking for the "no" to get to the next "YES." To be able to do this, you must separate yourself emotionally from the "no." Do not take the "no" personally but see it as your next step to get to a "yes."

If I stopped dancing because someone said no when I asked or stopped teaching when a student didn't buy a private lesson, then I would not be in business today.

If you don't ask, you will never get what you want.
Therefore, keep getting told "no" until you find a "YES!"

Dance Life 6
Helping People
No Earning Without Learning

To get where you want to go in life and business, you need to surround yourself with people who have qualities you want in yourself. You should surround yourself with people who are hungry for knowledge and growth. For example, if you desire to be a well-managed business owner, then surround yourself with successful business owners who manage their time well.

Successful people will say, "I would rather have 1% of 100 people's efforts than 100% of my own efforts." This saying rings true because if the person giving 100% can't work, then the business doesn't make money. Although, if I have 100 people giving 1 percent of themselves, then the business will still be able to run.

In network marketing, I can get the one percent from people, instead of requiring 100% from myself. This allows the business to go beyond me and run on its own. That's what initially attracted me to network marketing: you do the work once but get paid out repeatedly. Therefore, if you build enough business, network marketing can be sustainable and profitable.

In the dance world, I had two choices when clients master the skill I taught them: look for a new client or teach the current client the value in continuing lessons. If I look for a new client once the client learns a set of patterns or moves, then replacing that client would cost me my time and money. Instead, I would rather remind the student of the value in lessons and explain new patterns and techniques they can learn if they continue lessons.

As long as you keep these three things in mind, success should come:
- Helping them learn. Help your employees learn the responsibilities and duties of their new role, so they do not feel overwhelmed.
- Helping them solve a problem. Some examples are learning new moves, time management, or how to save money.
- Care about the people. Caring about people will allow your employees to be loyal to you and your company.

The Dance Life 7
Recruiting Steps

A. Recruiting
1. You want to look for **quality** not **quantity** when it comes to business partners or associates for your team. Quantity will come as your team grows.
2. Work smarter not harder. Ensure you are working strategically so that you do not work hard unnecessarily.
3. It is easier to work with willing, like-minded, enthusiastic people, rather than try to push, sway, manipulate or sell someone on a business or service. Even if the client may **need** the service, if they do not see the value or have a desire, then it is not worth the energy convincing them.
4. Work with the living, not the dead. If you are working with someone who is unmotivated, then find a new person and watch your business take off.
5. Stop trying to resurrect the dead; if someone on your team is not working on the business or is pulling you down, then let them go and find a new person.
6. You are just one new person away from being a big success. Keep pushing yourself to find that next person to take your business to the next step.

B. NaySayers
1. Be aware of those trying to thwart your dreams, goals, and business. These people want you to fail; therefore, you should be cautious around them or avoid them if possible.
2. If you have friends that are negative towards your business and they are not open-minded to be a positive supporter, then change your friends. You need a healthy support system.
3. If you help enough people get what they want in business or life, then you will likely get what you want out of business and life.
4. Pay yourself first, no matter how much you make. Take 10 to 20% off the top for savings, 10% for taxes, 10% for an emergency fund, then live off the rest. By doing this, you will pay the necessities while saving. By living below your means, you'll hopefully never get into a financial struggle. Then when your business takes off, you can adjust those percentages accordingly.

5. Tying into the previous point, spend less than you make. Don't buy unnecessary items you don't need. Live below your means so that you can invest in your business.

The Dance Life 8
(B I I Y) Believe and Invest in Yourself

1. **(B I Y)** Believe in yourself
2. **(I I Y)** Invest In yourself
   You have to Believe in what you're doing in order to invest in the Process.
3. You have to **Believe** to **Achieve.**
4. If you think you can or you think you can't, then you're right!
5. Read a motivational book daily, even if it's only a few pages. Or, listen to inspirational CD's or audiobooks while driving to and from work or appointments.
   You will be surprised at the results of your improved attitude and inspiration.
6. Below is the: Leg Weights Method System by **Blake Elder Dance.**
   Sometimes people have trouble learning certain patterns, moves, combinations, frame, connection, etc. As a teacher, after showing them a set of patterns or a certain pattern combination several times, I will switch gears and start to show them a different, more advanced pattern or a combination. When that occurs, the student usually doesn't pick up the new move, but that's expected. I don't expect the student to have perfected the move, but after trying the new and very difficult pattern several times, I will switch back to the much easier pattern they were having trouble with before. Now, the original pattern that was once difficult seems easy and familiar because they begin to remember the pattern and feel more successful than when they tried the harder set of moves. It's like wearing leg weights while running or working out; when you take them off, you feel lighter and more energized. This way of teaching can be a great way to help students learn.
7. You must push students to learn. Begin to challenge them and review material to check for understanding. If a goal or task is completed and the student understands, then continue to progress. If not, repeat the difficult task until the student finds success.
8. Always be kind and encouraging with your team, associates, students, and recruits. Do not only instruct by word but lead by example; show them a step by step path to success, and you will find success as well.

The Dance Life 9
Quotes I Like by Blake Elder

1. You will never dance if you don't ask someone to join you, or say "yes" when someone asks you to. Start saying "yes" and taking chances.
2. If you must take action, then you must take it with proper coaching and guidance.

3. Moments of clarity or inspiration with opportunity are few and far between. Therefore, being able to recognize them as an opportunity and act on them can make you a winner. In the end, some money and success may come, or you'll be able to help others achieve their goals and dreams.
4. Remember, only you can change you. If You Choose To.
5. In Dancing, People always come up and ask me after they see me dancing at a high level with one of my Dance Partners and say: WOW! That looks great! I want to Dance Like that. How fast can I learn that? Thinking they can come in and do a few lessons and be great or competing in a month or less, what they fail to realize is how many hours of Practice time it takes to learn the moves or patterns in a specific Dance to certain types of Music, and how many thousands of hours of floor time out Dancing and Perfecting your craft, plus rehearsal time to always try to improve whatever style of Dance you are working on.

They see the Finished Product of Smooth Moves and Musicality, the SHOW, not the Blood, Sweat, and Tears; the CORRECT REPETITION it took to get there and make it look easy, effortless and as close to "PERFECT" as you can. Anyone can learn to Dance if they are willing to put in the time.

Closing

Thank you for reading my chapter, I've devoted my Life and Career to teaching and helping others to achieve their Goals and Dreams, whether in Business or to learn the Beautiful Art and Joy of Dancing. I've stayed committed to my Passion of Dancing, Competing and Teaching Dance through Good and Bad Times and wanted to share these experiences that have truly made me successful, to help and inspire others.

BIOGRAPHY

Blake Elder is driven and defined by his Faith in God. A Higher Power is always at work within him to do better. His happiness comes from helping people, whether it is a student learning to dance, a young couple perfecting their wedding dance, or the success of a business partner.

CONTACT INFORMATION

Facebook: https://www.facebook.com/BlakeElderDance/
LinkedIn: https://www.linkedin.com/in/blake-elder-b2b66122/
Website: http://blakeelderdance.com/

Chapter 11

POSITIVE ENERGY BEHIND CLOSED DOORS

By Calvin Bennett

There I was, sitting in another personal development training session, telling myself, "I can do this, no problem." I hadn't been more excited than I was at that moment. With every training session I attended, I felt more and more motivated, thinking *this is my year*. I would go home and tell my wife, "Honey, you will be proud of what I am about to accomplish!" When I would go out with my peers, I was always the ambitious, positive, ready to do it guy. Then, I would go home and use that positive energy for myself.

I learned a few things growing up. The man of the house must wake up every morning and go to work. Then, come home after work, spend time with the family, go to bed, and do it all over again tomorrow. He doesn't take risks because that could be a risk for the family. This was my subconscious thinking. I had some ideas and ventures I wanted to try just like anyone else. The problem was, I found myself using work, family, and sleep as my life pattern. I would make excuses like, "I can do it tomorrow," or "maybe brainstorm a little today, and act tomorrow because I'm too busy today." I found it very easy to say, "I can" and come up with excuses why I didn't! After 12 years in a profession I felt I would retire in, I was promoted to a role in outside sales. This was a role I looked forward to for many years. Finally, I told myself, "It's my turn!"

I was also part of an awesome network marketing company, and I felt I could do both since I now worked from home. I thought I had time to rule both worlds. There were days I could have made my big break by merely going out and meeting with potential customers. Instead, there I found myself watching hours of television, surfing the web, or playing games on my phone. Once I realized half my day was gone, I would convince myself it was just too late to start any work anyway. Excuse after excuse, until one day, I started thinking from a very negative point of view.

It's a way of thinking that we all get caught up in but need to stay away from. I found that if you have any negativity in your life, it is easy to keep thinking negatively. My family had little to no money while I was growing up. My mom and dad divorced when I was young, and my brother, sister, and I lived with my mom. She did the best she could for us, but a single mom of three does not have all the money in the world. Being a parent, I reflected on my childhood many times. I think mom did an excellent job with what she had, but I want a different life for my kids. There were times I would wonder if that was how life was supposed to be for me. Am I destined to be someone who doesn't get ahead and lives paycheck to paycheck until I retire? Am I supposed to struggle in life? I was losing my positive way of thinking. I used self-pity and negativity concerning my own goals. I would ask myself questions like, "Do I want to take risks? Does a guy like me deserve the rewards? Can this opportunity be something I can succeed at?" When I was not doing well in my current position, I would blame others for things I should have done. The positive energy was fading fast without realizing it.

Mostly, I felt happy with my life. I am a husband to an awesome wife and a very proud dad of two wonderful kids. I have a great family and a set of friends that most people could only dream about. I was always Mr. Positive when I was around them. As far as any they were concerned, I was handling all my business and then some. My attitude around my friends gave them no reason to ever worry about me. Business was the only area where I had problems. I now realize I was slipping into work depression and then one day, it finally happened. I had a breakdown and avoided everyone without understanding why. I didn't want to talk to customers, friends, or family. It wasn't easy to tell my wife this, but I needed to be alone for a while. I locked myself in my room and sat there trying to understand why I felt so bad. That was when I realized that my positive energy was just gone! Why? Where was it? After thinking about it, I realized that I only showed my positivity around others. I guess I felt as if energy for others would translate to energy for myself as well. I never once felt the need to work towards using that positive energy for myself.

Why would this guy need positive energy for himself? I was arrogant about it at first. "Not this guy," I would tell myself. "I am the most positive with the best energy in the room," then I started thinking about my daily activities. "When am I good and when am I bad? When does the negativity hit me the hardest?" I asked myself a few questions and thought hard about the answers. When it comes to business, what makes me produce positive energy? What's the positive element for me? When am I the most negative? Why am I negative at these times? How do I turn the negative days into positive ones? Can I do this on my own or do I need help?

Personally, some of the answers were easy, and others were hard. As far as business was concerned, I had the most positive energy during the personal training sessions. That is what the training is for; it is energy-filled to help you move towards and accomplish your goals. It did it for me, but why? I remember how they would post random quotes on the screen for everyone to read. It always surprised me how so many quotes could be used to motivate an individual, but the trainers knew how to open our eyes. One I remember well is, "Every struggle in life has shaped you into the person you are today. Be thankful for the hard times; they can only make you stronger," was a quote from Keanu Reeves.

I would read things like this and think, "These guys really know how to reach me." That pumped me up so much. Also, when I am just kicking back with my friends and family and talking, laughing, and cutting up, it makes me feel good. I feel like that ambitious go-getter who has the energy to do anything in life.

Once I was alone, I started letting my negative thoughts enter my brain, and would resort to no action, with no results. Why was alone time my negative time? That was a hard question to answer. I felt it was easier to draw on the positive energy around you to create positive energy yourself. So, now, I needed to figure out how to create my own positive energy when alone to match the same positive energy I have in group settings.

I started by analyzing why I wanted to be successful in the first place. It was an easy question to answer. My wife is a smart, strong, successful woman, but she still depends on me to be stronger. I know I need to be that man for her. My kids are so pro-dad, and they wouldn't care if I picked up trash for a living, as long as I can kiss and hug them every day and tell them that I love them. Being the man of the house, those are easy tasks to accomplish. There is a lot more to it like making sure they don't need or want certain things as well. That thought gets me pushing through my day, so I never have to tell my kids I can't afford to take them for ice cream or can't buy them new school clothes this year. I don't want to tell my wife we can't afford to go to dinner for our anniversary. I don't want to tell the family we can't afford to go on vacation for another year. I want to provide for my family. I want the needs and wants to be handled without worrying about how to pay the next bill. How do I make that happen? How do I turn on that light and make the negative days turn into positive days?

Now that I learned to be honest with myself, it was time to be honest with friends, family, and mentors. I had to let them know I needed some help, and that meant opening up and asking them to help me. Me, the guy that is always there for everyone else now needs help of his own. It is hard to admit it, but you will feel much better when you do! I have several friends that call me up on a regular basis to make sure I am having a good day. We might talk business, we might just cut up a little, but that helps me out. When I need a quick motivational quote to remind me that I can do this, I will get on Google Images and type in the word 'motivation.' There are many quotes and memes that pop up specifically for me to find and read. I downloaded several to my phone and pull them up regularly to read. I will print some out to make them constantly visible and write others down to read in my own handwriting. When taking phone calls, I get up and pace the floor. My blood starts flowing good and by the time I am done talking I feel good and motivated. Now, I leave the television off during the day. I don't need to fall into a sitcom marathon of shows I probably watched at least once before. If I need background noise, I use the radio as I can work and listen to it at the same time.

In life, you need to find what stimulates your energy and make it work for you. Be honest with yourself. Lose whatever ego you have built. If you need help, please find someone to open up to and work with, so you too can stay positive and become the successful person you want to be. Let's all be positive and successful together.

BIOGRAPHY

Calvin Bennett's career in sales and marketing has opened his eyes to success and leadership in a whole new light. His passions include spending quality time with his wife and children, and helping others become successful by opening their eyes to what is not always understood.

CONTACT INFORMATION

Facebook: http://facebook.com/calvin.bennett13

Chapter 12

HOW BIG IS A SILVER PLATTER WITH TRAGEDIES?

By Carol Eberle Peterson

While growing up, my mom was a very laid back, patient person. She was extremely kind and loving. I see those traits in me. Mom and I had a close relationship and a relaxed way of reacting to life. For example, situations never seemed to bother my mom or me, and neither of us liked to be rushed. We preferred an analytical problem-solving method before making decisions. My mom would always receive compliments at church on how well her daughters were behaved. I was often shocked at this praise and contemplated those accolades. *Me? Really? Minding my manners?*

In contrast to my close relationship with my mother, my dad and I exhibited a strained relationship. However, he taught me several vital life lessons. One that has deeply resonated with me is, "never call in sick to work unless you absolutely must." He devotedly worked for a drug warehouse, and I don't ever recall him missing a day until he was really sick.

While my peers were glued to media, I never really was able to watch TV as a child much because dad always sat in his rocker and monopolized the TV. He hardly had any friends, so he succumbed to a couch potato lifestyle. So, what else was a child supposed to do? I loved talking on the phone, but we didn't have cell phones back then. As a result of my phone addiction, I got in so much trouble with long-distance phone bills. I also wrote tons of letters to my cousins and a couple of Aunts. I also cherished my time playing outside with neighborhood friends.

Due to my parents' lax rules, I never had a curfew in high school. Strangely enough, I usually came home when my friends 'curfews expired. As life passes and as a person grows up, I suddenly found myself feeling quite stressed. I initially was clueless about what was really happening to me and struggled to pinpoint it. People always asked me how I could seem so calm through things, but I wore a mask at times.

According to the Oxford dictionary, the definition of stress is – "a state of mental or emotional strain or tension resulting from adverse or very demanding circumstances." I then started assessing if stress was impacting me?

In 1996, I thought life was going to end. In January of 1996, my close high school classmate, my romantic crush who shared the same birthday as I, decided to commit suicide. Then in May of 1996, my father passed away, followed by my grandmother in November; and subsequently more Aunts, and Uncles, a couple of older cousins, and a few friends in the course of 18 months. In turn, I attended 13 funerals of mostly relatives. After all of that loss, I fretted about what would happen and who might pass away next. I had to seek solace in my Bible, and that's where I found peace and the faith that life could persist resiliently.

In 1996, I also started working for my "dream" job in aviation. My work/life platter started to fill. I even gained more confidence and freedom since I could travel when and where I wanted to freely.

Then in January 2015, my silver platter became laded with heaviness. My aviation employer sent me a letter by mail saying that they would lay off 1600 people and outsource my job. Accordingly, I worried about what my life would look and feel like after this tumultuous change?

When March of 2015 struck, I sadly got laid off from my aviation job of 19 years. Also, in March, my sisters wanted to sell my mom's house (where she lived for 50 years because my mother developed Alzheimer's. I was overwhelmed and stressed that my silver platter was starting to overflow. I became extremely bitter, angry, and sad. What did I want to do when I grew up again? What career path do I want to assume next? I was asking myself so many questions. My childhood house of 50 years was being sold, and I began pondering if I wanted to remain in Aviation again? Did I want to secure a whole different career? I took about four months off to expedite the unemployment process.

Then in July of 2015, I decided to work with the vendor who had taken over my job but only part-time. As some of you may know, one has to write down all these jobs that they advertise, so I didn't have a clue where I wanted to work or where.

As January of 2016 approached, I had been offered another part-time job in aviation again. So, now I held two part-time jobs since I also liked to pet sit on the side part-time. My sisters and I chose to take care of my mom, so I assist there when I can. Next, I decided to try and pursue getting my own business going with a network marketing company. I brainstormed what my life would resemble with five jobs now and assessed my sanity with all these obligations? How big was my silver platter now? What else could I fit on it?

I slowly tried to work out a routine for all the financial stresses and anything else that life threw at me. While still quite hectic, I noticed that I was getting better gradually.

Then while at work one day in April of 2019, I was devastated when my husband was involved in a severe motorcycle accident. The ER doctor revealed that he would be transported to a Level 1 trauma unit hospital. What? Level 1, oh no, here we go again! More stress! He had to ensure two major surgeries, and he was unable to put weight on his lower body for roughly six to eight weeks.

Oh, my gosh, I wondered, how big is my silver platter now? It was starting to rust and accumulate with stress. Five jobs and now adding a second caregiver job, so six jobs? Now more questions manifested. Do I take a leave from work? Do I just take a couple of weeks off? Do I seek home Health care? When do I sleep? When will bills get paid? UGH!

Have you faced this situation before? What about a friend? What do I do now? Do I quit my JOBS? He was in a rehab facility for about a month or so. When they determined it was discharge time, more questions arose: Where are we going to live? He can't ascend stairs till the middle of June. Thank God for friends to let us live in their living room with no stairs. All I can do is smile, look up, and trust at this point. Take one day at a time, was my mantra to survive at that time.

In my spare time, I like to go to the mountains and listen to the waterfalls. I also like to sit amongst nature to think, hear the birds chirping, and relax in a recliner. It felt like my silver platter was full.

Hopefully, one can find insight through my personal experience and recognize that life can go on amid all the struggles that end up on your silver platter.

Biography

Carol Eberle Peterson is an author and life coach. She has over 24 years of experience in Aviation. As a proud world traveler, she persevered through life despite many struggles and tragedies. She still finds time to help people get through hardships and add passion to traveling amid life's storms.

Contact Information

Facebook: https://www.facebook.com/ceberle310
Instagram: https://www.instagram.com/ceteddybear
Website: https://www.caroleberle.worldventures.biz/

CHAPTER 13

5 STEPS TO BECOMING A GOOD ENTREPRENEUR

By Jasmina Cernilogar Mihajlovic

Have you ever asked someone what he or she thinks about you? How does he see you?

Do you want to know why people treat you like they do?

What if you asked people what they think about your work?

Maybe you are scared to hear the truth, and it seems easier to hide and be invisible.

If you have asked, then you know how it feels and if you haven't you should try.

It's worth the try. I am always surprised and honored because people around me see me like the person I always wanted to be. They see my dreams and my fears. It's nice to hear from people that I live my dreams.

People often tell me, it's so easy for you, you are so confident, you know what you are doing, or you are so determined and always find a way.

Who, me? Are they really talking about me? It's like I don't know that person. I am a little girl who doesn't know how to react and then when no one does anything I try to find a way. I am not confident. I am just determined to succeed; I want to make a better day, a better year and a better world for everybody.

I can share my knowledge and help people. I can share my experience and my common sense to help people from stress so that they don't go through the tough times I did. Maybe, I can help them think differently and open their mind to positive and beautiful things in life and business. It's bigger and stronger than me.

Many times, I want to quit, and I hide from everybody, but it's always just for a short time. I am here to tell what I must tell. I want to change the world.

My mission is to teach common people how to be an entrepreneur and how to organize their administrative activities, books, taxes, money, and finances. I enjoy every moment of it.

From idea to business success is a long journey. Nobody can do it for you. You'll have to do it yourself.

Everything starts with your first few steps. I've done things differently for more than 15 years. I've had to figure out a lot of things through trial and error.

You must learn new things constantly, be focused, determined, and not fear failure. If you fail, try again till you succeed.

If you have an idea, project, or a dream; and want to become an entrepreneur, you have to go through these five steps and learn the fundamentals of entrepreneurship.

1. How to open a company
2. How to do business
3. Costs
4. Business report

5. Marketing

Let's discuss the five steps in more detail.

Step #1: How to open a company

The laws are different depending on your country. You may need to get familiar with the rules in your country, the costs, the benefits, and your applicable taxes.

It's important to understand the taxes you need to pay, your obligations on book-keeping, invoicing, employment, etc.

Understand as much as you can before you start your business. It's important to do your due diligence, understand the laws in your country, and ask as many questions as possible before you even start.

Step #2: How to do business

This step involves taking care of administrative activities, organizing work processes, making sure that you have enough finances, opening a bank account, calculating profit margins, doing your bookkeeping, handling taxes, dealing with clients, suppliers, and employees.

It might be hard to think about all the activities in your business before you even start. You might want to figure things out along the way, but the process will be less painful if you prepare yourself. Preparation will help you stay more focused on your business without losing time and energy figuring out processes while you are on the run.

Step #3: Costs

An entrepreneur needs to know his costs. He should find legal ways to reduce taxes. He should know the difference between costs, expenses, outflows, revenues, and inflows.

Distinguishing between these terms is important. Not knowing these terms can land you in trouble. It's like driving a car blindfolded.

Imagine your business is doing great, you have several orders, you are selling good, but if you are not going to track your expenses and revenues, you will never know about the financial health of your business. So, learn about economics, read stories about other entrepreneurs, imitate them until you are ready to innovate and experiment with new things on your own.

Step #4: Understand business reports

As an entrepreneur, you will need to deal with banks, clients, and suppliers. It's important to understand the language of business and know the rules of the game.

It's important to know the difference between a balance sheet, income statement, cash flow statement, capital gains report, and how you could optimize these for your business.

You may not be an expert in economics, and you need not become one. But you must know at least the basics of running your business.

It's your business, and the responsibility of its success depends entirely on you. A startup is like a newborn baby, and you'll have to nurture it through the delicate initial stages where the business can be vulnerable. You can't learn everything, but you can gain just enough knowledge necessary to understand the fundamentals of business and economics.

You may think that you can do without it. But I suggest that you learn as much as you can before you start. A few mistakes can set you back by several years. I believe knowledge is everything and a person without knowledge is at a significant disadvantage.

Step #5: Marketing

You might have a great product, but what if no one knows about it? Marketing is one of the most important cornerstones of a successful business. All you do, write and say about you and your company is marketing.

You have to find the most appropriate way to inform people about your business. Your customers must like you and your product. My coach Lenja says "You must first tattoo yourself in your client's hearts and then their wallets."

You need to know some things about internet sites and how you can spread the word about your business. You have to learn a lot about social networks and how to use it for your business.

Advertising is the key to success today. How can you use it for your business to attract more clients?

You have to think about your marketing plan, and maybe you don't even know what it is.

It's not enough to just have a business idea, but you should also have a strategy on how to do it. And to do it you need the knowledge that makes you better and more prepared than your competitors.

These are just a few things you should know about entrepreneurship before you start. I have to admit I didn't even know half of it when I began. If I did, my entrepreneurial life would've been much easier, and I would've reached my goals much faster.

My sincere suggestion to all of you is to chase your dreams, don't stop if you come across obstacles because there will always be something that seems difficult to overcome. Everything can be done. Things that seem impossible are not always impossible. Things will come to you if you truly desire them, work on it, and don't let other people discourage you.

Fortune favors the brave. That's the entrepreneur in me talking.

BIOGRAPHY

Jasmina Cernilogar Mihajlovic is an entrepreneur with a heart. She's been running a tax consulting and accounting business for the last 15 years. Her mission is to teach people to become good entrepreneurs. She has her own way of giving knowledge that comes from her experience of helping several entrepreneurs.

CONTACT INFORMATION

LinkedIn: https://www.linkedin.com/in/jasmina-%C4%8Dernilogar-m-a5941552/
Twitter: https://twitter.com/jasminacermih
Instagram: https://www.instagram.com/jasminacernilogarmihajlovic/

Chapter 14

UPLIFT YOUR POTENTIAL

By Christine Powell

I come from a second-generation black Canadian pioneer family. My father learned how to make money brokering junk by being a scrap dealer. Although I admired that he made thousands helping to rid the world of garbage, his money always disappeared through his poor financial management and lack of business skills. My mother stayed at home to raise us for as long as she could, and to provide for our family, she advanced her education and secured a government job. My extended family consisted of single mothers, family members on government assistance, and tradesmen. The saying, "The apple does not fall far from the tree," scared the hell out of me. The odds were against me from birth.

I was the youngest of four girls. We lived in a three-bedroom, one-bathroom house. There were times when our heating bill wasn't paid, and we had to keep the oven open to warm up the house. And, we joked with friends about our phone being disconnected every few months. My parents were horrible with money, and there was never enough income. Now, in their retirement age, my parents are still working as their pension is not enough to live on.

As you see on TV, lottery winners who win big, end up where they started. Generally, impoverished people are not educated in financial literacy and find it hard to change their way of thinking.

Being the youngest, I felt pressured to please my parents, and they had high expectations to live up to. With an eager eye, I watched my older sisters' achievements and wanted to aim higher. My eldest sister was the first to start her own business, where she made and sold novelties at a flea market at a young age. I struggled with not having enough, so at thirteen years of age, I started working to make money. I enrolled in college straight after high school and took the quickest degree I thought earned the highest salary so I could find a job and work till retirement. I graduated with honors but did not end up following my field of study.

I have entrepreneurial blood in my veins. So, I was attracted to several network marketing companies. I signed up to sell health and wellness, as well as beauty and household products. These businesses had a structured plan, but I did not put in the effort to see the financial returns. However, I did enjoy the tax benefits that increased my yearly tax return.

In my early twenties, I met my significant other, who was an American professional athlete. Shortly after, he retired due to injuries. His transition from earning a high salary to finding a second career was difficult, with no college degree. My husband did not know much about managing money and he did not have a retirement plan set up, aside from the basic 401K. As a couple, we began investing in ourselves by taking self-improvement courses. My husband worked in security and I moved up the corporate ladder into management, but we were not truly satisfied with our career choices. Then, we got pregnant.

Everything changes when you know you need to do better to create the best upbringing for a child. When I was seven months pregnant, my husband and I relocated across the country. For a short time, we lived with my parents on little savings and a maternity leave income. Within a few months of our son's birth, my husband started an automotive recycling company, and we moved into our own home.

My maternity leave was ending, and we were faced with a hard decision whether to move back across the country to my previous corporate position or start a new chapter in our life. We could not get ahead solely on my husband's income. I wanted to raise my son, but I had to do something to create a legacy other than helping my husband with his book-keeping. I had two goals; to be a stay at home mom and contribute to our family's financial security.

With these goals and a business idea, I created my SUCCESS plan.

Serve a product or experience in which customers find value
Uplift your potential and value
Connect with experts
Clearly communicate visions and goals
Educate yourself and self-develop
Set up strategies and plans
Set tangible goals - 6 months, one year, two years, etc.

I started my first company with faith, zero money, Kijiji, and Facebook. My father taught me the value of people's junk. In my case, the junk I collected was beautiful, sentimental, and still very valuable. I had little experience in starting a business but taught myself the basics. I obtained a business license and registered a trade name, and off I went. I researched similar businesses around the world and felt confident I had a niche market to provide a service to. With no training in setting up an eCommerce website and no funding for commercial premises, my business developed from a home office.

It was a challenge managing the business with an infant around, but I vowed to be an inspiration to my children. The time was now to make a change. From the day I decided to start my own business, my mindset evolved, and I uplifted my level of success.

When you start a business, the worst thing that could happen is ending up where you started. It is important to remember, 'what doesn't kill you makes you stronger.' One of the things that worked for me was talking about my business to others as if it had been around for years. I believed in the power of thought and manifestation. With the right mindset, you encourage yourself and feel empowered. Create affirmations that you are successful and creative. I performed more job descriptions and roles than before when working for another company. Everything I did was intentional. I was professional in every task, in how I answered calls and replied to emails while having a part-time work schedule around my sons' needs. My brand would be created along the way, but my mission was always to 'share the love.'

It is important to surround yourself with the right people who are positive and encouraging. Ray Gofor said, "There are two types of people who will tell you that you cannot make a difference in this world; those who are afraid to try and those who are afraid you will succeed." I have a great support system in my husband and immediate family.

To attract clients, I put free listings on Facebook, Craigslist, and Kijiji. I purchased software to create a logo and marketing material, and dedicated every spare moment in developing my business.

Our home boutique experience was a great success. I offered an experience to clients like no other boutique. You visited our boutique as a guest and not just a customer. I also did not have the stress of overhead business operations expenses.

Being a housewife, managing my husband's business admin, and stepping up to the demands of my company was physically and mentally exhausting. My first year of business was not profitable but I became an expert. I completed my degree in "create it or fake it until you make it."

As an entrepreneur, the hardest part at first was accepting the sacrifice in time for little to no money. I had to accept I could not do it all. I enlisted an accountant and other like-minded people as business advisors to help with the financial side. I was too busy on the battleground to manage the back end office. Successful people are excited to share their experiences and knowledge, which can help your company's growth.

In my second year of business, I turned a profit and had my second son. While staying home with the children, I continued to build my brand with part-time operational hours and full-time business planning. It was at my five-year mark when I reached six figures in sales and far exceeded my old corporate salary. I reached my goal of being a stay at home mom and contributing to our family finances.

Even with the recession, our company strived. I created new goals and set forth new plans to accommodate the growth of my business. I created new sales targets and built up company-owned inventory. I am very proud to have personally reached seven figures in sales in the comfort of my own home while raising my children.

With the limited space and clientele demands, it was apparent my home boutique and family could not dwell under the same roof. I needed to work smarter and not harder. I needed a commercial location and employees.

It was time to make a location change. We took an unconventional retail location that had the feel of my home boutique. Since the new premises, our business continues to grow yearly, and I continue to learn more about customer service, retail management, and employee training every day.

Now, I am involved in several businesses that allow me to add value to other people's lives. As I plan for my retirement, the importance of several income streams is essential, as most millionaires have more than one stream of income. I've gained knowledge and skills through owning a company, and by getting involved with a network marketing business, it was a great way for me to follow a proven successful business system.

Being an entrepreneur has allowed me to have the confidence to try and go beyond my fears. God gives you the means and creates the opportunity for your success. You must create the mindset and uplift your potential. Success is more than the amount of money in your bank. Success is measured by your quality of life and the memories you make with your loved ones.

Biography

Christine Powell started her career as a business owner with faith, zero funds, and a passion to build a business that supports and celebrates women. It was a difficult concept to take on with selling boutique products out of her home a few days of the week, with a baby in tow. But with ingenuity, smart marketing, and a winning attitude, Christine doubled her business profits every year.

Contact Information

Facebook: https://www.facebook.com/upliftedbychristine
Instagram: https://www.instagram.com/upliftedbychristine/

Chapter 15

POSITIVE THINKING

By Douglas Dendy

I believe Positive Thinking is the key to a successful life. To achieve the goals, you set for yourself in this world; you have to envision them. Once you visualize your goals coming to fruition, the universe will help you make it a reality.

Every situation in life has a positive and negative aspect. It's your job to choose which perspective you see, which one to follow, and which one to live by. Choose to look at the negative, and you will get negative in return; choose to focus on the positive, and you will see positive results.

I am nobody special. Like many families, my siblings and I were taken to church regularly. We were taught to honor and respect authority and to respect our elders. So, that is how I lived my life. I listened to my teachers in school, paid attention, did not skip or disrupt any classes. I suppose you could say I was an average student. I didn't excel at any one subject, and I certainly didn't retain much of the thought-provoking books I read in High School English. I did pass, but just barely.

I was extremely shy and introverted. If I even thought I liked a girl, I could hardly say her name out loud. It was difficult to have a conversation with that young lady as I couldn't even make eye contact with her. I was picked on a lot because I was not a cool kid, certainly not part of the popular clique. I even toted my bible to school every day, which made me different and not well-liked. I was not forced to do that, it was my choice, and so I endured the reaction from others.

Skipping forward a few years, I joined the United States Marine Corps, which was one of the greatest decisions of my life. The corps has my utmost respect because they took this shy introverted kid and transformed me into a hardworking and fun-loving extrovert. They made me into a man! The discipline, respect, and dedication that I received both growing up and as a Marine, helped me build the foundation for my positive thinking today.

I believe the human mind is very powerful. It is capable of extraordinary tasks and ideas when given the right incentives and knowledge to fuel its growth. Yes, the mind has to be developed just like any other muscle in the body. Think about it this way: could you do everything you can do now when you were born? No, you had to learn. You had to be taught either by trial and error or by someone smarter than you. Feed your mind with information and valuable knowledge to enhance your way of thinking. There is useless knowledge that we all know little of, but the more you study thought-provoking ideas and information, the more you'll advance your mental compacity to understand the profound.

What is positive for you may not always be positive for others, but everyone else is not the main concern here. Your obligation is to yourself. Do what is best for you, choose what is best for you. How life affects everyone else should not be the deciding factor for your mental intentions. Your mind is yours alone, and you are the director of its thoughts.

Life is about choices. You make good choices, or you make bad choices, as well as positive and negative decisions. But the requirement is, you have to make a choice. Not everyone will see things in the same light as you, so they may not understand your choices.

I am not saying it will always be easy, nor am I saying it will be obvious. Sometimes the negative option is so blatantly visible, that it's hard to see the positive aspect of a situation. Now, this is where it gets tricky. This is where it will challenge your mental strength and determination to make that positive decision. And, it is all about your perception of the situation. To someone else, it looks negative, so therefore they make negative choices. But if you have the mental prowess in choosing positivity in your decision making, you will find the positive aspect of a particular situation. Sometimes you will have to search, search, and search some more. The negatives in this life are out to divide and conquer your positive potential. Nobody says it will be life-altering. Sometimes you go with the flow like the masses, but it's all about how you mentally perceive the event. When you choose to look at life positively, even when it is an insignificant event, the simple awareness of wanting to think more positively can transform the situation into a positive event in your thought processes.

Continue to collect these positive thoughts in your mind, and it will change the way your brain naturally thinks. Again, it's a choice, and the choice is all yours. No one can make you choose differently unless you allow them. POSITIVE THINKING IS A CHOICE!

Mind over Matter

We have talked about the power of the thinking mind, so now let's think more about the physical mindset. The human brain has more potential than what most people use. Mind over matter is a true inspiration. It is not just a cute catchphrase. There are many examples of how, through the use of the mind, people have accomplished incredible tasks. For example, the movie, 127 Hours, which is so thought-provoking. The character is trapped in a remote canyon with his arm crushed under a large boulder. He was trapped for five days as he contemplated whether to wait for help that may never come or cut off his arm with a pocketknife to save his life. Had it not been for his mental strength to make the decision, endure the agony and pain, and have the general survival knowledge; he would have surely perished. My question to you is, "Could you have done it?" Do you have that strength of mind to make such a drastic decision?

I recently read a story about the historical figure, Alexander the Great, who set out to conquer the world. Would he have been able to conquer the world of his time and build a vast empire if he had mediocre thinking? One of his impressive strategies is when he was fighting head-to-head with his enemy; not making any forward movements, he ordered the middle of his frontlines to retreat. The opposing army thought they were winning the war and followed. Suddenly, Alexander the Great turned about-face and flanked the enemy forces and broke their frontlines, allowing him to conquer the entire opposing army. It is said that his mental capacity for strategy and leadership inspired his troops to follow him with loyalty to the death. I'm not a historian, so I offer no factual data, and this is my perception of what I've read about him.

How about Love? Most people would argue that love comes from the heart. And yes, symbolically I would agree. But love is an emotion. The heart is just a muscle. Without the signals from the brain (aka the subconscious mind), the heart will stop beating. So, love actually comes from the mind. We all know the power of love, which makes us do crazy things. That alone should be an example of how influential and strong the mind can be.

I heard a statistic that the subconscious mind is infinitely more powerful than the conscious mind. It is the foundation of how you think. So, are you stuck with how your mindset evolved as you grew older? Absolutely not! You can retrain your subconscious mind!

Earlier I mentioned 'mind over matter.' I do not relate this to physical mind control. You can't move objects telepathically without some physical force. That's impossible as far as I know. What I am referring to is using the power of the mind to control certain physical responses of the body. Let's take pain for instance. Not saying you can just will it away, but you can make it manageable. How you choose to respond to pain plays a big part in how your body reacts.

For example, as a young boy, my cousin, my dad and I were working on a vehicle engine. When lifting it out the frame for better access, it fell, catching my dad's hand right across the palm between the engine and oil pan. I never saw nor heard him utter a sound, not even grimace. Once we got his hand loose, we found there were no broken bones, and his skin wasn't even scratched as it should have been. If he had reacted differently, I'm sure there would have been a different outcome.

All my life, I tried dieting to lose weight. Nothing worked, but up to that point, I had never mentally committed to the decision to lose weight. So, my subconscious always derailed me. Not until after two knee surgeries and two back surgeries when I realized I needed to change. I made that 'Do or Die' type decision in my mind: "I WAS going to lose weight!" Only then did my body respond and I lost 70+ lbs in under five months. I'm not saying it was just that alone, but that allowed other factors to support and help my body's response.

It's the choices we make in our reactions to life that command life itself to bend to our influences.

I will say that being positive does not prevent you from negative stresses in life; it just guides you to handle them better.

Choosing positivity is never a negative reality.

Summarize

How you feel, how you act/react, how you display your attitude is all about choices. You can choose which parts of your personality to strengthen and which parts to change. I choose to have a great day, so therefore I do. I choose to be happy about being single, so therefore I am. I choose not to get angry when someone does me wrong or says bad things about me, so therefore I don't. And I choose to be positive in my daily thinking, so therefore I will. I have a very upbeat personality. I am positive in my daily intentions. I am now extroverted and enjoy talking to others. I choose to have a blessed life, and God honors that in me!

What do you choose?

Positive or Negative?

It is your choice!

Biography

Douglas Dendy is a retired and disabled Marine, who has seen and felt the negative aspects of life. Doug has traveled to all 50 states in the United States, 18 foreign countries, lived in Japan, and is a Mississippi native who strives to improve his mental strengths every day. He is a truck driver, heavy equipment operator, scuba diver, and shot expert eight times on the range. He once held the record of -325 degrees for 3 minutes in Cryofreeze Therapy. He loves riding his Harley Davidson.

Contact Information

Facebook: https://www.facebook.com/Doelde
Instagram: http://www.instagram.com/gradescraper

Chapter 16

SUCCESS IS BEING ABLE TO LIVE A LIFE OF PRIORITIES NOT OBLIGATIONS

By Dr. Jim Storhok

Success is so many things to so many people. Perhaps it's a fat bank account, a large home with acreage, or a fancy sports car for you. Or, perhaps it's a loving marriage or a large family. For others, success is living a life of service through missionary work, public service, or growing a large, successful company. I feel all of these things are very worthy of being considered "a success." For me, my definition of success was to never "haveta." What I mean by that is that I despise having to do something when it's not in line with my priorities. It's not that I'm not grateful or feel blessed for my Doctoral education in the field of Orthopedic Physical Therapy, but I hate feeling like I "haveta" go into the office and treat patients to earn a living and provide for my family.

When we have a sick child at home, or when my wife is stressed out from being up all night with a crying, fussy infant, I always feel bad about leaving her and my family because I "haveta" provide for the family by going to a traditional 9-to-5 job. Again, to be clear, I'm honored to be able to serve my clientele in our clinic. I gain great satisfaction and take pride in the fact that I'm providing a service that can change a life by providing better physical well-being and a life with better function and less pain. However, as I've always said, I love my family MORE than I love my patients.

My priorities are 1. God, 2. Family, 3. Business, 4. Fitness/Health. My ultimate definition of success, and my reason for getting into network marketing, and more recently, digital marketing, is to be able to help others live lives based upon their priorities, not their obligations. Even more specifically, my passion is to inspire other men to want to lead their families to the best of their abilities. I'm striving to inspire other men to want to create a life from which they don't need a vacation. That's what intrigued me so much about the network marketing profession. Once you put together a sales organization properly, and back it with appropriate systems to create duplication, you can create true wealth, according to Robert Kiyosaki, successful entrepreneur and author. That translates into both time and money.

A problem that I see in society today is that we have two to three categories of men. The first type is the guy who is satisfied with putting in his hours, doing the minimum to get by and live a comfortable existence. He may raise children, but it's more like a couch potato raising the next generation of tater tots. There's lots of entertainment, watching sports and T.V., video games, and not much vision, except for maybe two weeks off for vacation (when he gets paid). Now, I don't think there's anything wrong with a little TV, playing an occasional video game, or relaxing from time to time, but I do wish that more men were striving for excellence, not just exist in the home.

The second category of men I see is comprised of men who are operating at full force, out to prove something and are striving to score big time in corporate America. They are the go-getters, willing to work 80-100 hours per week to earn enough to hit the next status symbol: move into the larger home, purchase the latest sports car and have all the toys so they "look the part." The problem here is that these men may be providing financially for their family, but at what ultimate price? These guys may be present in the home physically, but often they are preoccupied with the next quota to hit or the next deadline to meet, and they aren't emotionally or even mentally available to their wives and children. Again, don't get me wrong; I don't feel that any of these desires of "success" are all that bad in and of themselves, but I don't feel that trading a healthy marriage or a relationship with your kids is worth it.

What I'd like to do is influence a third type of man –the ultimate family man. Am I personally there yet? I don't think so, but I do work tirelessly every single day to move closer to this reality. The type of man that I'd like to influence and inspire lives for his family. He isn't willing to settle for either providing for them financially by working 80-100 hours per week, or just being there physically, but having no motivation or inspiration to provide more than just getting by. My dream is to awaken in men the desire to live lives of priority, not obligation. This would be a life in which they can provide a secure financial future for their family but do so on their own terms. This would be a life in which they can build a business of their own, but do it in a way that the income is systematized.

This is what attracted me to network marketing because I met people in this industry that had those types of results. My first mentors in network marketing were living my definition of success. They have a wonderful faith life, a large home on a very private, exclusive lake, and they have a wonderful marriage as well as relationships with their friends and teammates. They lead by example and take responsibility for failures in their lives. One member of this couple has been free of his engineering job for well over a decade. To me, they were an example for me to follow and they personified my definition of success. There was just one BIG problem...they built their organization in the early 2000's in an offline fashion, and I came into the industry in 2010.

The internet and social media were changing the profession right under our noses, but I was still being taught outdated strategies, which did not help me build the same types of results that they did. The result was I got personal results early in my network marketing journey because I earned the respect of people in my market and they joined me in business. Many of them fell away over time because they weren't willing to "pay the price" and do what it took to build a business in network marketing offline: endless home and hotel meetings, one on ones, out of town seminars and national conventions. The pain of change was greater than the pain of staying the same, so they went back to the lives in which they were comfortable. Their dream wasn't big enough. I struggled for the next six years in my network marketing journey because my dream was big enough, but I was getting more and more frustrated with my lack of results due to outdated strategies and tactics. It wasn't until a cold winter day in 2016 when my business took a major turn for the better, and I found my "missing link."

My wife had run into the grocery store after church on a bright, sunny, and very crisp December Sunday. I pulled out my cell phone and started flipping through my

Facebook newsfeed to pass the time. What I saw next has changed our lives and is the reason we are where we are today in business. I read a post that talked about a stay-at-home mom who built an organization of over 8,300 customers and distributors, earning a multiple six-figure income, and she did so entirely through prospecting and recruiting through Facebook from home! She was a mom to two high energy boys and wanted to be present in her home and available for her children and her husband, and she was tired of running around town doing meetings in coffee shops all the time. Long story short, I clicked on what I found out to be an advertisement for a mentorship company that specializes in teaching network marketers how to transition their business building skill sets from offline strategies and tactics to online strategies and tactics through informational products and mentorship from six, seven and eight-figure earners in the internet marketing space.

    I dove head first into mentorship and haven't picked my head up for the last 16 months! In my mind, THIS was the information I was missing. This was the reason why I was stuck and struggling. I was sold a HOME business, but after working my 9-5, choking down a quick dinner, and kissing my wife and kids goodbye again to do a meeting, I was never present in the home. And if I was in the home, I was mentally and emotionally somewhere else, lost in the business frustrations as well as the financial stresses. What I saw in that Facebook ad was my chance at freedom and success, which was to be debt and financially free and have the time to spend with my wife and kids.

    When I got started online, I didn't even recognize that what I was looking at was an advertisement until I got to a sales page. I was clueless to the fact that there were people out there building sales funnels, which were running largely on autopilot, and were generating leads and sales for people, including network marketers! I was also amazed and a bit angry to learn that the key to building a business that will last long after you're gone is to build a personal brand. I was never taught this! It's not about branding your company and spamming your company logo and latest incentives all over your Facebook wall, in order to "advertise." It is also not about sending copy-and-paste messages to people that you just "friended" in an attempt to get them to ask you what you do, and then prospect them for your business. It is about becoming an expert in the field who demonstrates leadership by having a vision for their lives and their teams, building influence by providing value into the marketplace consistently, building "know, like and trust" with their tribe, and developing a soft heart for people. That means loving them where they are, but at the same time having a thick skin to be able to handle the haters and the naysayers. What I've learned over the last 16 months is that it is possible to prospect and recruit largely on autopilot, leveraging social media platforms and the internet to get your marketing message out to very specific, targeted people in the world. In network marketing, not everyone is your prospect. The "3-foot rule" is garbage. The skill sets to learn, in my opinion, in 21st century network marketing are getting comfortable going live on a Facebook live video, learning copywriting skills to develop a marketing message through Facebook ads, blog posts, and emails that are captivating, influencing, and entertaining, and learning some of the technical skills that it takes to build an online sales funnel. This way, when you are talking to a prospect online using a video chat such as zoom, they are 1. targeted, 2. qualified, and 3. already interested in your product, service, or opportunity. Say goodbye to having to overcome the pyramid objection!

Since beginning to learn these skill sets, from scratch with zero online or technical experience (remember I'm a physical therapist for crying out loud), I have been able to achieve some pretty cool results. I built a Facebook fan page from zero to over 7,000 targeted fans, built an email list of over 1,100 targeted subscribers, and generated five figures of additional revenue into my business within the first six months of learning these skill sets.

I even got my website/blog set up and started generating leads and sales on nearly a daily basis! Now I don't say this to brag, but to inspire those who are reading this chapter to know that you, too, can get these results. It just takes persistence, grit, and a willingness to learn some new skill sets. These skill sets will be valuable to learn because once you master them, you can literally print money. What I mean by that is that you'll know how to generate customers and sales on autopilot with leverage in any niche or business you want in the future! How exciting is that? You just have to get a big enough dream/target, learn some stuff, and get to work! I have recently been asked to become a mentor to incoming students in the same company that I got started mentoring with 16 months ago. How cool is that? The information works and is valuable if it can propel a no-tech physical therapist from no results online to becoming a leader and expert in online network marketing in 16 months!

I'd like to conclude with this thought for you. I hesitated to write about my results because I didn't want to come off as bragging. I know I don't have it all figured out, and I'm nowhere near the results that I'm looking for in my life or my business career. However, the path is clear. I have focus, direction, mentors, and a strategy that flat out works. And the end result will provide my definition of success, which is to be able to live a life of my priorities, not my obligations. I'm never going to "haveta." And, you don't "haveta" either. If you have a target, are willing to learn some skill sets, are willing to mentor and grow into your leadership potential, you too can design your ideal life. That can be the kind of life from which you don't have to take a vacation. That can be the kind of lifestyle that was probably promoted to you when you got started in network marketing or business in general in the first place. It's time to move into 21st-century business, and the internet and social media are already playing a massive role. Are you ready to skill up and lead your family? I hope you are. I'm in your corner, and I'm cheering you on to your victory and your personal definition of success.

Biography

Dr. Jim Storhok is a 21st Century Network Marketer who specializes in coaching and training other network marketers to utilize the internet, especially social media, to create automated leads and sales for their business. His passions include spending both quality and quantity time with his wife and children, improving the professionalism of network marketing through improved processes and systems, and inspiring other men to live lives of priority, not just obligation.

CONTACT INFORMATION

Facebook https://www.facebook.com/DrJimStorhokpage/
LinkedIn https://www.linkedin.com/in/drjimstorhok/
Twitter https://twitter.com/DrStorhok
Instagram https://www.instagram.com/drjimstorhok/
Website http://drjimstorhok.com/

Chapter 17

IN AN INSTANT

By Eric Maddox

Imagine sitting in a hospital, five hours from home, after battling debilitating symptoms for the past two years; symptoms that you hid from everyone, including those closest to you. Your doctor confirms why you've been experiencing these symptoms. He informs you that you have a rare terminal condition with no cure.

How would you react to this news? What would you do next?

As I sit on the edge of the exam table, I watch as my doctor turns towards me with tear-filled eyes. He rolls closer to me on a stool and places his hand on my left knee. He looks at me eye-to-eye and tells me that he is sorry, I have a rare terminal condition. I told him it was okay because I already knew what the results would confirm. He looks at me with confusion as his eyes begin to tear up more and says that I don't seem to understand what he is telling me. He explains that not only is it terminal, but there is no cure and my condition will kill me, that it could have already killed me and that it could kill me any day. I explained to him once again that it was okay, I didn't fear death because we all have an appointed time and as great as a physician as he was, he didn't have the power to change that date.

I told him he'd done me an excellent service by confirming the diagnosis that explained the excruciating pain and unbearable symptoms. I added that my appointed time didn't suddenly change after he confirmed my condition. It was the same as it was, as it is and what it will always be. He was quite shocked by my response, but he thanked me because no patient of his had ever responded that way to such devastating news. I said I had made my peace with death long before meeting him.

I spent the better half of my life as a police officer. I was still employed as a full-time police officer at the time of the diagnosis. As a police officer, you know that any day could be your last. I was well respected and trusted in every jurisdiction I worked, as well as in the court system, various agencies, with fellow officers, and the general public. As a veteran officer, I held a collection of certifications and qualifications. I was told by all who knew me that law enforcement was a perfect fit because of my natural leadership abilities and instinct to protect others. I was the officer who was requested when things got dangerous and chaotic as I was able to perform well and excel in the most treacherous conditions. Throughout my career, my colleagues often said they wanted me to be the officer who responds if anything terrible happened to them or their family. I was the officer that wanted to be the first on the scene to confront the danger and ensure the protection and safety of everyone involved. I was also frequently asked to train new officers.

When faced with the news of having a terminal condition, it forced me to reflect on life. I was always considered a freak of nature from a very young age. People were often shocked by my physical abilities. I would use my hands to lift my body up from my school desk and hold it out to the side and then swop sides before lowering myself back in the chair. It was all upper body strength, and it became a popular request in school. In my early teens, I started lifting weights and acquired a love for boxing. I was always the dominant male in life even from a young age.

As a freshman in high school, I weighed 160-165 lbs. I could bench press 395 pounds. As I got older, my strength and bench press weight continued to increase even when I stopped working out. I had a naturally large muscular physique. I was also accused of steroid use even years after I stopped lifting weights. I was told that I got my strength from my grandfather. When people first came to my house, they would usually ask how much I could still bench press and then prove it.

Before I started writing this chapter, I only allowed a select few to know what I was capable of. Once I destroyed my left shoulder so badly that I nearly had a complete shoulder replacement. I grabbed 550 lbs and pressed it six times before racking it. I felt my shoulder tear on the first press, but I was too stubborn to stop until all six repetitions were completed. I didn't tell anyone I destroyed my shoulder until six weeks later. Finally, I had surgery to repair it, and they discovered my rotor cuff and labrum were torn. I had bone spurs, and there was a 90% reduction in my bone lining, so my shoulder joint had to be repositioned. Even this didn't stop me from bench pressing mass amounts of weight. I remember people always asking me how I was able to lift such extreme weights. My response was the same every time. I never told myself that I couldn't. I used to lay down and visualize myself pressing the weight in my mind before I even grabbed the barbell. I always excelled at everything I chose to do in life, and I credit that to my mindset.

Because of this mindset, I won several awards during my teens, law enforcement training, and career. I was battalion commander over the entire JROTC in my senior high school year. I received one award for being a positive role model and leader at the law enforcement academy, which was due to my attitude and conviction. In the state where I live, it's required to complete basic training at the law enforcement complex. Several recruits complained about the military style training with getting up early and meeting physical fitness requirements. I told them if they didn't like it then maybe they should go back home and not be in the police. When they asked how I stayed so positive, I explained that I didn't think about whether I wanted to be there or not. I didn't give myself that option. I knew that to be in the police; I had to graduate from the law enforcement academy. It was merely a task I had to accomplish.

I also reflected on all the events that led up to the day I was officially diagnosed. As mentioned earlier, I hid my condition from everyone for two years. I was hiding it well until one cold morning, I got up for work at 4 am and collapsed to the floor which woke up my wife. She jumped from the bed, ran over to me and started crying. She asked what was wrong as she watched me struggle to get up. I didn't know the answer. I just knew it was getting progressively worse and becoming harder to hide. She watched in tears as I strained to get ready for work. Routine tasks like getting in and out of the shower, getting dressed and putting on my duty belt were now difficult to perform. She begged me not to go to work, but I told her I didn't have a choice. I was the only officer on duty that day who was covering the day shift. She cried as she watched the sweat pouring from my head while I fought the excruciating pain to get into my patrol car. The only two ways you can tell I'm fighting pain is when my head sweats and my blood pressure goes up. Obviously, one is easier to hide than the other.

For those of you who don't know, when you marry a nurse, there is no arguing especially when they discover you have serious health issues. The lengthy process of going from specialist to specialist began immediately. I was tested for everything imaginable. I gave what seemed like enough blood to sink a battleship. I even had a biopsy where they cut a three-inch segment of muscle from my upper thigh. All of these tests finally led me five hours from home, in another state, to be told I had a terminal condition.

My doctors recommended I get my affairs in order before the condition gets rapidly worse. Too stubborn to give up on life, I began the process of doing everything I could to protect my family and make things easier for them when my time came. I planned my funeral, completed my Will, my Living Will, and the Power Of Attorney papers. I've experienced a lot in my life especially during my career. I've had several people try to kill me and one late night as a young officer; I was attacked by a group that tried to kill me. I never told that story before, but I was asked once by the officer who responded to my distress call, how I survived that night. I told him that my desire to live was greater than their desire to take my life. Through all I've experienced, the most surreal was picking out my own casket.

I was forced to retire from my career due to the diagnosis. I was never angry at God or questioned "Why Me," but I did wonder why I would be taken from a career I excelled at while I was still relatively young. I got my answer one year after I was diagnosed when I got involved in network marketing.

I achieved success at a swift pace, which led me to a Regional Training event where I was asked to speak on stage. Once I began to tell my story, I could have heard a pin drop in that large crowded room. After my talk, several people approached me throughout the day to thank me for telling my story. It was a huge inspiration to them. I've had many people approach me at national events telling me how I inspire them to make rank advancements. I learned that by allowing myself to be vulnerable, I was able to help others. God didn't end my career. He simply changed my path so I could help people on a global scale instead of only in my community. The way I see it, as long as I'm still alive, I haven't fulfilled my purpose yet. I plan to continue helping others in any and every way I can. I would love to become a life coach and inspirational speaker, and share how my mindset helped me make it this far in life. Remember, you control how you view every situation in life. You can make it an opportunity or a problem. I prefer opportunities.

BIOGRAPHY

Eric Maddox is a retired police officer who uses his traumatic life experiences to give readers a glimpse into his warrior mindset. He explains how this mindset helped him survive life-threatening situations and achieve the unthinkable.

CONTACT INFORMATION

Facebook: https://www.facebook.com/profile.php?id=100012139116971
Instagram: http://www.instagram.com/thebeardedtraveler77/

Chapter 18

RESCUED INTO MANHOOD

By Frank Mbanusi

One decade ago, I sat in a jail cell. Looking up at the rusty underside of the top bunk, I could only focus on the fear. I was filled with so much anger towards myself. I was no longer worthy of belonging. "How in the world did I get here?" The success I claimed fatally crashed back down to earth under that cell ceiling. I was now a nobody with my future hopes gone. The worst part? I had done what I had vowed never to do, become like my father. I walked in his very footsteps; creating the same results.

I am opening up about my story with a new hope that sharing a part of me will speak to any man out there who thinks, "I'm the only one with my problem," or "there's no hope for me," or "I have failed as a man, a father or a husband." Whatever your situation, you're not the only one. How I got to jail, that doesn't matter. But what I learned after hitting rock bottom, makes me the man I am today.

My Story

I am the oldest son in a single-parent family of five kids. Let that sink in. Five kids. One mom. If you asked her today, she'd tell you, "I couldn't have done it without my Heavenly Father." My mom gifted me with a profoundly spiritual, Christian faith shaping my path to purpose.

I have only scattered memories of my father. On one end of the spectrum, I remember the surprise McDonald's kids' meals he'd pick up for me on his way home from work. On the other, I remember angry yelling and pictures shattering. I would cower and cry. Somehow, those broken family pictures would always make their way back up on the walls, taped up and in new frames purchased by my mother. The very last time I saw my father I watched him be dragged away by officers. That 7-year-old vowed, "I will not be that man."

From that age, my experience of negative masculinity haunted me. I grew up angry at my father for the things I experienced and blamed him for his absence in my life. Every day, led by my mother, we would pray for him; praying he would change his ways and come back home to be the father we needed. Needless to say, there were other plans God had for our family; great plans, even through tragedy.

As best I can tell, my middle-school years were pretty much the typical middle schooler's experience. I didn't really have an identity. I wasn't popular, and kids made fun of me at times. I tried to fit in where I could, choosing to be unnoticed above excluded. And yet, rejection reared its ugly head over and over. At the age of 12, I didn't have the skills to manage pain, and the world of pornography easily sucked me in; addiction proved to be a stronghold for many more years to come causing a ripple effect into many other parts of my life.

Surviving middle school, I found status in high school sports; most notably track & field. Bent over, with my feet pushed hard back into the blocks was the only place I felt like I meant something. I was good, and everybody knew it. I loved being recognized for my accomplishments in the ink of school announcements and newspaper publications. I desperately performed for that love and attention.

I carried the same desperation into relationships. Without a foundation or guidance, I went in and out of unhealthy hookups. I felt the need to please everyone else just to get a dose of being wanted and liked. My self-worth was dirt-low. Without a father in my life, the best blueprint to manhood came from TV shows like Family Matters, Full House, and MTV. I did not realize at the time how much that had molded my thoughts, feelings, and actions for the next phase of my life.

False Start

When 9/11 rocked the world, I found my next purpose. Being from Jersey, the destruction of the Twin Towers hit way too close to home. I enlisted in the United States Marine Corps. Talk about growing up fast. At the age of 19, this was exactly what I needed. I thought.

Fast forward a few years. After a successful enlistment full of accolades and recognition from family and friends, it led to a rare opportunity to jump into the corporate world to start a dream career. I felt like I had it all. At least so I thought. By the age of 25, I was at the top of the achievement table by most standards with an over six-figure income, a home mortgage with a couple of years already paid off, and traveling the country consulting in high-powered corporate environments.

It was all a facade. Drugs, alcohol, and sex engulfed me. I lived a life I had idealized, but I had not attained real meaning. It was a false, self-created interpretation of reality. I took it to another level. I crossed the line and made choices that affected others greatly. And it put me in jail.

Dysfunction

We, as men, don't always share our struggles—the addictions, the guilt, the perceived shame. American pop culture tells men, "be tough" but pairs this message with images of dysfunctional behaviors. To rise above takes a willingness to seek out the resources required to foster accountability. Most men are in this same boat. I had a first-class seat on that trip.

This cycle of dysfunctional behavior comes to work on autopilot, no thinking involved. We just do, do, do. A mentor told me once, at a deeper level, we as men are looking to fill a void in us, "Our internals are never at peace." We are always attempting to fill our void by any means possible. The words of philosopher Blaise Pascal hit home for me: "What else does this craving, and this helplessness, proclaim but that there was once in man a true happiness, of which all that now remains is the empty print and trace? This he tries in vain to fill with everything around him, seeking solace in things that are not there, the help he cannot find in those that are, though none can help, since this infinite abyss can be filled only with an infinite and immutable object; in other words, by God himself."

I tried to fill a void. I disconnected from those who loved and supported me. I found pleasure in a materialistic lifestyle. I engulfed myself in pleasures, destroying my sense of reality.

Now here I was, sitting in a jail cell reflecting on my actions and their consequences. As quoted from another great and late mentor, "Results... often harsh, always fair."

My journey to being a better man began on that lower bunk ten years ago. I challenge you to take this journey. It has been a fulfilling one for me and has pushed me further beyond what I thought success would look like for me.

Manhood now means taking personal responsibility for my actions, thoughts, and feelings. Manhood is the wisdom to identify the dysfunction in my life and taking the courageous steps to shift to a higher purpose. Manhood means choosing to be a leader in every challenge life brings my way. This is beyond success.

Some of the struggles I've mentioned may resonate with you. If so, know there are others who have been there. Remember, it does not define you!

Rescue

While the journey started in that cell, it took me years to break the destructive thought patterns in my life. I have not "arrived" by any means. As human beings, we are always growing and learning. It required taking an in-depth look at myself and participating in my own rescue. I took responsibility for my poor choices in life, learned empathy, truly knowing and understanding who I am, and walking in that truth with the power to make the right life choices moving forward.

Today, I am a more successful version of the same 25-year-old businessman, with more figures in my income and houses to my name. The outside achievement does not bolster my manhood now. I operate from a flipped mindset, changing me on the inside—making me a better man—leading to higher levels of success and satisfaction then I knew existed.

In 2013, smack in the middle of this journey, I had a life-altering insight. After years of looking at myself in the mirror, day in and day out, God showed me what I am meant to do in this lifetime. My purpose became simple: to help create better men in this world. This journey supersedes success. It's beyond money and toys. To me, becoming the best man I can be leads to true fulfillment. This motivates me. If living my values can influence at least one person become a better version of themselves too, the pain I went through will all be worth it.

Tools

I'm here to tell you poor choices you have made do not define you. True hope exists for your future, beyond the mess. I want to offer you some tools I used along the way:

- Awareness, Awareness, Awareness – I've found it is easy to slip and fall. Awareness anticipates the signals ahead of the curve. Stop. Breathe. Take note of what you are thinking from day-to-day and in your interactions with other people and situations. Experiencing the abundance of negative thoughts during the hard times, gave me the aha, "to think is to create." Get that junk out of your head! What you think of the most will only expand, so take inventory of what you are thinking!
- Open, Responsible Communication – Seek out accountability. I am a believer that men should hold other men accountable. Build a support team

around you of men who will lift you up, but are not afraid to call you out on your stuff. To be successful, you must be accountable!
- Prayer – I am a man of faith, and I believe in the power of prayer. Through my journey, prayer has been a significant part of my success. Prayer was and still is an integral part of my success.

Practice

Purpose is the reason for which something exists or is done, made or used. Finding my purpose brought significance to manhood for me.

What is life all about to you?

Why does it matter?

How do you find your purpose?

From my experience, you find it through a great deal of introspection. It starts with awareness, then proceeds into a breakthrough and choice shift.

Here's an exercise that I will leave with you in helping to find your purpose:
1. Take out a blank sheet of paper
2. Write at the top, "What is my true purpose in life?"
3. Write an answer (any answer) that pops into your head. No judgment. The words do not even have to be a complete sentence.
4. Repeat Step 3 until you write the answer that makes you cry. This is your purpose.

This may take you 30 minutes. Or it may take you three months. Or it may take ten years. When you get there, you will know. What purpose will you give your life to moving forward? Grab a hold of that and make it happen. Participate in your own rescue!

Biography

Frank Mbanusi grew up in a household with four younger siblings, raised by a single mother from the age of seven. Through hardships and tragedy, he stepped into manhood very quickly. On this journey, read how he finds purpose beyond success; and walks the path to becoming a better man.

Contact Information

Email: frankmbanusi@gmail.com

Chapter 19

LIVING AN INSPIRED, PURPOSEFUL, AND AMAZING LIFE

By Jeremy Hoort

My family was as far from normal as it gets, with my two Fathers both working as drug dealers until I was 13 years old, but still, I grew up surrounded by love, faith, and discipline.

After I turned 13, my biological Father went to Federal Prison, while my other Father chose to follow a different path, one that I consider being much harder. He gave it all up, the drugs and the crime, and instead focused his efforts on his faith. For a while, we lived relatively happily, albeit modestly, until the divorce of my father and mother.

After the divorce, my mother took care of three children all by herself. Neither of my Fathers supported us financially. And so, from a young age, I started to learn about the corruption of people, governments, police, and I began to see what money does to people and society. It's destructive.

My life was like something most people only see in the movies – we would hide silver and gold bars in our laundry baskets and wait until we could launder it through a business. We were constantly playing cat and mouse with the police and the federal government.

In a way though, I was lucky, because despite the illegal activity, my siblings and I were always loved. We were always disciplined and taught right from wrong. And I was also lucky that my fathers weren't tied to any organized crime, so they were able to walk away.

My biological Father served five years in a federal prison for possession of 200 pounds of marijuana. He was set up by his own friends in a federal sting operation. While he could have shortened his sentence, he served full time, because he refused to snitch on others, and for this, I was proud of him. He did the crime, without tattling on others to get a lighter sentence.

My Step-Father raised me while my biological Father was in prison, and I consider him just as much a Father as my real Dad. He made the hard decision to give up the illegal life for good and left the drug trade after finding his faith in the bible.

I plan on writing a detailed book about my Fathers and my childhood, where I'll divulge all the dirty details, but here I wanted you to see that our lives are about choices and our thoughts. I chose to be the direct opposite of my Fathers when it came to my schooling, career life and my time in the military. I never allowed myself a failure or even sub-par performance, ever. I could have followed in my Father's footsteps and lived a life of crime, chasing cash, but instead, I decided to focus on High School and afterward, on my military career.

I learned that regardless of our history, we choose who we will become. Living in the past, and holding grudges will lead to becoming consumed by negative thoughts.

Everyone has one main choice: to be a victim of their circumstances or to take control and be a lion of their own lives. I chose to be a lion and so far, I've reached my goals, and been successful in most aspects of my life.

My life after childhood and high school was one of many tough choices, but by age 18, I was out on my own, and I chose to join the United States Air Force. I only signed a four-year contract, but I made the mistake of not having a lawyer look over that contract, which made be obligated to serve for eight years, if the government needed me. It was a lesson learned that you must be careful what you sign.

I completed four successful years working on the fighter aircraft of an E&E specialist but went to complete a total of 10 years' service, working with and around fighter jets like the F-111 Aardvark fighter-bomber (whispering death), F-16 Fighting Falcon, and F-15 eagle. I also completed five years of extra duty in the Air Force Base Honor Guard.

With commanding officers talking highly of me, and several awards and medals under my belt, I could have returned to the military as a commissioned officer, and that was my initial plan. However, my first son was born just after 9/11, and then my plans changed. Instead of returning to the military, I finished my business degree at the University of South Florida in 2015.

I can honestly say that I think all of my current success is due to me being the best father and husband I could be for my family. I now have three beautiful boys: Bryce, Grayson, and Vander who are all the light of my life. I also have my wife, Meagan, who is the rock of the family and is the most beautiful and intelligent woman I have ever met. I'm so happy to have her in my life – it looks like my prayers were answered, because I now have my lioness, and I love her more every day.

I think it's important to create our world in our own minds first, and then it's up to us to decide what's important to us as individuals, and what we're going to do in this life. I think we create our futures long before they happen through what we think and how we act, so keep those negative and limiting thoughts away from your creativity.

Now that I have achieved my success, and created my perfect family, I now try to make a difference on a local level. I started Dash Health Consulting so that I could make a difference by helping one family or business at a time.

We all only have one life to live, a life that's ended with a (-) dash. None of us know when that dash is going to come, which is why it's so important to live every important moment.

I was inspired by many family members, mentors, and my faith to create a lasting legacy and make the world a better place so that by the time my dash comes, I've done my bit to help others achieve success and happiness. I want to help the whole person, from health to wealth while allowing individuals to leave a legacy that will last for many future generations. Legacy in this sense isn't just about wealth, in fact, wealth has little to do with it. My legacy will be the life I lead, Legacy may seem like wealth, but that isn't the case at all. My personal legacy will be the life I lead, my family, and the book I leave for my family and sons along with my charity, CHILD Charity USA (www.childcharityusa.com).

CHILD Charity USA stands for:
Children
Health

Investment

Learning

Development

The goal is to educate children about finance and health. We work with schools for a better tomorrow and help deliver education that will help our children to be successful. Denzel Washington once said: "Don't aspire to make a living, aspire to make a difference" and that's what CHILD Charity USA is all about.

Wealth isn't guaranteed, not for me, not for anyone, but I believe that I've already achieved success and that this is just the tip of the iceberg.

I've always been good at numbers, and so I tried to base my corporate career around them, but I struggled to find a career I agreed with. Every role I tried seemed to be based around selling clients services or products that weren't always right for them.

I became fed up with businesses only promoting the products they were able to sell, rather than genuinely helping clients with a dilemma or pointing them in the right direction. So I created Dash Health Consulting so that I could help people succeed, from Health to Wealth. It's a unique business, the first of its kind.

We focus on what the client needs, bringing businesses together to work for and with clients, rather than just promoting one type of product or service. I hope that Dash Health Consulting will disrupt the market and help millions of people succeed. I created a company that has a huge amount of products and services at its fingertips, for those that want to build their own business.

As well as putting entrepreneurs and businesses in touch with the right services, we're also delivering business and finance education through our website. This is something I haven't seen any other financial advisor, company or business do! I am so excited to share my one-of-a-kind company with the nation.

I'm writing my book to inspire others to focus not on instant rewards, but on the journey towards success. Everywhere you look, you'll see people trying to sell 'get rich quick' schemes that don't necessarily work, but I expect more. I believe that by helping each other as well as ourselves, we'll solve a lot of nationwide issues, and we can all benefit and find our success together. If all you want is a way to make quick money, so you can live the life of a millionaire, I suggest buying a lotto ticket and a prayer.

We need to make new services and products that don't just help one person or business. There's some amazing technology out there that can be used to make this world a better place; it's only our own creativity that's limiting us.

Is success based on a paper currency and the ability to hoard as much as we can as quickly as we can, not caring what it might do to others? Sure, pursuing money might work short term but what kind of damage will we be cleaning up? I believe we'll find ourselves back where we were in 2008, with more bubbles in the economy.

My book and my business aren't about get-rich-quick plans; they're about the truth and a different way of looking at things. I've built a business that offers a number of solutions to a huge number of people.

The business world today is a house of cards, and if you don't just want to take my word for it, there are many other experts much smarter than myself warning us that it's unstable. The trouble is that no one wants to admit it, because admitting it would make the economy even more delicate. But it is bad, and we need to admit this to ourselves so that we can move on to a more controlled economy.

I was once good at poker. I could have pursued it further, but I chose to help others first. I might play poker again one day, but I fully understand that it's gambling. What I don't understand is how people can think the stock market is any different. Rather than putting money into gambling, I believe people should be looking to create products that protect the economy and earn money as well. There are so many different ways to do this, so many different ways to protect people first, and genuinely help them, rather than just selling regardless.

We all have greatness inside us, and we can all excel in life, we just have to access our talents, develop them, and put them to use. Your job doesn't define who you are, it's just a means to an end, a tool.

I challenge you to live an inspired, purposeful, and amazing life. Your life is a ship that only you can captain. Remember not to view failures as a bad thing, think of them as clues. Each failure is a clue that you're heading in the wrong direction, and in its own way, it will steer you in the right direction.

Listen to the strangest secret by Earl Nightingale.

"Do not go where the path may lead, go instead where there is no path and leave a trail." - Ralph Waldo Emerson

Biography

With over 20 years of experience in customer service, ten years of USAF Honor Guard structure, Jeremy Hoort brings amazing talent, taking care of the client from health to wealth to a whole new level. The one of a kind platform of experts in one location at https://www.dashhealthconsulting.com/ is truly unique and inspiring. It changes lives forever while giving back through their charity CHILDcharityUSA.com.

Contact Information

Facebook https://www.facebook.com/jeremy.hoort
LinkedIn https://www.linkedin.com/in/live4life/
Twitter https://twitter.com/ReachDashDCH
YouTube https://www.youtube.com/channel/UCM9A0b9JTL41tTEWYD7OGVQ
Instagram https://www.instagram.com/reachdashdhc/
Website https://www.dashhealthconsulting.com/
Blog https://jeremyhoort.wixsite.com/website
Pinterest https://www.pinterest.com/craighoort/
Charity https://www.childcharityusa.com

Chapter 20

TRIUMPH THROUGH A BUMPY ROAD

By James Mbele

Have you ever asked yourself why some people live a luxurious life and why they attract almost all their heart's desires, while others barely make it? It's a question I used to ask myself growing up.

"The moment of enlightenment is when a person's dreams of possibilities become images of probabilities. Nothing in this world brings ecstasy into a dreamer's life than to see the most cherished images in his mind and heart transformed into something tangible." – **Vic Braden.**

As you go through this book, you will understand that you have done yourself a great favor by investing in one of your greatest assets; "**You.**" It's my honest desire that as you read this book, your mind will be renewed and transformed.

I grew up in a remote rural village coming from very humble beginnings, but, of course, like any other child, I had big dreams and always imagined a great life for myself and my family. Life was hard then, and we were just surviving, for even a simple meal was hard to come by and more often than not, we were forced to beg for food from our relatives.

My high school principal, **Father O'Toole**, saw greatness in me and pointed out to my dad that I was called to transform lives, and that has been the pillar of my life. "If one advances confidently in the direction of his dreams and endeavors to live the life which he has imagined, he will meet with success unexpected in common hours." – **Henry David Thoreau.**

I had dreams of living a luxurious life. While in employment, I specialized in marketing through the Chartered Institute of Marketing (CIM) – UK. I qualified as a chartered marketer. Demand for salespeople with my qualifications was high, so job offers were plentiful. I finally landed a role in a company which had branches in several countries, and this provided me the opportunity to travel to different cities in Africa and overseas.

However, as an employee, I didn't have time and financial freedom, and it dawned on me that I might never realize my dreams of bigger and better things in life. I knew that for me to live the creative vision for my future, I had to break out of my comfort zone. As the famous quote states, "**opportunity meets the prepared.**" I was so ready for change, and that's when I met a friend who introduced me to the world of multilevel marketing.

The first day I attended their presentation, I was mesmerized by the tuition given by the person who had invited me. It opened me up to a world of possibilities just by listening to the testimonials of the speakers. We learned how to leverage on people, and I was excited beyond belief. I saw my dreams come alive that day.

The income levels of the top earners in this network marketing company shocked me. I was however patient enough to remain in full-time employment while doing part-time network marketing. At this point, I knew I had to *do* more to *become* more, and that's when I started reading books and watching videos from top speakers.

I now wanted to achieve a much higher income and decided to research the best strategies to apply to this end. I looked for the top earners in the network marketing industry, and I was shocked to learn that some of them were even earning one million dollars monthly.

I had to act fast; I consulted Google for the secrets applied by these top earners. I gathered a wealth of knowledge by reading countless books and watching a huge number of videos produced by the world's top motivational speakers, such as Tony Robbins, Les Brown, Jim Rohn, Randy Gage, and Matt Morris, among others.

Within five months, I qualified for overseas trips with this part-time job, my income increased tremendously, and my presentation skills improved enormously, and it was time to 'fire' my boss. At that moment, my childhood dream of owning a car came true.

A Chinese proverb says, "Studying is like sailing against the current. A boat must forge ahead, or it will be swept downstream." I was competing with my goals by attending all the company events and seminars within my country and abroad. I never missed a single training opportunity. I also had acquired the skill of inviting prospects to business presentations. The secret to success became easy to find, you only need to look for successful people in your line of business and do what they do, and within a short period, you will be successful.

Within two-and-a-half years in network marketing, I had a team of 10,000 leaders in Africa. By this time, I became a sought-after leader by various network marketing companies globally. Word spread like wildfire of how influential I was, and many business owners wanted me to lead their organizations.

Being a leader, I took up the role of investing in my business partners and bookings for meetings and catering for all expenses. I would pay for halls and spend the whole day inviting people for meetings through social media and word of mouth, and most people confirmed their attendance. One day while in my own country, I called a meeting and, with excitement, I drove with my son to the meeting's destination armed with all the necessary materials. Upon arrival, my son went straight into setting up the projector and arranged the tables and seats. At that time, no one had arrived for the meeting, "it's still early," I would tell myself. So I imagined it would only be a matter of time and guys would start showing up any second, and besides the African Leader (myself) is here! No one would miss this training opportunity; I would chest-beat.

One leader came after one hour of waiting, and late, two others came. Disappointment started slowly setting in, I encouraged myself, and I rose up from my seat, took the mic, and began to teach the three gentlemen and my son. I was shouting at the top of my voice. I refused to allow the low turnout to dictate my mood. I trained them for hours, and later we all went back home satisfied. I learned from the best; my mentors taught me never to give up because of the low turnout on my presentations. It's never about quantity, but rather the quality of the leaders you produce.

"Read the biographies and autobiographies of great people, and again you discover that each of these people went through setbacks many times." stated **David J. Schwartz**. However, through focus, consistency, vision, and persistence, you will get there in the end. I remember one time promoting a business while in Nigeria, and it did not go well, finances were not flowing, and paying for accommodation and meals proved difficult. I even thought of looking for a job. However, my dreams were much bigger than mere employment. As **Robert Schuler** would say; "TOUGH TIMES NEVER LAST BUT TOUGH PEOPLE DO"; tough as it was my strong desires made me overcome the challenge.

I had to pick up the pieces and move on. I believe when we look at the length of life, greatness begins with our inner attitude irrespective of whatever level we can find ourselves in. Great people have great attitudes even in doing small things. I teach my audiences, "Traits of Millionaires", including Attitude, Learning from the Past and Never Giving Up, among others. I knew it was time to apply them in real life. I came across an audiotape by **Matt Morris** on "7 Secrets to 7 Figures," which I listened to religiously, making me rise against all odds to cross the boundaries of social mediocrity.

Dreams can take you to territories far beyond your comfort zone, **Goethe** once said; "Dream no small dreams for they have no power to move the hearts of men." Just as the fetus develops in the womb, dreams also develop as we grow older; my dreams grew so big they scared me. I needed to refuel, re-strategize, and work even more smartly for my new aspirations.

Given my good reputation and integrity, I was sought-after by another company. I took the lead as the coach and business was booming, money started flowing in, and I was able to pay all my outstanding bills, and my lifestyle changed drastically.

I was gaining popularity, and I quickly expanded my network of trusted partners in many parts of Africa and Asia. Life became fun; flying to different places, holidaying with my family. It was also at this time I was able to move houses from a middle-class environment to a home on a leafy suburb near the city center which I paid for in cash. I now drive my dream cars, and I have elevated my parents and my siblings' lifestyles.

"Change your focus from making money to serving more people, and more money will come," said **Robert Kiyosaki**. I have shifted my focus into touching lives and empowering others for the world remembers people who gave their lives for the welfare of others through unconditional love and service.

The sweetest and biggest adventure you can take is to live the life of your dreams. Nothing compares to living a fulfilled life of not only accomplishing most or all your dreams and living beyond success by making the world a better place. Being able to turn failures, setbacks, ridicule, and past mistakes into victories are the greatest weapons we can possess in the world of business and all areas of our lives.

According to the author **Willie Jolley**, "a setback is a set up for a comeback." I have gone through setbacks that were to damage me and my reputation seriously but, as a result of reading books and listening to top motivational speakers, I learned to learn from disappointments, grow from them and bounce straight back.

I believe that after reading this book, your life will be transformed and that your perspective on life will change. You are well equipped to face life again with more determination, and confidence with new dreams in your mind and a higher standard of self-belief.

One thing I know for sure is that God's intentions for us go beyond anything we can imagine. The truth is that you are powerful beyond comprehension, beyond measure, and that you can be anything you want. I am a living testimony of this. I made up my mind growing up never to settle for anything less in life than my destiny.

I dare you to start finding that greatness within you. If we nurture our human spirit, it can explore the deepest depths of human potential. We are all born winners regardless of our religion, race, status, or background. The only difference is who we become is the choices we make in life.

Onwards! Decide to hunt down your dreams and beat them mercilessly into submission.

Exploit the talents and gifts given to you freely by your Creator and do not allow any limiting beliefs to hinder you from achieving your dreams.

Always create time every day for meditation, be honest in all your endeavors, be generous in everything you do, compliment others, and avoid giving criticism. Avoid procrastination by all means and face your fears with boldness. There is no future in the past, so don't dwell on it.

Set your goals promptly and follow them through. Make sure your goals are massive and write them down. Keep the company of like-minded people.

I have followed all these tips to the letter, and I have managed to climb the ladder of success, it's my prayer that you will be transformed too.

Biography

James Mbele's career in sales and marketing spans various companies in Africa and abroad. He earned his chartered marketer certification from the UK's Chartered Institute of Marketing, applying his expertise for more than seven successful years as an entrepreneur in the direct sales and network marketing industry.

From humble beginnings in Kenya, James Mbele's enormous potential and willingness to help others was first recognized by his high school principal, Father O'Toole. To this day, he's remained true to his philanthropic calling to inspire others to rise to their highest potential.

Rising quickly in this global arena and traveling to more than fifty countries to speak and motivate others, his service above and beyond the call of duty has been rewarded with numerous accolades. His visionary leadership has mentored many around him to experience massive success in business and life.

He is married to Christine since 1994. They are blessed with a son, Brian, and a daughter, Linnet.

Contact Information

Website: https://jamesmbele.com/author

Chapter 21

HOW I WENT THROUGH THE LOWEST OF LOWS TO BECOME SUCCESSFUL

By Jamie Lester

Even though I was raised in what would be considered a white-collar family, the value and ethics of hard work were drummed into me from a young age, and my father wasted no time in teaching me the value of a dollar.

From the age of thirteen, I would spend every vacation working in my family business which was never a chore because I was always passionate about the business. We lived in Martinsville, VA and my family owned a company that produced building components for the housing industry. I always knew that after I finished college, I would join the family business.

I graduated from Virginia Tech in 1986, and a few years later my father's health started to decline. As a family, we decided that the best option would be to sell the business. I was 25 years old at the time, and for the first time in my life, I had no idea about my future.

I went back to business school at Wake Forest University, and after I graduated I took a job at a certified public accountant (CPA) firm, formerly Coopers & Lybrand; now PricewaterhouseCoopers.

During my time there, I worked with a variety of different businesses that were facing bankruptcy, which equipped me with the skill set and confidence to buy back my family business when it began to struggle financially. I originally had a partner who was an investment banker, but the partnership did not work out. We both wanted very different things. My long-term plan was to restore the business to the way it once was whereas my partner wanted to sell off the assets and then close the business down. I ended up buying him out only to discover that the business was in far worse condition than I initially thought.

I had to invest all the money I had at the time into the business, and for about ten years things were going very well; however, everything changed in 2008 when the mortgage crisis hit. We could not weather the storm this time around, and I ended up having to file for both corporate and personal bankruptcy. I lost everything except my retirement accounts. Other than losing my mother, it was the lowest point of my life. For me, having money and losing it was worse than never having it at all.

After the business went under, I moved to Charleston, South Carolina to start afresh. Things started to change when I spoke with my 72-year old cousin who had been in the real estate business for some time. He had lost everything and rebuilt it several times. He told me, "If you haven't gone broke at least once in your life, you don't have any lead in your pencil," and that I could make more money but I could not make more time. The advice he gave me made me realize that as long as time was on my side, there would always be opportunities to make more money and I took that to heart.

The one thing that I was sure of was going on someone's payroll wasn't an option. I was prepared to work as hard as I needed to, but I wanted the reward to be mine and no one else's. I founded my present business in 2011, and since then I have never looked back.

If my new business has taught me anything, it is that you will only be truly successful if you are completely passionate about what you do, and you put your heart in it. If you do not believe in yourself and the value that your business offers, then others are not going to believe in you either.

Another key to success is that you have to be a great leader. You may not think that this is something which is inside you, but I believe that it is something which is in everybody. If you do not have good leadership, then it does not matter how good the rest of your business is. Only good leadership will bring real success.

I believe that there are eight key steps to becoming a great leader.

#1 Planning

You need to focus on the things that are the most important and be decisive when it is needed most.

The true champions have a plan, commit to the plan, and then establish a routine to execute that plan. Ramon Floyd, past champion of the Masters Golf Tournament, was interviewed about his preparation for that tournament because of the uniqueness of the golf course. He said months before the tournament he would write down his strategy and the way he was going to play every shot on all 18 holes. What he found out was whenever he had a bad shot or had a bad hole, he was able to jump right back into his game plan and not waste another shot or hole. He had committed to it, so when something went wrong, he was ready. He said preparation and committing to his plan was everything.

#2 Motivation and Passion

You need motivation and desire. This is what is going to carry you through the days when things get tough.

Maintain a positive attitude and enthusiasm. Charles Swindoll said, "The longer I live, the more I realize the impact of attitude on life. Attitude to me is more important than facts, more important than the past, more important than education, money, circumstances, more important than failures, successes, what other people think or say or do. More important than giftedness or skill. It will make or break a company."

#3 Hard Work

You are always prepared to put in the hard work to get things done. I believe you can beat 50% of the competition just by showing up, another 40% by doing what's right which is looking people in the eye and being honest, and that last 10% is a dogfight, having desire, loving what you're doing, rolling out of bed with a blueprint and ready to go after it.

#4 Passion

If you're going to be effective, you have to set yourself on fire. You must do something, get uncomfortable, and work like you have never worked before for a good amount of time. You have to create a fire in your organization, and it's hard to do that if you haven't first created a passion inside yourself.

#5 Be a Good Listener

Sometimes, people on the ground know a lot more about the business than you do. It's okay to acknowledge the fact that a leader does not need to know everything. He can take the counsel of wise and able people.

#6 Hire people smarter than you

When two people agree on everything, one of them is unnecessary. Surround yourself with great people with a vision who are ready to fight for their success and do it positively; people who are tired of sitting on the sidelines and are ready to go out and make their mark.

#7 Know the ins and outs of your business

Be a student of your business. Know your subject. Leaders don't go to sleep at the wheel. They know everything that is going on in their business.

#8 Know when things are not working

Recognize when things are not working and be ready to change course.

If you know it is going to hurt when you don't meet your goals, you will work extra hard to achieve them. It is okay to take failure personally because this is what is going to spur you on to do better the next time.

Your attitude is also going to play a large part in your success. When you wake up each morning, you do not know what challenges you are going to face. However, what you do know is that you will be facing these challenges with a positive attitude and this is half the battle.

Successful people have fear just like all of us. But they do things in spite of the fear. I believe that fear should not stop you from achieving your goals. You should take fear head on and do things that you fear the most. Tom Cruise in the movie Days of Thunder says, "I am more afraid of being nothing than I am of being hurt." That's how I've lived my life.

Closing Thoughts

To be successful in business, you must be willing to go through the dump, just don't hang out there. Losing and not accomplishing your goals must hurt and be so offensive to you that you are not going to accept it. We have a choice every day regarding the attitude we will embrace for that day. We cannot change our past; we cannot change the fact that people will act the way they want. We cannot change the inevitable. The only thing we can do is play on the one string that we have, and that's our attitude. Life is 5% of what happens to us and 95% of how we react to it. We are in charge of our attitudes. Sometimes you have to go through the absolute worst to get to the best times of your life.

BIOGRAPHY

Jamie Lester has a B.S. in Marketing and Finance from Virginia Tech, and an MBA from Wake Forest University. Whether he's interviewing someone to join his business or sitting with a client, he is always looking to uncover their pain and find a solution. He takes a hands-on approach to solving problems by getting down in the trenches with people rather than sitting in an ivory tower.

CONTACT INFORMATION

Facebook: https://www.facebook.com/The-Lester-Agency-873623722798474/
Twitter: https://twitter.com/Officelesterag1
Instagram: https://www.instagram.com/office132/
LinkedIn: https://www.linkedin.com/in/lester-agency-344105160/

Chapter 22

THE SECRET SAUCE TO NEVER QUITTING

By Jayde Martinez Santana

We've all had those moments where it felt like the odds were against us. Maybe we experienced fear or felt we should just give up. What is the solution to overcome those thoughts and keep climbing until you succeed? Even successful people have to face their fears and surmount obstacles. So, how do they accomplish that? How do they overcome their fears? What's the secret sauce? The secret sauce is believing in yourself and staying focused on your purpose throughout your journey. Whenever you feel like quitting, it simply means you are not present in your purpose and you're unaware of the difference it can make if you persist in accomplishing your goals. All you need to do is refocus and continue to believe that you will succeed.

From the age of 14, I always dreamed I would serve my country. I knew I would be a soldier one day, although I never knew what it entailed, I just strongly believed that day would come, and it did.

In 2013, I was enlisted in the army. I signed a ton of paperwork but what stood out to me the most was a statement that revealed 18 weeks of vigorous training was required. It stated we might experience physical pain that we've never felt before, such as severe pain in our knees, ankles, and back. As I read this, I thought it couldn't possibly be as bad as they're making it out to be. I exercise regularly and do CrossFit, so I doubt I'll experience any of that. Little did I know how this vigorous training was going to impact my body.

In January 2014, I shipped out for basic combat training. Day Zero, as we call it, began with an obstacle course immediately upon arrival. I ended up rolling my ankle twice during the course. I was so focused on finishing and wanting to make a great first impression, that I disregarded the fact that I rolled my ankle and continued running to the next obstacle to crawl under barb wire, climb up and over a net and a wall, and then jump off a cliff into muddy water. I promised myself that no matter what challenges were ahead, I would face them because quitting was not an option.

In the following days, we started every morning at 4 am with physical fitness training, which consisted of running anywhere between 2-4 miles, then push-ups, sit-ups, squats, jumping jacks, and anything else our drill sergeants could come up with. One morning, despite it being 7 degrees outside, we woke up for our usual 4 am routine. It was so cold that my gloves were practically useless. My fingers began to freeze and go numb during the run. I wanted to go back inside but I kept thinking to myself, I didn't come here to quit, so I carried on running. After a mile and a half, my fingers started heating up and felt like they were on fire. The pain was brutal, but I swallowed hard to avoid choking up and crying. I knew then I had frostbite. I didn't want anyone to know because they would force me to go to the emergency room and the drill sergeants made it clear that going to the emergency room meant missing a day of training and having to restart. I already set my mind to never quitting because i knew that stopping and restarting would be worst than finishing, so I continued to run. Finally, we reached the barracks and were allowed to go upstairs and get ready for our missions. Once I got upstairs, with my fingers still in pain, all I thought of was to thank God that I am mentally fit and was able to get through that. If my mental attitude could get me through that physical pain, then I could get through anything.

Throughout our training, we had several foot and ruck marches. We started with foot marches, where we walked between 3 to 5 miles to our mission. The foot marches were building us up for the ruck marches, which required us to start off with 30 lbs on our back for 3 miles and increase it to 45 lbs for an 18-mile ruck march. This has by far been my biggest challenge, not just in basic training or the army, but in life.

Never have I felt like I wanted to give up so badly as I did during those marches. I will tell you why. I've always heard of people who ran or walked every day and got shin splints but never thought it would happen to me, and I never understood how severe it could be. Shin splints are micro-tears in muscle tissues, which occurs when muscles tendons and bone tissues are overstrained. By my second week of basic training, I experienced shin splints for the first time.

I was one of the shortest people in my platoon, and when marching or running, I was the shortest to lead the front. If we couldn't keep up, we were told to step out of the formation or "fall out" as we called it. I witnessed several people falling out, but I told myself no matter what happens, no matter how fast we're going, no matter how bad I feel or think I can't keep up, no matter how tired I am or how weak my legs are, I will never fall out.

One day, during a foot march, I started experiencing a sharp pain on both my shins. The more I walked, the more pain I had to the point that my shins felt like flames were against them. I never felt that physical pain before. Everything in me was saying fall out and tell the drill sergeants what I was dealing with. I had a legitimate reason, but I just wouldn't do it. So, sometimes, we have legitimate reasons to give up, but I was aware of the consequences if I prolonged achieving my goals. I knew that sticking through this would make me feel better in the long run rather than giving up now.

Finally, 45 minutes later, the drill sergeants called for a 15-minute rest. At that moment, I was so grateful to give my shins a break and some relief from the pain. What I didn't know was stopping is worse than continuing. After the break, we fell back into formation and continued our march. Two minutes in, I started to feel the same shin pain as before, only this time it was worse. I noticed every time we stopped to rest before continuing the march, the pain would increase. I began thinking, I rather push through the pain to reach my destination instead of having to repeatedly stop and experience more pain than if I just kept going.

Since I was following orders, I complied with the plan of action set out for us, which meant rest periods during the marches. So, unless I wanted to quit, I had to deal with everything as it happened.

I completed the march as painful as it was. I was relieved to make it through day one of shin splints. I knew the pain did not end here. There were still six weeks left of basic training, and the only way to heal from shin splints is to stay off of your feet, which was not an option. Ice and painkillers would help, but I had no access to either since I refused to let anyone know what I was going through. I know that anything we focus on increases so I chose not to focus on the pain. I was willing to do whatever necessary to make sure I graduated with my platoon.

It was time to take my second physical fitness test, which consisted of doing as many pushups and sit-ups as possible in two minutes and then running two miles. I knew I would pass because I was physically fit and already passed the first. However, with shin splints, it was going to be a huge challenge. The second I started running, I felt the pain in my shins. Halfway through the first mile, a drill sergeant yelled at me, "Martinez, speed up. Why are you running so slow this time?" I thought if only you knew. It was tough keeping a steady pace and running fast, but I had to complete my run in 18 minutes, and I was already 6 minutes in. I told myself I can do this.

The faster I run, the sooner it's over. Let's get it. I started to pick up my pace, and even though the pain was relentless, I just kept thinking about the finish line. The drill sergeant noticed I sped up and said, "That's what I'm talking about, Martinez. Keep it up." I managed to finish my 2-mile run in sixteen minutes. I wanted to throw myself on the floor and curl up and hold my shin but as they say, "We have to maintain our military bearing." So again, I sucked up the pain and held my head high.

The days started to get colder, and soon, snow began to fall. I was experiencing frostbite frequently and so became accustomed to the numbness. The snow delayed our schedule as it was too heavy to march in. This made it tougher because then we had to squeeze our marches into two weeks to make up for what we couldn't complete when it snowed. My shin splints worsened during this time because of the excess of training in a short period. Eventually, the more I dealt with it, the easier it seemed to manage mentally.

I had one last ruck march to look forward to completing, which was our longest march with the heaviest weight. It was a total of 18 miles with 45 lbs and we would be marching for hours. At this point, it would be the biggest challenge. I thought it's been eight weeks of running and marching daily with shin splints. I got this far with only two weeks left and the last ruck march. There's nothing I cannot conquer at this point. Our ruck march was referred to as the Victory Forge, and upon completing, it felt like victory at last.

When we arrived back at the barracks, we were called down for a ceremony. There were over a hundred soldiers in my platoon, and none of us were aware of what was going on. A drill sergeant started speaking, "Congratulations to everyone for making it to this phase. This is a ceremony to acknowledge and promote two soldiers from our company. We are only allowed to choose one male and one female. We chose based on the performance of these two soldiers from Day Zero until now. Private Martinez, post." My heart raced as I ran to post in front of the drill sergeant. I felt so accomplished because no one knew the physical pain I endured. I felt honored earning that promotion. I believe the challenges I faced were worth it.

What I suggest throughout any journey is to be patient, become mentally fit, and believe in your purpose. If your actions correlate with your purpose then keep pushing, no matter how rough things get. Learn to be resilient and committed and fight through the discomfort and obstacles because if you want it, you can have it. Just stay motivated and work hard, and you will be rewarded.

Biography

Jayde Martinez Santana has been serving in the Army reserves for six years. She is a non-commissioned officer with the title of sergeant. She is also an entrepreneur in the travel industry. Jayde has a passion for writing about relatable events in her life to inspire others to learn from them and apply action in their lives. Her latest work motivates people to push through the obstacles that they face without giving up so that they can accomplish their goals.

Contact Information

Facebook: https://www.facebook.com/JaydeMartinezSantana
Instagram: https://www.instagram.com/jaydelivinlavida/

Chapter 23

HELPING PEOPLE AND CHANGING THEIR LIVES FOREVER

By Jim Cusick

I was born and raised in a council estate village called Oakley, near the City of Dunfermline in Scotland. Oakley was an old-fashioned mining village where everyone knew each other's families and businesses. During the time of the famous miners' strike in the UK in the early 1980s, there was a lot of bitterness and violence.

But in all honesty, Oakley was a good place to grow up. Everyone looked out for each other, and it was a safe environment to raise a family. I had five siblings, three brothers and one sister. We were blessed with the most amazing and loving parents who taught us love, discipline, and respect. To this day, we all remain extremely close and live within 3 miles of each other.

At age 9, I stumbled across something that would change my life forever. One Monday evening, I arrived earlier than usual at the local children's youth club. I walked into the building and saw a bunch of lads finishing their boxing session. On impulse, I marched right over to the guy who was coaching. I'll never forget that short conversation. My exact words to him were (which now gives me the shivers), "Hey Mister, could I be a boxer?" He looked at me and said, "Aye of course." I asked, "How much?" and he said, "Ten pence."

My eyes lit up, and I said, "That's great! I think my dad will be able to give me that."

I was so excited. I worked extremely hard and never missed a training session. Skipping, shadow boxing, and running were some of the activities I practiced in my spare time. It wasn't a natural talent, but my determination made me believe I'd be a champion.

I was committed, dedicated, and I totally loved it. By the time I hit my teenage years, I had become the national schoolboy champion. I developed self-discipline, belief, and desire. I remember training hard and then suddenly catch sight of friends looking in from outside the youth club windows. They would all be smoking and hanging around.

Boxing helped me avoid smoking, drinking, drugs, and all the other bad distractions. I went through all my teenage years without touching a drop of alcohol. I was terrible at school and learned absolutely nothing that's been useful on my journey. I never took it seriously, and on three occasions, I was excluded for antisocial behavior. My academic competency was inadequate, and I left school at 16 with no qualifications.

My father and his brother were co-owners of a car garage in our village. When I left school, they offered me a mechanic apprenticeship in the family business. I worked hard through my 4-year apprenticeship, working six days a week and boxing in my spare time.

Throughout my teens, I was keen on going out to our local town Dunfermline. I enjoyed going out stone-cold sober, chasing girls and having fun. I also loved waking up fresh the next morning and reminding my friends of their drunken antics.

When I was 20, I knew I wasn't destined to do more with my life. I became a time served mechanic after four years but hated fixing cars. I was a senior-level boxer by this time and trained with brilliant boxers who inspired me.

One guy, in particular, was Charlie Baird. Charlie was a brilliant full-time fighter in the Royal Marines, he often said, over the years, "You should join the Marines. You could box full-time like me and travel the world".

This sounded perfect for me. Shortly before this, my big brother John joined the Elite Parachute Regiment in the British Army. He was enjoying it, and I often thought about following in his footsteps. He advised me to join the Royal Marines instead of the Paras as it was the best avenue to pursue my boxing.

It was one of the best pieces of advice I've ever been given, and I thank him so much.

So, on the 22nd of March 1999 at the age of 20, I joined the Elite Royal Marines. I was terrified and extremely excited at the same time. I knew I was ready for this challenge and a complete change of life. By this time, I had over 90 boxing matches and a great record under my belt.

The 32 weeks of recruit training was to be the toughest thing I'd ever experience in my life. Nothing could have prepared me for the eight months ahead. From not having time to eat while rapidly depleting calories every day, the constant pressure challenged me mentally and physically. There was little time to learn new skills, and personal and kit standards were extremely high. Massive sleep deprivation over 32 weeks was also a huge factor. At times, I felt I was going to pass out from exhaustion and dehydration. I went through Marines training weighing ten stones (64 kg) and sometimes carrying nine stones (60 kg) of kit.

When I graduated from the Royal Marines on the 19th of November 1999, it was one of the proudest moments of my life. Over 80 of us started and only nine finished. I went from being a boy to a man and was a completely different person at the end.

I spent many great years in the Royal Marines and served my country for 14 years. I met amazing people who I'm honored to call friends for life. I went on two operational deployments during my time and attended over ten funerals for fallen comrades in those 14 years. Some of my good friends still suffer from PTSD. I've seen families torn apart by the hurt and pain of this terrible condition.

I was one of the lucky ones and spent four years of my career as a full-time boxer. I became the British Military Boxing Champion in my first year on the squad and remained unbeaten for four years in the military. Our boxing squad traveled the world competing against different counties and teams, including the US Marines.

I was now boxing full time for the Marines and Scotland's national team. I fought in Olympic qualifying tournaments and went on to complete 150 fights in my career. I fell short at the highest level but did my best for over 20 years.

I proudly retired at 26 years of age after failing to make the Olympics. I've witnessed good friends fight on for too long and ruin their lives.

In the second half of my military career, I transferred to the physical training branch of the Royal Navy. This was very different from the Marines, and so were the people I worked with. They weren't as loyal, and I never felt the same bond with them. As much as I met great guys during my time in the Navy, I learned more from my superiors' poor leadership and their poor people skills.

I discovered personal development from a good friend of mine who I served with. He was severely affected by PTSD and was trying to rebuild his mind. He got my attention and I started to study this condition with him along with positive mental thinking and the law of attraction. I thank John constantly for introducing me to this because it changed my life's focus. I decided to apply for redundancy from the forces when I was 34 years old. For the first time in my life, I believed I could move onto bigger and better things without any qualifications.

John asked what I would do when I left, and I said I think I can help many people and become rich! He asked, "Doing what?" I replied, "I have no idea."

I just knew I had this burning desire and believed I could better myself by helping others.

Only eight more years of service would guarantee a full military pension for life. However, my newfound ambition forced me to take a risk!! I believe that anyone afraid to take risks will accomplish little in life. During this time, I started giving outdoor fitness classes in the local park. It took off and the numbers grew fast. On the Sunday morning of 12th August 2012, my life took an unexpected turn.

A complete stranger knocked on my door and asked if I heard of this company. I replied no. I was skeptical about his whole sales pitch. For some crazy reason, which I always wonder about, I invited him into my house to tell me more.

I agreed to try his health and nutrition products. I believe my positive attitude attracted this opportunity. I fell in love with the products almost instantly. We quickly formed a great relationship. He helped me get great results. He also gave me the option to help others do the same.

His name was Scott Walker, an ex-accountant, who had been involved with the company for six months at the time. He invited me to a local company event to see the potential on a larger scale. I also reviewed their marketing plan on how they paid their members. I knew I could do it.

It was that same feeling I had as the little shy 9-year-old boxer. I knew I was going to the top of this company. I made up my mind and built a life-changing business within 12 months. I helped all my friends and family achieve great results and showed them how to build a profitable part-time income.

I love helping people. It was the opposite of what I had always done before. Within three years of joining, I reached the top 1% of the company, which meant I was now earning a 6-figure income.

I recruited many ex-Marines and Navy personnel, one of whom was my best friend, Kevin Green. Kevin now has a 6-figure income and can afford a private education for all his children.

I now travel the world and work with the people I want. This is the career of a lifetime for me that allows me to work around my children and personal commitments. I have presented to around 20,000 people. In my opinion, having time and financial freedom along with good health, are the most rewarding things in life. Furthermore, this opportunity led me to meet my beautiful fiancée, Natalie. Life couldn't be better.

Our company has a presence in 96 countries around the world. I want to help more people everywhere. My two children will have the best possible chance in life. I am very grateful and blessed, and I'm just getting started.

I've never been so happy and now know where my destiny will take me.

Biography

Jim Cusick came from a tough and humble beginning to building the life of his dreams. He achieved this by finding a way to serve and help people change their lives. Through tough challenges in the military and competing in high-level sport, Jim found belief and desire to carry him through a rollercoaster journey. After all his life experiences so far, he now has serious ambition to help change many more lives around the world.

Contact Information

Facebook: https://www.facebook.com/jim.cusick.526
Instagram: http://Instagram.com/cusickjim

Chapter 24

SMALL TOWN GUY, BIG TIME WHY

By Joshua Holland

I am from a small town in Middle Tennessee called Defeated Creek. It is your average town, with average people and a few who are a little crazy, but mostly all earning a modest household income. However, I noticed that few think about leaving a legacy for their families, whether it be a financial legacy or valuable text that is passed down the generations.

It is my BIG TIME WHY, not only to leave a financial legacy but also, to leave a book of encouragement for others to read so they can realize God's intention for them and be filled with hope and determination for a better future.

About six years ago, I was up late and unable to sleep. I prayed and asked God to provide me with purpose and passion in my life. The answer did not come immediately, but two months later, an acquaintance called me to ask if I would be open to exploring something. I was open and ready for any business opportunity. The idea presented to me was a Network Marketing company that I never heard before, and I had never been approached me with anything like this before, which was a business that could provide Financial Freedom and Time Freedom. I did not join the business that night, but I did two weeks later.

To give some background, I graduated from Cumberland University with a bachelor's degree in Business Administration and majored in Accounting. I was the first person in my family to graduate from college. I have been a corporate Accountant for the last 16 years. Being an Accountant, you learn about numbers, not people. So, I hadn't developed my social skills. I was a shy guy, and this was the reason no one ever approached me about the Network Marketing business model. Many people probably thought Josh is so timid that even if he joins my team, he won't be able to talk to others about the business as he barely talks to anyone. They were right in that I barely spoke to anyone. Mostly, I kept to myself and didn't socialize much with others. Hence, I had no personal development in my life and knew nothing about stepping out of my comfort zone to grow personally. I had no idea that this Network Marketing business was also a personal development business. All I knew was that I had an entrepreneur spirit, and I was ready to dive into this new business presented to me.

I invited family and friends to a presentation to see this great business. Before this, I had already hosted fourteen of my own presentations. Sounds ridiculous, right? But at the beginning of my entrepreneurial and personal development journey, few people joined my team while others said it would never work and chuckled at the business model. I did not understand why so many people kept saying no as I believed it was the best business model ever created.

Not a lot of people have a passive income or the desire to make necessary changes to achieve this type of income. The 'Nos" began to pile up, and my list of names started to dwindle. I took this rejection personally, which was a mistake on my part because I doubted if the business was right for me. Then, I received my first personal development book, "The Magic of Thinking Big," by David Schwartz which was the catalyst for starting my personal development journey that changed my outlook on life and my mindset so I could accomplish my goals to create a better future.

As I began to read more personal development books and listen to daily positive affirmations, I could feel my mindset change from negative thought patterns to positive beliefs. It was during this time that I started to grow.

A noteworthy incident to mention is during one of my presentations where a lovely couple, known through family, joined my business, The gentleman said, "When can you go to Mississippi with us to show the business to an old friend of mine." I said, "Let's pick a weekend and make the trip." The two men did cattle business together and needed to trade longhorns anyway. We scheduled a weekend and drove 12 hours one-way to Southern Mississippi for me to do a presentation. On the way, I asked my team member what he had mentioned to his friend about our company, and he had told him he had a business to present when we got there. When we arrived and got out of the vehicle, my colleague introduced me to the older gentleman who asked me what type of business I'm going to show him. While briefly describing the business, he stops me and says, " Wait, are you talking about…" And unbelievably, the older gentleman and his family were in the specific company I was about to present and had been for several years. Naturally, this took me by surprise yet also deflated me. I wasted a whole weekend, but I will admit, I met some fine folks even though they were not going to be in my business. Now, if it had not been for personal development and the ability to shake off that situation, then I would have been finished with this business.

Later, I attended a company event, and one of the team leaders asked me to share my experience with everyone. As mentioned before, I was a shy person, so being able to speak on a team call could only happen through personal development and help from God. After reading 30 books on Network Marketing to learn the industry and spending thousands of dollars on training courses to develop the personal skills and gain the confidence to speak publicly, is a huge accomplishment and movement towards SUCCESS. On the team call, I talked about what I had learned from the event. The word POWER came to mind. Let me expand:

P: Persistence - get through the disappointments, pay no attention to being discouraged, laughed at, or scolded for being in this profession.

O: Obstacles - there are many variables that can keep us from being successful in this profession as life happens to all.

W: Winners - everyone is a winner, so look on the inside and pull that winning mentality out.

E: Encouragement - without encouragement, you will not make it in this business. You must be a leader and positively encourage others to become leaders too. Small successes are positive actions, such as setting a meeting, and leaders praising the teammate's initiative.

R: Reward - everyone should set a reward for every success in the business. Small rewards for small victories and big rewards for big achievements. Let the reward be strong enough to instill the desire to achieve it.

Question for you: A pool or a river – which one are you? In a pool, you can swim around or float, but you don't really go anywhere. Most people live their lives like a pool, and they don't even realize it; they stay in this circle and never get out. There is no current in a pool to take you somewhere new, somewhere you've never been before. You just float around through life with no destination in mind. It may be fun, but there's no real excitement with a limited area in which to invite new people. In a river, you can swim and float around, and the current of the river will force you to move to a new area. Few people live their lives like this and have a plan to get to a new destination. If you can show people how much fun you are having in the river current, they will want to join you and go somewhere new; which is a lot of fun and super exciting with unlimited areas in which to invite new people.

I choose the river. Let me know your answer.

Being consumed with personal development these last few years has led me to a concept I did not think would work, but did. It is to take some time and write down what you want in life and be specific. Let's say you want a specific vehicle, then write down the make, model, color, wheels, and anything else you may want on this vehicle. Before you know it, you will see the exact vehicle you described going down the road, and when you see it, all you must say is "Thank You." This is referred to as the Universal Law. The reason you will see your vehicle is that the Universe is letting you know your dream vehicle is on the way. I recommend you do this in all aspects of your life.

What will people think about me being in the Network Marketing Industry? Most people won't think much about you throughout your life; let me expand.

Statistics show that on average, about ten people will cry at your funeral, and the determining factor whether or not they will even go to your funeral is the weather. Being a hot or cold day will determine their attendance.

Let that sink in.

All the people you hang out with during your life won't be there at the end. So, stop worrying about what others think about your Network Marketing business. I am working on a better and brighter future to help future generations. We are all here to help one another and create a better life for each other, so let's make a change for the better.

Network Marketing, along with personal development, has allowed me to develop the people skills necessary for a successful life and to think about my life's core purpose, which I want to share with you now.

MY CORE PURPOSE IN LIFE

My core purpose in life is to seek GOD and allow HIM to fill me with his power, mercy, and glory. To help my family in any way possible to prosper throughout life. I am in good health due to staying active and a successful person by improving myself, which inspires others to do the same. Seek to help others and leave a legacy of Financial Freedom for generations to come. Live my life with a positive attitude, honesty, and integrity. Desire to emotionally touch and help millions of ambitious people find Time Freedom and happiness. Live a fun-filled life that most people only dream about.

I encourage you to write your own purpose in life, record yourself saying it, listen to it often, and see what happens in your life.

I sit here in my cabin in the woods, my second home. I am not bragging but providing hope that you can achieve the goals you set to have a better future for you and your family. The Network Marketing Industry allows you to have relationships with people you would have never met otherwise, and to me, that is priceless. I want to thank my family and friends who have supported me throughout this journey and a huge thank you to Matt Morris for allowing me to share my story. I hope and pray my story will help many people realize how powerful they are and how great this industry truly is.

Biography

Joshua Holland is a graduate from Cumberland University with a bachelor's degree in Business and also the first in his family to do so. Joshua has studied and researched personal development and the Network Marketing Industry for the last six years and found many techniques and strategies to overcome limiting beliefs to become the person he needs to be to achieve success. Joshua works and lives in Middle Tennessee and spends his summers going to the gym, hiking, and golfing.

Contact Information

Facebook: www.facebook.com/joshua.holland.543
Linkedin: www.linkedin.com/in/joshua-holland-53214a7a

Chapter 25

WE ALREADY HAVE ALL WE NEED

By Juan Enamorado

Tears were running down my cheeks. I was trying to make a phone call from inside one of the old telephone booths. I seldom cry. But here I was, sobbing loudly and uncontrollably. I was desperate, anxious, and feeling depressed and confused about my future.

Then something began to emerge in my mind. I recalled seeing the words, *"Go Beyond the Impossible,"* a few days earlier on an Anthony Robbins webpage. The impact of these words had been growing in me and stirring something within me. I anticipated that something good was going to happen. It was tiny in the beginning, but I felt it growing. The word *"impossible"* also motivated me. I was often attracted to hard and challenging things.

My emotions had changed, and my tears were gone. One thought was growing in my mind. Our brains have about 100 billion neurons, and experts tell us that is as much as about 1,000 times the number of stars in our galaxy. I knew that our brains in themselves are amazing computers with almost unbelievable possibilities.

I think because some of these things I already knew, I was feeling an unexpected hope. My imagination was expanding to the possibility of a bright world taking shape within my brain. I was beginning to feel I was in the very beginning of my preparation for the greatest adventure of my life. It was an illuminating moment.

I wasn't surprised I had a desperate urge to write about what I was feeling. When I walked back to the car from the phone booth, I sat down and began writing. My writing was fast and some of it illegible, as later, I had a hard time deciphering what I wrote.

Several times during our lives, we've produced compelling moments. At times, we had glimpses of the unmined vast treasure of dormant capabilities and aptitudes within each of us. What happens is when time passes, some of these memories fade away, which often happen to be the richest ones. What we do is that we unearth the memories blocking the way to our inner wealth, which is why we must search, find, and root out our powerful memories. They are there, so we must relive them to their full intensity and splendor. And then, take it a step further by continually rehearsing them mentally.

The powerful emotions that accompany them will shield us from the surrounding negativity, and instead, it will strengthen our state of mind and our self-confidence. It has the potential to make us unstoppable, and we can increase our winning edge exponentially in whatever we choose to do.

I have a burning desire to help others. I want to help them feel and experience the glory of their greatness. I want them to intensely feel and be excited about the greatness that lives within them.

When I'm helping others in this way, I feel a rush within me. It is a mixture of excitement, happiness, and euphoria. I must be producing some sort of addictive, natural *'feel-good'* neurochemicals in my brain.

I compare it to a drug addiction because doing this gives me a rush. It also makes me feel healthier and fills me with energy. It inspires me. I have difficulty explaining even to myself why and how this happens. It must cause my brain to create high levels of dopamine and endorphins. But with the utmost certainty, I know that helping others in this way is my calling in life. I have become like a *'Crusader.'*

From the avalanche of emotions catapulting inside my mind, some memories stood out. I felt like I was living in an ancient world. There were a lot of molasses slowing down everything, especially the people. The people here didn't have inquiring minds. They were not curious. They were not interested in personal development. Their minds were closed.

In the other world, the new world, people were full of curiosity. They were starving for personal development. They wanted to help others, and their minds were fully open. Maybe I was overly optimistic. But that is the way I am, and I like being that way. Perhaps it helps me to have a thirst for knowledge and helps me be more open to many different possibilities.

I remember when I was a young boy back in Cuba, I saw something in my father that he wasn't even aware of. Mr. Frian, the owner of the construction company where my father worked as a laborer, was looking for a foreman for a different project, but none of the other foremen knew how to go about it. I told my father he could apply. Even though he didn't believe me, I insisted and persisted. One day, when he came home from work, he told me Mr. Frian had hired him for the job. Every day, during construction, I walked to the job site. It was fun to watch him and the progress of the construction. For my father, it was a big unforgettable moment in his life and mine. I was very proud of him and his progress.

In high school, I had to select some of the subjects in my curriculum. I picked German, Statistics, and Trigonometry. My two closest buddies, George and Dominique, selected Spanish as one of their courses, and I couldn't understand why. Spanish was the language we learned in our childhood, so I felt I already knew it, so why take it as a subject? When Mr. Fuchs, the school counselor, learned of my choices, he told me I would never amount to anything. This increased my desire and motivation for the challenge.

I remembered reading *Jonathan Livingston Seagull*. Like me, Jonathan also wanted to leave its present life. And like me, Jonathan also felt life had to be much more exciting and rewarding. This is the reason why I strive to learn from the great teachers and leaders. They stand on the shoulders of others who're even greater. I crave for a little space on their shoulders. I want to help others become aware of what abilities they already have and then to assist them in their improvement.

When I watched the movie *Happy Feet*, I identified with Mumble. He needed to sing but couldn't. I was behind everyone in school. I only had one year of schooling when I immigrated to the US, and I was already fourteen. Like Mumble, I felt I didn't belong and was out of place. But eventually, I became aware that the one capability I had was that of a great desire to help others become excited about themselves and develop their abilities.

When in college, a girl came up to me. She was crying profusely. I believe the reason she came to me was because I was a proctor assisting my psychology professor. She told me she couldn't keep up with her class and that she was quitting. I felt terrible for her and told her I knew she could do it. She ended up not quitting and getting a B in her report card.

In my first Tony Robbins seminar, one of the top two learning challenges was to climb up a tall telephone pole, the *Pamper Pole*. Then, stand on top of it and jump to a swinging trapeze. The turn came up for a young lady, and the team began cheering for her. When she was midway up, she lost her hold and fell to the net below. We ran up to her as she was getting down from the net. She was crying, saying, *"I failed! I failed!"*

The only thing that came to mind to say to her was, *"You succeeded. You didn't fail. You succeeded!"* Others in the team picked up on these words, also telling her she succeeded. With a surprise look on her face, she looked at us and said, *"I did?" "Yes. You did. You succeeded!"*, I was saying to her. The entire team picked up on it and began cheering for her. And, as we were cheering, we all fell on the ground together with her as a group. It reminded me of seeing this type of celebrating when a team scored the winning point in a championship game. I feel great emotion in my entire body when I remember this moment. It was a big victory for me in my life to help transform her feeling of failure into one of success.

A few years later, when my wife died, my life was in turmoil. I was confused and at times, felt I wanted to die too. Instead, I chose to go on a trip to Costa Rica. I rented a little apartment in an area where some expatriates were living, and most of them spoke very little or no Spanish. Some were trying to learn how to speak it from books but were having a terrible time with the pronunciation. A few of them asked me to help them out. But I was getting frustrated because they were still not learning. Eventually, I started telling them to look at my lips as I pronounced the words in Spanish. When they began to do so, I was surprised at the results. Their pronunciation was almost like that of native speakers, and they too were amazed, which inspired me to create an online *Spanish Online Academy*. I wanted people to feel happy about their learning and ability to communicate better. Later, I learned this was because of something called neuroplasticity. But I had very little income, so eventually, I returned to the US, still feeling lost and with no real reason to exist.

Then, by chance, I saw my friend, Ed Reid, looking through Facebook. Being extremely curious, I saw the face of a certain lady. I asked Ed to let me look more. I was highly attracted to her face in her profile. I went to my laptop and wrote to her, *"Can I respectfully ask you for your Facebook friendship?"* She replied, *"Yes."* Jaunice pretty much saved my life. We communicated often and got on so well that I had to visit her in her country, the Philippines. I was with her and her family for two years, and they were happy moments in my life. Once again, I was motivated to live. I didn't want to die anymore.

My life began to regain focus. I felt happy and full of hope, and I wanted others to find the love I had found. I created an online dating site, *FilipinoWomanDating.com*. With Jaunice, I video-interviewed Filipino ladies and uploaded the videos to Amazon S3 and YouTube. However, this project also brought in very little income. With my newfound love and the need for a stable financial future, I couldn't continue with it. And my visa to stay in the Philippines already had expired, so I couldn't do more live video interviews.

However, I remembered once reading something the Dalai Lama said, *"If you want to be happy, practice compassion. Our prime purpose in this life is to help others."* I always felt a powerful urge to help others. It's not just a desire. It's more than a need. It's a craving.

My number one challenge is that I get easily sidetracked. It's like being a child in a candy store. I see so many things I like. I read a quote from Steve Jobs that said there were so many great ideas, and the problem is which ones to ignore, which is something I must continually do. I must train myself to correct my seriously bad habit of spending so much of my very finite time on this planet, on things that don't serve me or my purpose in life.

But I do fully realize and recognize my gift. My gift is my burning desire to help people become more aware of their abilities. When they realize these abilities, they can develop ways to sharpen them. There is happiness in doing what you like and doing it well.

I am genuinely obsessed with this desire. My life has been spilling all over with so many events that I labeled as failures and disappointments. Yet, something drives me forward in what I know is the right path. It's similar to a gyroscope forcing me to continue in the right direction. Steve Jobs once said, *"Have the courage to follow your heart and intuition. It somehow already knows what you truly want to become. Everything else is secondary."*

I know the subconscious part of my brain is 30,000 times more powerful than the conscious one. I know everything is coming together. What was once a puzzle has now become a bright, panoramic, and colorful picture. And I desperately want to help others with their growth and their own realizations.

BIOGRAPHY

Juan Enamorado is a public speaker and a self-development coach specializing in empowering people to become excited about their greatness. It started early on with his father and continued with him in high school, college, seminars, and through the creation of the *SpanishOnlineAcademy.com*, and the dating site, *FilipinoWomanDating.com*. His formal education is in psychology and sociology. His additional training includes *Mastery University* with Tony Robbins; *Date With Destiny,* and *Unlimited Power Within*, also with Tony Robbins.

CONTACT INFORMATION

Facebook: https://www.facebook.com/JuanGrowthCoach
Twitter: https://twitter.com/john_anselmo
YouTube: https://www.youtube.com/user/JuanEnamoradoChannel/videos

Chapter 26

MY DEFINITION OF SUCCESS

By Kadri Kristelle Karu

How do we define success?

Is it a lot of money? A rich lifestyle? A big house? An expensive car? Luxurious trips? Is it enough, or do we need something more to be happy?

Yes, success can be counted like this too. But success could be growing as a person, feeling happy, finding inner peace, having influence, helping others, a happy family life, good health, etc.

Often, we think of ourselves as successful or unsuccessful by comparing ourselves to others. But there is always someone who has more expensive things than we do and there are still people who have less. At times, rich people are unhappy, and financially poor people are happy. Which of them is more successful?

What is success about? Is it equal to a happy life?

When I was in my 20s, I thought I'll be successful living my dream life when I could manage my time effectively, earn good money, live in a beautiful home, have a nice car and travel a lot. During the journey of my life, I added much more of what would qualify as success for me: a happy family life, good friends, positive emotions, good health, helping other people and living a rewarding life by growing and enjoying every minute of life.

It took me years to understand what I really want and what makes me happy. People said I was successful, and I saw all these external things that proved it, but I was not happy. I was looking for my happiness in other people, money, travels, and ended up with an understanding that all we need is self-love. I think people should do whatever it takes to love themselves, live a happy life and encourage others to do the same by being an example. People who value and love themselves are an inspiration for other people.

I was not born into a wealthy family, I grew up with my grandmother, and later saw my mother's struggles with her business, depression, and difficulties. I just wanted to know if there was possibly another way to live, succeed financially, and have fun and enjoy life at the same time.

Now I know by experience that it is possible, and it's based on our own decisions. We can make decisions at every moment of our life; it does not matter where we live or how old we are.

Was it always easy to achieve it? Certainly not. Was it worth it? Absolutely!

I studied in different schools and was looking for what I really like to do. I completed my education at secondary school level, worked in a kindergarten, during studies I worked in a hospital, then trained and worked as a secretary at a bank. I liked the job, but I realized that the most important thing for me was missing – my freedom. So, I decided to study International Business and started to work as a manager and later personnel manager in a big company.

At that time someone showed me options in Network Marketing and direct selling. I was somewhat skeptical about business, but I really liked the products, so I shared my experiences naturally. People grew interested, the company paid me money, and when it was equal to my salary, I thought maybe this is an option to become the hostess of my time and be truly free. I understood by then that I had no good ideas for creating my own business and saw the difficulties in starting ordinary businesses. But I liked the freedom, the teamwork, managing my time myself and the income that Network Marketing allows you to achieve.

When I started, I had a full-time job, my son was three years old, and I just had to find extra time for my Network Marketing business. But I knew what I wanted – freedom. It's wonderful that I've enjoyed direct marketing success for 20 years now and I am really happy about it, it taught me more than what I learned in 5 years of business school. I met many wonderful people, enjoyed great self-development, fantastic travels, freedom, a good income, and these opportunities are limitless.

I am glad to share the experiences I've learned on this fantastic journey. I am still learning but also using the skills I've learned so far because they work in every area of life.

The most important thing I've learned is that you are enough, love yourself and enjoy life! All the advertisements on TV and magazines show us that if we buy this or that we will be better, more beautiful, more complete. It's not true. We are complete as we are and worthy of love. There's nothing bad in good things; it's great to enjoy life, but these fulfill us just for a moment. Very often we think other people need to give us happiness and appreciation. No, it's our job. If we love and appreciate ourselves, others will follow this.

Have a great relationship with yourself, and you will have great relationships with others.

Love yourself; then you can love others and will be loved by others.

We are used to comparing ourselves with others, but we should compare ourselves and our growth with ourselves, this is success.

People are conditioned to live in the past and regret what happened in the past, or they are looking forward to the future where their dreams or fears exist. Life is happening here and now, be present, enjoy it, be curious and open minded.

In being present and curious about life, we can see that life is full of opportunities. Often, we need some courage to catch them, but they are all around us.

People are walking on the street; there is €100 lying on the sidewalk. Many people are passing by without noticing it. Suddenly someone sees it and will pick it up — the same with opportunities around us. There are always opportunities around us. Notice them!

With every opportunity I see, I listen to my intuition; do I have a good feeling about this or not? Even when there is a good feeling, the mind is there, and the fear is pumping up.

It needs courage to deal with it.

My method for this is to figure out as much as I need about this opportunity to be sure, and when it still feels good then make a decision and start. After starting and having made a decision, the fear begins to recede. We have everything we need – the feeling and the information to convince our mind.

On the way, we encounter a lot of people, circumstances and many gifts; we have to be present and see them. The journey is the same or even more important than the destination. Sometimes during the journey, the destination will change, and this is completely okay because during this transition we will be more aware of what we want in life.

Do things that you FEEL you are attracted to, even if your mind is not supportive at this moment. Sometimes our inner voice knows more than our mind. Figure out more about it and don't let your worries sap your energy. If you feel good, you attract positive experiences.

The opportunities are always there, but you cannot see them when you are not opening yourself to them. How do you do it? My question to myself in these situations is: What is the worst thing that can happen?

Our life is all about energy. On some level, we are the sum of the results we achieve. When we are complaining and whining that life is bad, life proves it to us, it's bad, and the opposite is also true. If we feel good, life shows us more good things. This is all about the law of attraction. What helps to raise our energy? Being thankful, doing good things, good music, walking or being in nature, etc. Find out what makes your energy level go higher.

To keep our energy at optimum levels, we need to take care of our physical body too.

Pay attention to moving, nutrition, taking care of your body, and your level of energy will be much higher — the same with our mind. If we don't use it and grow, atrophy will take place. It can be a challenge in the beginning when starting out, but as long as we feel the difference, it's not possible to stop it.

If you feel good, you will attract positive results that will make you feel even better.

When your energy level is low, you can raise it by thinking of things you are thankful for right now.

We take many things in our life for granted until they are not there anymore. So, it's worth appreciating all the time that we have, and there is lots of it. There is a saying, a person is as rich as he (or she) can be grateful for. The person can be wealthy but if he does not appreciate it, then they will always feel it's not enough. There is a secret, be grateful for what you have, and you will have more of what you are grateful for.

Visualization and affirmations.

I've been in many seminars and courses, many tutors have said, write your goals on paper, set the exact date, visualize it and say it to the mirror out loud. I always wrote this suggestion down, but I never did it. Until... One day there was a goal I really wanted. It was the next level in the Network Marketing company I worked for. This title would give me a good income, but more important at that moment, the free luxurious trip to Mauritius with my partner.

It was a huge thing for me at that time.

I was so excited about this opportunity that I would do anything to achieve it. I wrote down the goal, set a date, went to the bathroom and stood next to the mirror. Before that, I was looking around to be sure that I was home alone. I even locked my cat out, then looked to the mirror and said, "I am a Leader." The first few times it was embarrassing, then I just said it, for a while I looked straight to the mirror, and I felt that I AM A LEADER. Finally, I was feeling and acting like the owner of the title; my self-image was changing day by day.

Guess if I took this trip? Yes, I did. This kind of affirmation and visualizing yourself achieving the goal really works.

There is just one BUT... it's better not to stick to our goal if there is a feeling of pressure that the goal is slipping away from you. The great feeling, looking in the mirror, saying in present form: I AM ... and visualizing as we achieve the goal, and then going out and doing your tasks with joy and focusing on helping people, not thinking about our goal but about assisting others.

When we are stuck, we feel pressure, and our energy goes down. People who we are talking to feel it too and it causes a barrier. What should you do when you feel stuck and under pressure? Just take your attention to something else. Go and work out, walk in the natural world, do something different and take yourself off for a while from this action and result. When you feel free about it again, go and act... and have fun with it.

Enjoy every moment of the journey. We set goals, but the most important is what is happening on the way, we may even change our goals when we grow or change the direction, so enjoy.

It's important to be the biggest fan of what you are doing. People can feel it if you are sincere and excited about it, or just scared or unconfident. Action, experiences, knowledge will make you more confident day by day.

Grow, learn from the people who have already achieved what you want to achieve. Seminars, books, webinars, mentors, coaches... there are lots of options you can use for it. Learn and teach what you found out. Teaching is the best way to learn.

Be flexible. Accept that changes are great and happening anyway, whether we want them or not. So be flexible and curious about life.

Investing in self-development is never about wasting time and money. Invest in seminars, books, traveling, etc., and we also need to choose who we listen to. Did they achieve what they are talking about or not, are they experts in this field or just reiterating what they read from books or heard from others. I prefer learning from experts.

We all sometimes feel that things are not going well, but in difficult times we grow the most because we need to find other ways and solutions what we haven't used yet. So, let's play down the difficulties and say to ourselves, "thank you for this opportunity to grow."

Listen to people and add value to their lives. The more we help other people succeed, the more successful we are in turn. If we have authority with people, they listen to us in many areas including what we are doing and the products we are offering.

One thing that is holding us back in achieving success is our comfort zone. Nothing bad about having a rest, but if it lasts too long, it's better to think, didn't I fall back into my comfort zone? Sometimes, we are just thinking and doing nothing; I think we don't need to talk about the importance of actions.

Success is a habit. Make yourself do more things every day and you will get closer to your goals and dreams. If we do something consistently for 40-60 days, it will become habitual. Therefore, we need to do the new habit until we can manage it instinctively.

Look who you are hanging around with. We have, on average, five closest friends. Are they positive, motivated, and encouraging; or are they negative and pessimistic? Who do you want to be? Remember, you will become the average of these five. Choose wisely.

Leave a legacy. Your experiences will help people make better decisions.

Lots of suggestions here, but life is easy. We came here to enjoy it and grow. We can grow by choice or life makes us grow. *Growing by choice is much better.*

Eighty percent of success and happiness is about mindset. Just 20% is about our skills. So we should guard our mindset.

And last, expect miracles and miracles will happen.

Biography

Kadri Kristelle Karu believes there is enough for everyone in this world and we are limitless. If we are ready to learn and grow, we can achieve everything we desire or even something better. Her formula works: **dream-goal-affirmation-plan-learn-act-receive**.

The most important thing in life is to *enjoy the journey*.

Contact Information

Website: BeyondSuccesswithKadriKristelleKaru.com
Facebook: https://www.facebook.com/kadri.karu.5
YouTube:
https://www.youtube.com/channel/UCDYbU5hYbQuvbZHYoMF798A?view_as=subscriber

Chapter 27

IT IS YOUR TIME

By Kammy Chibueze

"We have to let go of the life society has planned for us and create the life we desire." - Kammy Chibueze

I cannot recall when I started school, but I guess it was earlier than school age. My mum was a teacher, so she probably took me along to her class immediately after her maternity leave, which could be the reason I cannot remember.

However, I do remember the consciousness of being in school from primary grade three. It was the year I participated in training for the state primary interschool sports competition — the thought of being an athlete resonated with me. I was the only primary grade three pupil in a team with primary grade five and grade six pupils, so I was treated like the star kid. The feeling was so amazing that I decided from then to always do my best.

Then one day, the Headmaster of the school, who was my dad, called me into his office and said, "Son, you are very young and still have a lot of time for sports ahead of you but now you need to focus on your study. You can still play ball, but after completing your schooling."

That was my first encounter with the rules of society.

My first acid test for these rules came when I had to participate in a common entrance examination, which is a prerequisite test for admission into Nigerian secondary schools. The emphasis on the test was so intense that the night before the examination, I kneeled and prayed for God to help me excel, and I promised Him that I would study hard hereafter. God did His part; I passed with one of the least grades. Did I keep my part of the deal? Well, that remains to be seen.

Going to Boarding School

My first day in the boarding house was dramatic. I thought I was attending a secondary school in the area where my parents lived. However, my dad had other plans. He informed me that I would be attending Comprehensive Secondary School Nawfia in Anambra state, Nigeria.

On Sunday evening, that fateful day, my dad and I arrived at school and unloaded my luggage, after which he handed me over to the hostel prefect who I found so mean. There was no sign of a smile on his face, so I assumed he must be one of the wicked seniors. The story some of us were told by our friends who were in the dormitory was that secondary school hostels were filled with wicked seniors and prefects.

I was so troubled about how my life would be in this school that I started crying when my dad was about to leave. I pleaded with him to let me go back with him so I can officially resume on Monday. To my surprise, he refused even when I threatened not to take bread and provisions he bought for me, bread and tea was my favorite breakfast menu. Well, I guess this is why he didn't bring my mum along.

Well, after two weeks, I made new friends and began planning how to continue with my sports being a good distance away from home. But I was wrong. My secondary school father was the library prefect; I guess God knew I could not have kept my promise without proper support. Senior Hill, as he was popularly known, is a bookworm, so no wonder he was the library prefect. He noticed my great interest in sports and reminded me of the primary reason why I was there. It was the same rule my dad gave me a few years back in primary school. He expected me to be one of the best in my class and graduate with a good grade to gain admission into one of the best universities. Again, taking this from his sermon on the societal expectations of schooling.

To achieve the objective he already set out for me, he made me study with him in the senior class every early morning and every evening. It is against the dormitory norms for a junior student to have his evening class in the senior student class. But being a well-respected student because of his intelligence and his leadership, none of the senior students raised an eyebrow. So, I had no other choice than to study hard. At the end of each class, I had to share what I had learned first with him and then with other students in my hostel – a culture our school created to ensure students take their studies seriously.

This study routine helped significantly with shaping my reading habit and improving my classwork performance, to the extent that my teacher once commented on my report card that I was doing great and had big room for improvement.

Becoming a Science Student

My excellent performance lasted for the first three years in junior secondary, and when I entered senior secondary, my performance began to dwindle. Two things contributed to this; one, I passed the entrance examination into special science school, without knowing that sports were an abomination while playing to my heart's content. It took the humiliating comment by our principal, on the assembly ground, to be reminded about the essence of schooling, the education of the mind to solely focus on passing examinations, and not to seek endeavors that resonate with one's heart. My name was mentioned among the students who will not perform well in the upcoming West Africa Examination Council (WAEC). This message was conveyed to me by my closest friend, who we jokingly nicknamed Isiukwu due to his big head; he was a brilliant fellow.

Being an emotional person, I was so affected by the principal's statement that I swore to never participate in sports again. Subsequently, I started living a life of solitude, forcing myself to read, but I knew I was deceiving myself because the principal's negative comment never left my mind. It took the encouragement and support of my great friend to weather through the storm, and to the glory of God, at least I came out with a good result to secure admission into a university.

University Life

It seems that every time I started the next level of schooling, my affinity for sports resurfaced. Despite my prior honest and emotion-laden declaration never to have anything to do with sports, I still played a big role in the university football club.

However, I had to give up other sporting activities to cope with my studies. The university education mission was no different from the two foundational educations I had. The importance was still on passing all the examinations with a good grade to get employment in a company that pays well. If you call it an education of the mind without the heart, you will not be wrong.

However, on completion of my National Youth Service Corps, I tried once again to pursue my dream in professional football. I reminded my dad about our agreement, which he did not only honor, but he also took me to the person in charge of a football club I intended to join. But society never let me be, despite my dad's endorsement. While I was at the Rangers International football club, most of my relatives, who knew I was playing football after university, were disappointed in me. They said, after all the money my parents spent on my education, this was how I repaid them when I should have just gone and played football instead of wasting time and money on university. I finally gave up on my intention of following my heart and joined the rat race.

Getting Employed

The greatest disadvantage of the Prussian education system is that we are not encouraged to find our gifts and seek adventure but rather to solely be schooled to find paid employment as if it is the only means to exchange value in the marketplace. My job search followed the societal rule to look for a good company that pays well instead of the laws of the universe that say "Man know thyself" and do what you love.

This is not My Message

I am not trying to undervalue formal education. It is imperative for individuals to attend university because it is the new standard six of the olden days, especially in developing countries. As John Obidi, JO, as he is fondly called, wrote an article titled "On University Education," and said that no matter how smart you think you will be in the future, how talented you are, it will be hard to explain your value without a university or post-secondary education. I agree with this philosophy. But my point is that schools should focus their resources on educating us to draw out what lies within us rather than suppress it.

What use is it to work when the worker is not using his talent or being stuck in a job he hates?

Looking at the trajectory of my journey through life so far, it's characterized by a running battle between societal expectations and my desire to express the giant that lies within. Yet, from a historical review or statistic, successful or famous men and women, from all over the world, never became successful and famous through work they were not passionate about or had no meaning to them.

This brings me to Rules versus Laws in the philosophy of success

There are rules, and there are laws. The rules are made by men according to societal objectives that benefit a few, and they can change these rules at any given time when the prevailing conditions are no longer beneficial. Laws, on the other hand, are universal and natural as day and night, rain and sun, life and death, and they are unchangeable. Suffice to say, the cost of an unsuccessful life is rooted in following the rules made by men while beyond successful living is a result of abiding by the laws of success.

What are these laws of success? I will not be able to dive into all the 12 Laws of Success, as shared by the great Napoleon Hill, but the core of these laws of success is foundational; the law of love of thy labor whether seeking admission to university, or searching for work, or starting a business, obeying this one basic law will help you avoid struggles in life.

It was with this insight that I never let go again when I realized that I have a passion to inspire people to be intentional in creating the life they desire. I pursue this with all my heart, and the result is historical for me. Co-authoring with Matt Morris, author of the bestseller, "The Unemployed Millionaire," along with twenty other influential authors, is a personal manifestation of the power of passion over the rules of society.

It is Your Time

Now, it is your time to let go of the life that society planned for you and create a life you desire. It is your time to fight for what you believe you are called to do. If you missed the lesson from my story, here it is… It's more mentality than ability or talent; it is our resilience to continue in the direction of our calling to CREATE the *Beyond Success story*.

BIOGRAPHY

Kammy Chibueze is a writer, entrepreneur, and founder of the PassionCare Academy, a social enterprise that helps individuals reawaken their life purpose. He is a member of the National Speaker Association (USA) and an alumnus of the School of Eloquence, Nigeria. He has trained over a thousand people on work ethics, personal development, and quality improvement systems during his over ten years as a manager in a multinational company. He hails from Enugu and resides in Port-Harcourt, Rivers State, Nigeria.

CONTACT INFORMATION

Facebook: https://www.facebook.com/kammy.ude
Instagram: https://www.instagram.com/kammychibueze/

Chapter 28

THE FIRST TIME I FAILED IN MY LIFE WAS THE DAY I WAS BORN

By Kate Jones

I was born a girl, not a boy, and that was a huge disappointment to my father. As I grew up and became more self-aware, it became apparent that every time my father looked at me, there was a cloud of disappointment hanging over him. And as children do, I tried to make myself into the person that I thought he wanted me to be, believing that I would make him proud of me. So, I grew up attempting to be someone else and trying to please others. It was hard, and with each passing year, I buried my true self under layer upon layer of pretending to be someone else until the point where I began to believe the lie and lost sight of the real me.

I felt the only thing I was good at was being a failure, but deep down inside was a part of me that stubbornly refused to give up. There was a small voice deep within me that kept whispering, "I'm here. The real, true you. Let me out so I can be the person I was meant to be."

I refused to listen.

I continued to hide away and tried to be someone I wasn't.

So why am I telling you all this?

The title of this book is Success Unlimited, and here I am talking about abject failure.

Well, there comes a point in everyone's life where we draw a line in the sand, where the pain of being where we are now far outweighs the fear of any change. I reached that point. I had this toxic relationship with money. I desperately wanted more of it, but I hated the fact that no matter what I did, there was never enough. I eventually ended up in deep financial shit, stuck in an abusive relationship and in the depths of despair.

It seemed I was always destined to fail. And therein lay my problem. What I failed to understand was the Law of Attraction - like attracts like. Negativity attracts negativity. A belief in self-failure attracts failure. Limiting self-beliefs attract limiting results. When you constantly focus on the things you DON'T have right now, you will NEVER see the things you CAN have because the universe can only give you what you are focusing on RIGHT NOW.

Now, before you roll your eyes and tell me I'm going all "woo woo" on you, hear me out. Everything I am about to tell you now has its basis in quantum physics. Yep, that's right. Proven, researched, scientific fact. I am no scientist, and I won't go into a load of technical stuff about neutrons, electrons, positrons, etc. We, humans, are all, at our most basic cellular level, nothing more than pure energy. That's a scientifically proven fact. We are vibrating at various frequencies, positivity being high vibration and negativity being low vibration. That's also a scientifically proven fact. We have a measurable energy field around and within us. Guess what... that's a scientifically proven fact as well. Quantum scientists (Einstein included) have proven that all physical matter is made up of energy packets that are not bound by space and time. This energy field has no well-defined boundaries. Science has also proven that the mind has no boundaries.

So where does all this lead in terms of success? I'll take you back to the Law of Attraction. Like attracts like. What if, instead of being negative, and filling our lives with thoughts of failure, desperation and wanting things we don't have, we were to focus on the positive, look at and be grateful for the things we DO have and make the decision to love ourselves instead of allowing feelings of despair and failure?

How do you think that might change things? Surely, if the negativity in the past has brought about only more negativity, doesn't it stand to reason that positivity should bring about more positivity? Surely, if we are happy, we will attract more happiness? If we are grateful for the things we DO have, surely, we will get even more of those things? What if we put out feelings of self-love? Won't we get more love back? The answer to all of those questions is YES. The Universe only knows how to answer YES. Whatever you put out there you will get a YES back.

Negativity will return negativity. Believing you are a failure will only give you more failure. Worrying about debt will only bring more debt. Thinking you will always be alone means you WILL always be alone. Do you get the picture?

THIS WAS THE MASSIVE TURNING POINT IN MY LIFE.

I finally realized that the person solely responsible for everything negative that happened and was happening in my life was me. Boy, that was a really hard lesson to learn. Gone were all my excuses that blamed others. Gone was my justification for being angry with my father, my ex-husband and even my abusive partner.

Shit!!!!

It was ALL DOWN TO ME. Now notice, I'm not saying it was all my FAULT. I am not blaming anyone for where I ended up, not even myself. Blame is a negative vibration that only leads back to more negativity.

Instead, I've accepted that I did not make mistakes for which I could blame myself. I merely made decisions that had a different outcome to the one that I expected. And I made those decisions from a point of not knowing any better.

What this means is that success is available to every one of us. We must change our mindset, change our perspective and change who we are. We need to learn to control our natural monkey-brain that wants us to conform to what we have always experienced, to be who we have always been and to stay in our (dis)comfort zone. At this point, I am going to ask you a question. What is it you truly, deeply want? And what is it that is stopping you from achieving it? Do you want wealth, time, freedom, family time, abundance in your life, peace, contentment, fun, joy, health, to travel the world, to do whatever you want, be whoever you want, be the best possible version of yourself?

I don't think I can hear anyone saying "no" at this point. So, what is it that's stopping you from having all that? Limiting self-beliefs? Fear of failure? Disbelief? Thinking that it's only possible for other better people? Feeling you are not worthy of having all that? I can't afford to do it? I don't want to leave my comfort zone; it's too scary? What if I were to say that all those excuses were just your monkey-brain trying to protect you? What if I was to say you CAN have all of that and it's quite simple. Well, I've got news for you (and this is the MASSIVE lesson I learned that has utterly and completely changed my life).

The Universe (remember that scientifically proven stuff we talked about earlier) only knows how to say YES. So, if you ask for money, health, happiness, love, soulmate, success, peace, fulfillment, and whatever else you want in life, what do you think you are going to get?

Now I'll put a rider in here; it's not just a case of saying "OK Universe I want blah blah blah" and expecting to get it.

Remember the Law of Attraction?

Like attracts like.

If you want someone to love you, then you must learn to love yourself first.

If you want to receive love, give it first.

If you want more money, be grateful for every penny that is currently in your bank account.

You MUST develop a different mindset.

You must learn to believe in yourself and the fact that you CAN have everything you want.

Practice deliberate thoughts and intentions (positive ones not negative ones).

Clear out all the negative junk from your mind and your life (including negative people). Surround yourself with like-minded, positive, and supportive people.

Develop a positive mindset and wealth consciousness.

Be thankful for everything you have RIGHT NOW and stop focusing on the things you don't have. Become "I am" not "I am not." Become the person you want to be NOW, don't wait.

Educate yourself on how you can achieve the level of mindfulness that brings about true joy, wealth and abundance. Read, read, and read!

Start your day being grateful for everything in your life.

Every. Single. Thing.

Every. Single. Morning.

This is NON-NEGOTIABLE.

If you want the Universe to give you everything, start by being grateful for everything you already have. Apart from being the start of getting all those things you want, it actually makes you feel positive and happy.

When you are grateful and happy, it is IMPOSSIBLE to feel fear. (Again, a scientifically proven fact. Our brain is incapable of feeling fear and gratitude/love at the same time). If you have no fear, you can achieve absolutely anything in life.

Become acutely aware of your subconscious and what it is doing. Your subconscious is responsible for all your self-sabotaging habits, from your beliefs, values, emotions, habits, imagination, and intuition. Learn to become very aware of what your subconscious is thinking and doing because most of your self-limiting beliefs, negative values, feelings, and emotions come from your subconscious and you are not even aware of it.

Learn to listen to what it is doing and correct any negativity.

Stop all negative thoughts in their tracks and replace them with positive ones.

Stop all self-sabotaging thoughts and activities.

Raise your self-awareness to a much higher level, one that you can manage and control. Mindfulness and self-awareness are the two key things to remember and work on.

I am living proof that you CAN change your life dramatically for the better and I want to reach out to as many people as possible and show them and YOU that you don't have to remain in a poverty mindset, facing failure over and over again and feeling utterly shit about yourself.

It is ABSOLUTELY possible to change your life and have everything you ever wanted.

Success is NOT just about money. True happiness, wealth, abundance, and ultimately success comes from WITHIN YOU. It comes from aligning yourself to the one thing that connects everything and everyone – the Universe (remember it's scientifically proven and not woo woo!).

It comes from gratitude, giving and belief that you ARE worthy of having everything you want in life.

It comes from one simple decision to make a change. Don't you owe it to yourself to become the best possible version of yourself? Become the joyous, abundant, wealthy, healthy, grateful person that you have the opportunity to be.

I want you to feel the sheer joy that floods my life every moment. Even when I have moments of doubt or worry, I know how to deal with them, embrace them, analyze them, and then let them go.

I want you to have the wealth consciousness that will deliver you the financial freedom and peace you want, and deserve.

I want you to have the positive mindset that will give you courage, strength, optimism, belief, and gratitude for everything you have right now.

I want you to stop worrying about tomorrow's problems and start enjoying the peace and beauty of today, knowing that your future is secured.

I want you to understand that you CAN have everything you want and that ultimately you can have unlimited success in every single aspect of your life. And above all, I want you to learn to love yourself and know that you are loved in return.

The Universe only knows how to say YES.

What do you want it to say YES to today?

Biography

Kate Jones is a 55-year-old single mother and grandma who finally decided enough was enough. A lifelong self-limiting view of never being good enough in any sphere of life led to a decision to take a totally radical and different approach to life. What followed was a powerful process of personal growth and spirituality that has led to massive life changes and a mission to help others achieve the same.

Contact Information

Facebook https://www.facebook.com/kate.jones.55
YouTube https://www.youtube.com/channel/UCfDJBUR7J_tGR40xzVSRF4g
Instagram https://www.instagram.com/katejonesonline/
Website https://www.katejonesonline.com/

Chapter 29

DIRECTION AND PURPOSE

By Kenneth Hill

I struggle with the basics of daily time management. No matter how often I use my planner or try to take time off, I suddenly find myself wishing I had two or three of me to get everything done or help put out fires.

It's similar to the dog and the squirrel cartoon where the dog loses complete focus and is distracted when he sees the squirrel.

It seems more people today are struggling with the ability to find direction and execute objectives with meaningful purpose. So, let's get back to the basic training that gave me real exposure to "Direction and Purpose." I had no idea what it would take to become a soldier or what the expectations would be for me to fulfill that requirement. I was full of indecision with a lack of purpose, as was everyone else who was with me. But we had people there (drill sergeants) whose sole purpose was to transform us into the type of people the military needed.

Each morning, we were woken up before the sun to run two miles or do an hour of calisthenics before breakfast. This was all to teach us to find direction and purpose even if we had no clue what it might be. As time went by, we began to understand what it meant to be "HIGH SPEED NO DRAG!" (one of my favorite sayings).

Our objective became clear. We learned how to have a meaningful purpose in everything we did. Meaningful purpose is not always understood as it means different things to different people. To us, it meant giving our all in everything we did and sucking as much life out of every moment we possibly could! Hence the saying, "YOU PEOPLE NEED TO MOVE LIKE YOU HAVE A PURPOSE IN LIFE!"

We sometimes flounder on committing to the direction we chose, even though it is our heart's desire. We procrastinate by putting other things or people in front of what we want.

STOP IT! STOP IT NOW! Do not lose track of your direction!

Life happens and you must adjust, which is why the line to success is far from straight. But, by staying true to your direction and focusing on it as the most important thing you need to do is how you check it off the To-do list. But we can only do one thing at a time. Distractions and interruptions delay objectives making them un-realized. So, it's easier to give up or move it to the back burner, ultimately, robbing yourself of your heart's desires.

Remember when you first fell in love and that person made your heart skip a beat. Remember how you pursued them for that first date and every date after that, hell or high water could not stop your obsession or make you lose focus. This is the kind of direction you need to fulfill your life's aspirations.

The thing that people seem to forget is each direction they take has its own set of goals that must be accomplished for the objectives to come to fruition. As each goal is completed, you are closer to fulfilling your aspirations, but "SQUIRREL" can and does happen, and the impact is determined by the amount of importance you give it, so choose how much value it has in becoming a game-changer.

I worked with several veterans who faced setbacks, both mentally and physically, which could have taken them out of the game completely. A defining moment came when they decided to rebuild their lives in a new direction. So, they picked themselves up, dusted themselves off and got back on that horse, whatever that horse may be.

So, it is with every direction we take in life that requires us to make a decision and follow through to accomplish our objectives. We must obsess about it in a healthy and fulfilling way. You will only get out what you put into it. If it has no true purpose to empower it, give it drive and bring it to life, then it will wither and maybe even die or at least die in our hearts.

Here is a little secret to help keep your direction alive and well. Your direction is "a dream to be pursued wholeheartedly," or for those of you who are realists, it is a thought or possibly a desire to guide you in what you want to accomplish. To me, it is a dream of what I want to make real in my life and I pursue it just as I would pursue anything that matters to me. Regardless if it's a career or a life goal, you must breathe life into it.

In the military, most decisions are made for you, including the direction you will go. But you must have a purpose, breathe life into it, and do it for yourself, "Do or Die" so to speak. It's not to say you won't experience disruptions along the way, because you will. But, its how those disruptions define you that show the world who you have become and what you stand for. The military has some of the most effective ways to bring out the best in a person by teaching them how to make sound decisions and follow the direction set before them. Even if they only served for a short period, they learned how to make a decision and follow directions, so they were less indecisive and more purpose driven.

In the civilian world, someone who served in the military has a definite advantage in the "decision and direction" category; not to say it's always true but it's shown to be more often than not. The good news is that it can be a learned trait, so anyone can do it and become very effective given enough time and practice.

We are the directors of our lives. We decide how our day will go every time we wake up. I wake up and start my day (COFFEE). As the day evolves, I reflect on thanking God for giving me another opportunity to make a difference and set my course of direction. And, that could be finishing what I did not finish yesterday or working on the direction of my dreams.

It's now time to define the word PURPOSE!

Purpose, as defined by the Webster's New World Dictionary is:

"To intend, resolve, or plan
something one intends to get or do; intention;
resolution; determination
the object for which something exists or is done; end in view
Of set purpose 1 with a specific end in view
not accidentally; by design
On purpose by design; intentionally
To good purpose with a good result or effect; advantageously
To little (or no) purpose with little or no result or effect; pointlessly
To the purpose relevant; pertinent
Such a strong and dutiful word, it screams ACTION!"

In no sense of that word do we get to slack off or be lazy. It breathes life into anything that we apply it to. When we wholeheartedly pursue our dreams, it takes on an even more powerful meaning. Never back away from the things that we've committed to, binding us to our purpose, and directing us to follow through no matter what stands in our way.

There are some boundaries that should not be crossed ethically. Remember to stay humble and pleasant. Don't be pushy or arrogant when applying your purpose to whatever you want to accomplish.

While I was in the military, everything we did had a purpose even if we did not understand it at the time. It seemed like the same old, same old. But it prepared us for the things we had to do that helped ensure our survival in tough situations. It instilled a strong mental fortitude to make sure we would persevere to the finish, improvise, adapt, and overcome any obstacle that lay ahead.

As a civilian, the same holds true for our jobs and our dreams. We find ways to improvise, adapt, and overcome setbacks that come our way, even if it's not with the same fervor that military members may have. We too must have and apply purpose to our everyday lives if we want to flourish and thrive.

When we apply meaningful purpose and direction, our inherent abilities become even more useful in the pursuit of our dreams. It's our drive and that extra zest that pushes us a little bit harder instead of allowing ourselves to back out before reaching our goals and desires.

Biography

Kenneth Hill is a veteran of over 28 years with insight, discipline, and purpose, which are the envy of many. Kenneth is a business owner and adventurer. His lovely wife calls him "Mister Fix-It" and for good reason.

Contact Information

Facebook: http://facebook.com/KenHill

CHAPTER 30

REINVENTING YOURSELF EVEN IF IT WASN'T YOUR PLAN

By Laarni San Juan

The morning of my 44th birthday in October 2012 started with dreary skies. My husband and daughter greeted me with a handmade card and a warm cup of my favorite Bustelo coffee. My mind swirled with a strong mix of emotions throughout the day where I laughed but also cried. There was a cloud of guilt that floated over me. I celebrated four decades of achievements that certainly made my family proud.

My nursing career was draped with awards. I had a supportive, handsome husband with a thriving dental practice, a witty teen daughter, a home in a big city, and a great circle of girlfriends who cheered me on. I also have pretty good hair for my age, minimal wrinkles, and a car that runs. But why did I still feel incomplete? What was missing? Am I greedy to not be satisfied even after *making it*? Day after day, internet headlines and social media posts talk about being grateful. I am, dammit, but is it wrong to be grateful AND want more? Since I was young, I craved learning more than what was expected of me. The teacher assigned one chapter, but I read two. I always attempted extra credit on homework. I sharpened not just three pencils but the whole box.

The overachiever in me grew up with immigrant parents who chanted daily, "You are lucky to be in America, so work hard." So, I did. The mantra was uttered (or more like muttered) because they often compared their life to the impoverished living conditions of their upbringing. They left their home country because they knew opportunities were abundant in the United States. I witnessed my middle-class parents labor day in and day out to ensure that my older brother and I were comfortable.

It was my mother, who was middle-class. She got a college degree in chemistry in the Philippines and landed a job as a laboratory scientist at a big university in the 1960s. She made a decent wage in San Francisco where she lovingly supported the family, including siblings who also moved one-by-one to the US. My father who was 26 years older than my mom, barely finished his third-grade education. He worked as a janitor in the financial district and was fully retired when I was in elementary school. On our bus rides to school, he repetitively told the story of how he joined his buddies on a three-month ship journey in the 1920s that arrived in San Francisco. He earned 10 cents a day in the hot fields picking produce and then spent his downtime paying to dance with white women in dance halls. All these memories were the realities of their livelihood, and so those stories stay locked into my fabric and how I see the world.

It was from my parents' stories with underlying themes of struggle, seeking opportunity, acquiring a good education, and risk that pushed me to go to college where I eagerly got a Bachelor's degree in nursing, studied astronomy and human sexuality, and got a minor degree in Asian American Studies. I loved school so much that I pursued a Master's degree in public health. Soon after graduate school, I worked passionately as a community health nurse in the streets of San Francisco with high-risk children, often living in dire conditions and homeless shelters. I loved my job because I practiced the science of nursing, the art of helping, and the love of serving others. I often stayed after hours, never expecting overtime or a raise. I went above and beyond my call of duty. I secretly bought diapers for new mothers that couldn't afford them. I never expected anything in return.

For years, I put faith in the systems that took care of me, and I assumed those same systems understood and respected my passion. As time passed and as I matured in my career and in my ability to advocate, my moves got bolder. I worked my way to be on director boards, commissions, initiatives, movements, and classroom head. I mentored and provided support when asked. Giving was a natural expression of who I was. I spoke up against injustice. I stood up for those who didn't have the words to express themselves. I openly voiced my opinions and challenged the status quo. It became an addiction for me to be bold and stay bold.

However, the reality of how the world really works showed up. I learned that my perspective wasn't always favored nor accepted. When conflict and differences arose, I was victimized and bullied to weaken my stance and silence my voice. My mother didn't know how to support me because she never fully understood what I did for a living (I didn't hold a traditional nurse job in a hospital), nor did she understand why I had the nerve to speak out. "Laarni, stay quiet, and don't get into trouble." I got to a point of helplessness. I thought I was strong, but the bullying was hitting me in my core.

There were many times I wanted to give in and leave the profession. How dare the system try to take me out of the game even after I poured my soul into doing the right thing? My mind answered that it was a temporary crisis and that the mojo I once felt will eventually come back. I cried a lot in my cubicle and during intentional long walks to release tears and then quickly wipe up before I had to see the next patient in the queue. I came home with stooped shoulders and would make a beeline to the living room where I sat like a zombie in the dark. My family gently kissed my forehead, and I instinctively knew that was a sign they were running out of comforting words to say.

This went on for years. I saw from the corner of my eye that I was wearing out my husband and daughter all because of MY inability to handle MY stress, MY frustration, and MY anger. Here I am fighting against injustice and for the right conditions in communities, yet I was neglecting the conditions in my own home, including my self-worth. I wanted so badly to snap out of it, but it wasn't easy. My own mental funk was messing with me. My health started to fail. I gained weight faster than I could lose it, my cravings for junk food skyrocketed, my thyroid medication was increased to keep up with the physiological changes, and I was struggling to keep up with the cortisol that was flooding my body. I revisited old therapists, met with new ones, and had constant trips to my medical provider who seemed to be at a loss of how to help me and my despair. She ran out of referrals to give me. Psychiatrists offered me depression medication, but I knew deep down that the sadness I was going through had more do about unresolved frustration more than anything else.

I wore out my well-meaning friends because I was a broken record. I felt desperate. My life coach offered a piece of advice: stay in my lane, ignore the noise, and focus my mind on what I really wanted. That sounded simple enough. I liked the sound of it, and my overachiever self embraced it. I wanted to rekindle the joy and passion I first felt when I started my health professional career. I heeded the advice of my coach, but after a couple months I wondered which lane was she talking about? I have about five lanes to deal with on a daily basis: wife, mother, friend, woman of color, and nurse. Soft whispers from deep within my soul came in my ear every morning, "Laarni, you want more, so go get it."

I had no idea what that "more" looked like at this juncture of my life, but I knew that I couldn't possibly stay in this stupor forever. It's a lousy feeling, and all I kept thinking was that I was letting my loved ones and community down if I stayed in this miserable state. I instinctively knew I had to let go of the pain, hurt, and frustration that was wearing me down. I had to. I was certain that all the pain I felt stemmed from the stings of the job, my middle-aged body going through its changes, raising a child in this hectic generation, and wrestling with the guilt that I wasn't always present in my marriage.

To make myself feel better, I daydreamed about the happy parts of my childhood that filled my soul. Those days were carefree and stress-free. My cousins teased me that I often opted out of playing with them and instead chose to clean the toy room they left in disarray. It was there that I played store. I owned the business and organized the products meticulously, and I made price tags for everything. I also played the customer role who bought stuff. My cousins left me alone because they found much more excitement roughhousing each other until our grandmother said to quiet it down. As the business owner of my faux store, I maintained a ledger and kept track of my stock, prices, and store hours. I was organized, alert and a multitasker at a young age. Although I was drawn to the biological sciences in my formative years, I also embraced the business-minded soul that lived within me. I collected knickknacks that I re-sold for money. I was an entrepreneur at heart.

During those years of despair and emptiness, I managed to stay connected with my networks and the communities I grew up with. One of the ways I gave back was doing radio and sharing nuggets about different topics. I enjoyed doing segments on parenting, a topic dear to me as a parent myself, and I also referenced material I used when teaching parenting classes for over ten years. It was during that fateful weekend at the radio station in December 2015, when I met another guest speaker whose topic was about business and the importance of getting more women to take the entrepreneurial path. I couldn't believe what I was hearing: business, entrepreneur, and women in the same sentence. It was like soothing music to my ears.

I was shown a business venture that woke up the Laarni who felt defeated, tired, and apathetic. I got involved not knowing what it all meant, but there were undoubtedly two feelings that overpowered my senses: awe and hope. It was a powerful jolt that I wish anyone in despair can experience. When life feels daunting, burdensome, and overwhelming, it's difficult to see any future past the next 12 hours. The sensations of awe and hope revived me as if CPR was done on me repeatedly. As I dove into my business world, I rekindled my sense of excitement. Over time, I noticed my despair lighten up. I knew things were getting better because loved ones were noticing the pep in my step and a new kind of smile that beamed from my face.

This has been a journey of grieving my old self while also birthing a new version of my new self.

I hope the stories I share lands in someone else's heart. I hope my contributions inspire and put light into darkened spirits. It's only until we recognize our own context can we change, enhance, and motivate ourselves to transform.

BIOGRAPHY

Laarni San Juan is a nurse, community champion, and thought leader. She received her Bachelor of Science in Nursing at San Francisco State and a Master's in Public Health at UCLA. Her drive to continuously grow and lead by example got her recognized as one of the "100 Most Influential Filipina Women in the US." With over 25 years as a healthcare professional, she has a deep understanding of how communities thrive, and the struggles and injustices of the human spirit. Her journey filled with loss, grief, and disappointment, has challenged her to rise up and discover her true potential. On radio, print and mentorship circles, Laarni openly discusses how resilience and the will to win leads to personal growth and opportunities.

CONTACT INFORMATION

Instagram: https://instagram.com/sweetandfocusedlife

Chapter 31
SCARED OF BUTTERFLIES?

By Larysa Bednarchyk

Scared of butterflies? That's the question my son, who has developmental and intellectual challenges, will ask if you ever meet him. Aren't they attractive? When you see a butterfly, don't you want to extend your hand so it can land on your finger? But, to become a beautiful butterfly is not easy. They would not be butterflies if they didn't go through the whole process, and only the strongest can bring their beauty to the world, like the prettiest flower that grows through a lot of dirt before blooming.

I believe we can relate to this too. Life is not a perfect ride for anybody, even for the very successful. Your mindset, positive thinking, beliefs, and your attitude are key to keep going in life.

I was fortunate growing up with all the love and attention an only child can get. My dad was my role model, my hero, and my mom has always been my best friend and supporter. They were proud of me, and I was always the top student in school. And, after graduating from the best university in the country, I got a prestigious job in the big city, where my parents moved after my dad retired from the military. I got married, we welcomed three kids, and then everything changed when the country I grew up in, fell apart. At this time, many people didn't understand what was going to happen. My then-husband won the Green Card Lottery, and we moved to the United States with three little kids. This was 20 years ago.

Since I was the only one who spoke a bit of English, which I learned in school, I automatically became in charge of everything: housing, finances, school, sports, health, etc. We had few people who helped us at the beginning, and I am truly grateful. But, most of the time, while everybody was sleeping, it was me sitting up with the dictionary, (there was no access to computers or iPhones), paperwork and bills trying to figure out what to do. I started to work at the grocery store in the evenings and weekends to make ends meet. One of my son's therapists in his early intervention program referred me to one of the best ophthalmology practices in the country.

I started as a receptionist and the doctor I worked for was a great teacher. I learned a lot about the eyes considering my background was economics. Then, I decided to take a course in medical billing, which I did at night. After a few years, I was offered a full-time position at the main office of the same practice in downtown Chicago. Around the same time, I passed the citizenship test and officially became a US citizen. I thought I was finally on the right path to becoming successful. My ego was celebrating, but not my checking account. I was cleaning houses on the weekends, making and selling jewelry, and still trying to figure out how to get a comfortable income.

One morning, my son came up to me, looked me in the eye and asked, "Mom, do you still love us? Because dad said, you're working so much that you probably don't love us anymore." The realization that my husband is not being supportive was painful. I knew I would not stay in this relationship. But I also couldn't imagine if I would survive alone with three kids. So, I worked harder and found fulfillment at work where I had new responsibilities. I met new friends in coworkers and patients. Being an introvert, it was rewarding to feel a patient's appreciation.

A few years ago, a friend invited me to attend a workshop on personal growth. I found what I was looking for! There was a completely different atmosphere, and I was surrounded by likeminded people looking for something more in life. Working hard is good, but you need to work hard with a goal in mind and with purpose. I realized I never had a clear purpose. I work to make money, I had dreams but they were simple, small, and didn't excite me that much. I never allowed myself to dream big; my dreams were always limited by reality. Even watching fairytale movies, I thought it would never happen to me, only to other people.

One day, the schoolteacher called me in and read an essay my son wrote about superheroes. "For someone, the superhero is the Spiderman, or Power Ranger, for me - it's my mom." He raised the bar so high for me that I started believing I was able to be their superhero, their role model. I found my purpose and that was all that mattered. It helped change my thinking.

One of my favorite Russian authors is Leo Tolstoy who said, "If you want to be happy, be." That phrase stuck in my mind since school. So I decided that first, I need to figure out what it means to be happy. Everybody has their own understanding of success and happiness. Making more money would not make you happier because money is simply a tool to get what you want.

We always do what's important for us, but the problem is to set up priorities. Once I figured out that seeing the world, visiting new places, meeting new people, and experiencing new cultures excited me the most, there was no way for me to stay where I was.

With that said, I chose:

- Not to live in the past, because I can't change it. The more time I spend on whining about what happened to me, the less time I have to enjoy today and plan my future. My grandfather was a World War II veteran captured by the Germans. He was eventually released. But he hadn't seen his family for a long time. I remember him as a great math teacher, funny storyteller, and a big theater lover who sang opera songs all day! I found out about his past not long ago.
- Get rid of negative thoughts, and never let other people influence my mood. Ships don't sink because of water around them; ships sink because of the water that gets in them. Sometimes it means unlearning what I was taught. Times change and so do the rules. What worked when I grew up may not be relevant now. I am not talking about manners, kindness, or behavior, but about being open-minded and accepting new changes happening in technology, economy, and business. According to Benjamin Hardy, the average person has between 12,000 and 60,000 thoughts a day, 80% are negative, and 95% are repetitive. Let's change the statistics, and train ourselves to be powerful and control our thoughts because what we think, we become. Discover how to channel your energy. If you have a bad day, meditate, sing, dance, pray, read a good book, but don't get stuck. Get to the point where your thoughts and emotions don't change based on the insignificant actions or words of someone else.

- Turn bad situations into lessons and see opportunity in failure. I am where I am now because of the choices I made. There is nobody else to blame. Finally, I divorced, and a few months ago, I was laid off at work. Being busy with a lot of responsibilities at the office, I didn't see it coming. But lately, I wasn't happy there. At some point, I knew something had to change. So, I looked at this situation as my chance to change the direction of my life, and work on what I think is more important for me. When life gives you lemons, don't make lemonade, make life take the lemons back. I believe everything happens for a reason. You may not see it right away, but just when you think everything is falling apart, it actually starts falling into place. Your job is to keep going and focus on the light during your darkest moments. All of us are going through the yo-yo cycles, and the harder you hit the ground, the higher you will bounce.
- Open my mind to the enormous unreal dreams and become a baby who thinks everything is possible because it is. Dreams are not supposed to be realistic; that's why they are dreams. If you notice a lot of people who reached significant success in life, talk about dreams they had before their success. Without dreams, we would keep using candles; we wouldn't have cars, airplanes, or movies. I started to work on extending my imagination and create a bucket list that I wouldn't allow myself to previously consider and nurture my mind with great ideas. Live my beliefs and turn my world around.
- Take responsibility for my life, choose my thoughts, make a decision to chase my dreams with all my heart and efforts, live every day as if it's the best day of my life, and share my happiness with others. When you take responsibility, an urge and hunger develops to keep chasing those dreams to accomplish them. I am not where I want to be, but I am the only one who is personally responsible for the change. I cannot change my past or my circumstances, but I can change myself, my thoughts, my reaction, and my life.

We all have our purpose in this world that makes us significant. We are all different, and that makes life interesting. But, when we choose our thoughts and let our imagination work, our dreams unfold in front of us. They become our goals and our passion, and when we take full responsibility for our actions, we are unstoppable. Don't be scared of the butterflies. Become a butterfly and make this world more beautiful.

Biography

Larysa Bednarchyk is known for her smile and her love to dance to the music. Larysa was always interested in psychology but working with people at the medical office increased her passion for finding the keys to a successful mindset, positive thinking, and happiness. Living in Chicago with her three sons, Larysa loves to explore beautiful places in different states, countries, and cultures.

Contact Information

Facebook: https://www.facebook.com/larysa.bednarchyk
Instagram: http://instagram.com/larysabednarchyk

Chapter 32

WINNING THROUGH THE WRINKLES IN LIFE

By LaShonda McMorris

On the day you were born, you probably bore your first wrinkle. What? Really? How? We cried for the first few minutes after our birth. Who spanked you? The nurse or the doctor did it to get your lungs working. My understanding now is that doctors no longer use this practice. As babies, we can't verbalize, "Hey, why did you do that?" "What's happening?" or "Hey, that hurts," but our bodies can react. While we experience tears of joy, most tears come from a place of hurt, pain, disappointment or other traumatic experience.

At some point during grade school, you may have been the victim of bullying, teasing you about how you dressed, looked, spoke, what you didn't have, and called names like skinny (I experienced this), fat, dumb, or teacher's pet. You may have even been the contributor to inflicting pain and causing someone else to get a wrinkle. If you haven't had challenges in life, keep living as the saying goes.

Do you remember falling or getting knocked down in the playground? Did you stay on the ground, or did you get up and get over it? Gone through one or more divorces? Lost a job? Had a car accident? Hated with or without a cause, your partner broke off the relationship? Talked about? Lied to? I could go on and on. You reading this chapter is proof that you persevered. Someone will disappoint you, disagree with you, or simply fall out or stop speaking to you, but your pursuit towards your goals, regardless of obstacles, is the sum of persistence.

Not all wrinkles in life are bad because they also shape who you are. Different experiences influence and define your character, faith, motivation, drive, and integrity.

Giving Birth
Nine months of preparation and planning

You have nine months to plan expenses and necessities required for taking care of a baby. Some people can afford to purchase everything in one go, but most people are restricted financially. Planning for your success is likely to be in stages, but do you know what they are? The mother takes the time to write down every item she needs for her baby, similarly to what a wedding planner does for a bride and groom. Planning for your success should be happy times, but during the planning stage, wrinkles could surface too. As famously quoted, which I'm sure you've heard before, "If you can dream it, you can achieve it."

While pregnant with my youngest daughter, I developed Placenta Previa and frequently hospitalized. One night, after a church dinner, I began to experience severe abdominal pain.

My body was discharging something, but my ex-husband at the time prevented me from seeing it. I recall the paramedic saying, "We have a female who has lost a fetus appearing to be 2-3 months old". I remember praying and saying "NOOO Pooh bear (the nickname I initially gave her). Pooh bear you can't go and began to speak life into her. Although the paramedic said one thing, my belief was the opposite. I never saw what my ex-husband or the paramedics saw, but they said I discharged what appeared to be a fetus. The doctors confirmed it was not. My daughter is very much alive, graduated high school class Valedictorian and attending one of the big ten academic alliance universities. This event was one of the biggest wrinkles I had ever experienced in my life, but today all is well.

Babies are in the oven for nine months. That's the period it takes for them to develop all the body parts, organs, and internal makeup before they can be birthed into the world and breathe on their own. Drop any expectations that your success will occur overnight.

Here is the thing, when mommy gets morning sickness, gains then loses weight, the baby doesn't stop developing.

The next step is to plan. You may need additional education/training along the way but be mindful that wrinkles can manifest seemingly out of nowhere. Oh, oh – is there another wrinkle? What do you do? What is your mindset? Remain focused, positive, and motivated. Do not allow depression to creep in or begin feeling sorry for yourself and never start doubting yourself. Before you know it, your first milestone has been achieved, which motivates you to keep moving. Soon after that, you are in warp speed mode and then, oops – another wrinkle. This time you bulldoze right through it and then Walla Success. Celebration time begins! Remember, success, change, or anything New requires you to stay on the path no matter how many wrinkles you experience on your journey.

Time vs. Success

Yes, there is such a thing as a wrinkle when it comes to time and being successful. Time spent unproductively adds little or no value towards your success. Watching television shows all day or sports for hours on end does not add value towards dreams, ideas or goals that were penned on a piece of paper, in a notepad, or on your vision board for years? Now, I am not saying that you can't do these things, nor am I against movies or TV shows, but in the name of all these things that you want to do, how do they help? If several hours are spent daily and weekly talking on the phone about sports, or negative conversation, you are losing valuable time that could have been spent building your network and researching your next steps towards your vision. You need to get yourself closer to taking your business ideas from thought - to life - to action. Does spending hours of your day on Social Media help your idea? To be successful, you need time. If your time isn't managed wisely, you could end up on the phone or on Facebook, telling others how you Could've, Would've, or Should've been a????. Fill in the blank... The enemy of your time are the hours of the day or week doing things that add ZERO value to your ultimate goals and dreams.

Your background and past experiences, good or bad, don't have to affect your future negatively.

When you are knocked down by a life situation, don't just lie there, GET UP! Soldiers in the military are faced with life-and-death situations when the enemy attacks. When soldiers are in training, they train as if the situation is real. It's not a drill or a sequence of practice sessions. Reaching your goals and dreams should be approached as if your life depends on it. Why? If it is not treated as a priority, like "oh, I will get to it later" or "I'll begin writing my play next week" or "planning my new business in a few months when things settle down," it will never get done. I've learned to take action on an idea as soon as it occurs. I haven't mastered the technique yet, but it is something I am more aware of now than ever before. Demand more of yourself because no one else can make you do what needs to be done for your business, invention, education, or coaching program. You get it! Push yourself harder to assure a milestone, a task, etc is completed daily, no matter what!

Be your own success story, pray for something bigger than yourself and for something that's impossible for you to do in your own strength. What and who does your circle include? Are you surrounded by people who know more or less than you? Are they more successful than you? It is essential to increase your network and get to know folks who have made more than you and worked harder than you. If you hang around people who are always talking but not doing, where will you get your energy and support from when you are at a crossroads? Get a mentor. Find someone who inspires you to be a better you and who motivates you into action.

The year 2017 felt like a set up for me. I asked God to surround me with millionaires or those with a millionaire mindset. He did just that. Over the past three years, particularly in the last 12 months, I directly met ten people who are doing great things. And not just doing things to gain personally, but to help communities by giving their time to educate, contribute, share knowledge, wisdom, and skills that enable them to forever be able to FISH for a lifetime NOT just survive for a day.

Utilize your LinkedIn account like a professional showcase. I've seen many profiles that give off the perception that "I'm not really serious" or "I'm just here for kicks, so join me on my road to nowhere." I increased my circle with like-minded professionals, and I don't treat it like a social or hangout club. I don't manage my Facebook page that way either. Value yourself and the information you take in because the bible says, Proverbs 23:7 As a man thinketh in his heart, so is he. Surround yourself with go-getters.

Have you ever felt like, "man, I just can't get this thing, idea, business going" or "how do I start? I don't know what to do." Listen to Podcasts in your arena, get inspiration from others, and read books on the subject.

The Idea

I started my first business in 1990, making and selling jewelry to friends, family, co-workers, and my church family. I thought the products were pretty good only to find that after a few months, the glue that I used caused the jewelry to turn brown in some areas. It's funny how I recall feeling bad and making new pieces for free that did not require glue to compensate the affected customers. I figured, "ok, that didn't work. What else can I do?"

Then in 1995, I joined a company initially selling rendition fragrances door-to-door then opened my own office. I helped ten other people set up their own offices, and then I moved into my own distribution center. With this new role came a new set of challenges or what I consider wrinkles. After two years in business, I had to close the doors because the overhead costs far exceeded the profits. After many other wrinkles and more than 20 years later, I decided to give network marketing another try. My success is inevitable because my mindset shifted from "I can't" to "I will." Take a moment and think about your mindset, do you need a shift?

Do you have any ideas for starting or joining a Network Marketing Program? Do you want to start a business, write a book or play, publish a magazine, start a blog for a Not-For-Profit organization, construction company, or how to become a Ministerial leader? The ideas are endless, so set your goals. Even if what some would consider a failure has become a part of your journey, set them again, refresh them, and seek out what happened in your previous venture. Your success won't come without some teachable moments or experiences to help you grow. Sometimes building a reliable team or customer base can seem never-ending. However, the rewarding part is that you are sharing an opportunity or product that you believe in – otherwise, why else would you do it?

The financial rewards will come as a natural progression of your success. Be proud and don't be afraid when stuff happens. Share those times and ignore what else is said of you. Hey, think of it like this. If the person you share it with has something negative to say, ask them when was the last time they pursued their dreams and goals. Earlier in this chapter, I spoke about who was in your circle. If the right people are in your circle, you can be assured you will get the support and motivation if you fall, "Been there?" "It's ok - go for it again," "You can do it," and all the other encouraging words you need to continue your journey re-energized.

Wrinkled Thoughts are our Greatest Enemy

So, your big idea just sprung a leak, and you're thinking, "how am I going to recover?" "how much will it cost me?" "what will my family think if I don't succeed?." Think about this; what if these highly successful people didn't push forward and tried again after epic failures?

Thomas Edison was told by his teachers that he was 'too stupid to learn anything.'

Sir James Dyson who, after 5,126 failed prototypes for the bagless vacuum cleaner, amassed a net worth of $4.5 billion.

Steven Spielberg was rejected twice.

Walt Disney's editor told him that he 'lacked imagination and had no good ideas.'

Albert Einstein did not start talking until he was four years old.

Jerry Seinfeld was booed and jeered off stage when he froze during his first performance.

The creator of the first Dr. Seuss book was rejected 27 times, yes 27 different publishers, and now he sells more than 600 million copies worldwide.

Oprah Winfrey was fired from her first television job.

Elvis was fired after his first show.

Michael Jordan was cut from his high school basketball team.

All of these folks and many more in our history experienced one or more wrinkles in their lives. Their success came when multiple No's didn't deter them from continuing until they got a Yes. Failures are just wrinkles. Pull out your iron and dream, push, drive, and persist all the way.

Biography

LaShonda McMorris is a passionate communicator, minister, mentor, and empowerment coach. She lives a life of prayer, faith, helping others recognize the winner within them. She has built unforgettable relationships in her professional, ministerial, and personal life over the last 25 years helping people in their personal growth and spiritual development.

Contact Information

Facebook: https://www.facebook.com/MsLaShondaMcMorris
LinkedIn: https://www.linkedin.com/in/lashondamcmorris
YouTube: https://www.youtube.com/channel/UCAUHzfhvY9wotExiVPbEnmA
Twitter: @LaShondaMcMorris
Instagram: https://www.instagram.com/LaShondaMcMorris

Chapter 33

GOD IN MY STORMS OF LIFE

By Lilian Tsitsi Musa

"But those who wait on the Lord shall renew their strength; they shall mount up with wings like eagles, they shall run and not grow weary, they shall walk and not faint." - Isaiah 40 v 31A

Why do I begin with a scripture, you might be asking? However, I urge you to stay with me since it will all make sense in the end.

During my childhood, I mentally created my picture-perfect life story. I wanted to be happy, obtain a good education, be a successful businesswoman, get married to my perfect prince, have beautiful children, be an amazing wife, mum, a great leader, and have fun along the way. Big ambitious goals for a little girl, right? The only problem was that I didn't know how to make this vision a reality.

I didn't have a planned road map, so it wasn't a great start to this imagined fairytale life story. W Clement Stone says, "Definiteness of purpose is the starting point of all achievement."

I had a baby out of wedlock before I turned 19 years old. I was in the middle of doing my A-Levels. Not only did I feel like a piece of garbage, but I also felt like a total failure, a humiliation to my family, and my emotions were all over the place. Building a good track record wasn't getting off to the best start. However, with the help and support from family, I finished my A-Levels, went to college and studied business, and my little treasure was growing up, happy, and healthy.

On October 1st, 1981, my beloved mum died of cancer and my life was shattered. Again, it felt like my dream went out the window. Mum was a woman full of faith, loved Jesus, and taught us to trust in Him. So, why was God letting this happen? On February 23rd, 1983, my dad died and I asked myself, *where do I go from here?* Again I felt like this God of my mother had abandoned me. Storms struck, one after another, and I nearly reached the point of giving up. But when I gazed at my 3-year-old little girl, she gave me a reason to fight one more time.

I got married at 24, and at 25 years of age, I had my second child, a son. Then, my second daughter was born when I was 27-years-old. The marriage was rocky, but I was willing to try and make it work for the sake of my children. I don't know if my decision was good or bad, but I made a choice. My husband and I decided to quit our jobs and start a business to give ourselves more flexibility, time freedom, and financial freedom. At the time, my husband was an Assistant General Manager of a big building society, and I was a Credit Controller at a tobacco company. We had good, well-paid jobs, but it was time for us to move on.

We sold our house and re-invested the money into our new business. We also moved to an industrial city, which was a good fit for our manufacturing plant. Our co-products were pith helmets, police, army and air-force caps, and graduation caps, and we obtained all the contracts through the government tender board. The business took off and within three years, we were able to buy another beautiful home and privately educate our children. But, we didn't gain any time freedom we had anticipated, although we had the flexibility to work around our children, and we worked very long hours. Our marriage was strained and we were just co-habiting but to the outside world, we looked a happy couple. Seven years into the business, we had a staff complement of 146 with a gross annual turnover of over $2 million, but pressure was mounting from every side.

In my home country, any meaningful business attracts political pressure because they want a slice of what you have, and if you don't play ball, you are eliminated even though they can see your contribution to the GDP. By this time, my husband was very ill, so both the family and business pressures were on me. In August 1998, my second eldest brother passed away, and six months later, on March 18th, 1999, my husband died while I was in England. I flew back home to bury him and wind up the business, for I knew what was coming from the political powers of the day.

How I wish there was a manual on how to live a perfect life, but unfortunately, we discover as we plod along hoping for the best, so we tend to follow our hearts as our best guide. This time around, the storms were coming thick and fast from every direction, and soon the penny dropped and I knew that this was the defining moment where I had to either sink or swim. I hit rock bottom. My world had turned upside down overnight. While I was in that space, I remembered my childhood dream. Something deep inside told me to use that adversity as a stepping stone to rebuild my life. I got up, dusted up and gave it another shot one more time because I had my children to fight for.

Christian D. Larson says, "Believe in yourself and all that you are. Know that there is something inside you that is greater than any obstacle."

George Elliot says: "It's never too late to be who you might have been."

Great inspiration from both writers.

On October 23rd, 1999, I left Zimbabwe for the United Kingdom with nothing but my hope in Jesus. I had such a conviction and belief that God will see me through.

Before, it was all about me, but now I knew that the challenge was much bigger than me, and I had to turn to God like never before. I devoured God's word and literally absorbed everything from Isaiah 40 v 31A, Psalm 68v5, Proverbs 3v5, Philippians 4v6, and Romans 8v28. It became my daily bread.

My eldest daughter was already in college in England, so for five months, I left my younger son and daughter in Zimbabwe schooling while in the care of close family friends. My mission was to get a job, find accommodation, sort out work permits, and bring my children over as soon as possible. God was faithful, and on April 2nd, 2000 my children were able to join me. The next challenge was to get them into a good school. Again, God made a way and the children were granted 50% scholarships at Clifton College. I had to pay the other half, which was £18 000. I knew that £18 000 was a tall order, but God was with me. I just wanted my children to have some degree of normality.

Life was moving on with all its challenges and I was beginning to see a glimpse of light when another storm hit. January 12th, 2003, started as an ordinary day, I wasn't feeling very well, so I stayed in bed that day, but little did I know what was around the corner. At around 6.00 pm, I felt that I was losing sensation in my lower limbs. In a panic, I rushed to the bathroom, came back and sat on my bed and within an hour, my whole body shut down.

My girlfriend, who had spent that day with me, called paramedics, who arrived within ten minutes and rushed me to BRI hospital. I had all types of tests done including two MRI scans, which didn't reveal much except an inflammation in the spine. While I was in A&E at the BRI (Bristol Royal Infirmary), there was a white British Consultant called Chris Halfpenny, who was there for unknown reasons as a neurologist, and the BRI is a teaching hospital specializing in Cardiothoracic services. He came into my cubical and said to me, "My sister, your problem is a neurology one, and I will recommend that you are transferred to Frenchay Hospital, and I will look after you." I was baffled." Is this coincidence, or is God doing something?

The next morning, I was transferred to Frenchay and further MRI scans were done. Due to the inflammation in my spine, the surgeons decided to take me into theatre for surgery to explore more. This operation took more than five hours! The surgery revealed an infection in my spine that caused a spinal block which caused my sensory nerves to shut down — terrible prognosis. In layman's terms, I was told I had six months to live. If I lived beyond that then I would be wheelchair-bound for the rest of my life. "Ouch!" This was a valley of death. Now I am paralyzed from my breast to my feet. What was next, I wondered.

Science had failed and doctors had come to the end of their expertise. At that moment, I thought God raised the dead, so I turned to God to restore my broken body. I said to the doctor, "God will restore my health." He looked at me in disbelief and thought I was confused and in denial. However, that didn't matter because I knew God was in the business of fixing hopeless situations. From January to June 2003, I was now bedridden in hospital and my two children, aged 14 and 16.5 years old were at home alone and kicked out of school for non-payment of fees. Again all hopes were shattered. This was indeed the end of a very slippery slope with lots of uncertainty.

Six months later, I was still bedridden in hospital, but it was time to be discharged with a 24/7 care plan in place. It was the last week of June 2003, and I was crying to God to put my children back into school. At that moment, I felt prompted to find schools for my children. I had seven days to locate a school before the summer break. Long story short, God started to move mountains and doors began to open. I successfully secured school places at Queens College in Taunton. The fees was £15,000 per child per year, so I needed £30,000 for both of them. I owed the previous school £18,500, but God is infinite, He paid it all, and this is definitely too big a story to tell in one chapter, but I can confidently say my God is real and I have seen Him in action whether the need was big or small or in between. He showed up right on time.

The Board of Trustees at Queen's College gave my children a 100% scholarship for as long as they attended that school. The outstanding fees from the previous school was canceled miraculously. With God all things are possible.

Seven years down the line, God did it again and He healed me from paralysis. I started learning all the basics like a child. Today, I can do everything I did before and I'm getting stronger each day.

Now that God has brought me this far, I can testify of God's goodness in the land of the living. I believe in His grace, mercy, and love. I learned to hold onto the hem of His garment even when I didn't feel His presence. He opened doors that no man could open and closed the ones that needed to be shut. He paid school fees and put food on the table. He healed my sick body. He supplied all my needs, and above all, He kept me sane through the storms. He gave me joy in the midst of darkness. Having gone through the valley of death, I have come out stronger than ever before. I am thriving in every moment without remorse for the past or dread for the future because I know beyond a shadow of doubt that God is on my side.

He is truly a husband to the widow and the father to the fatherless. His word is trustworthy, and those who trust in Him will never be put to shame.

Biography

Lilian Tsitsi Musa is a Zimbabwean-born experienced entrepreneur with a demonstrated history of working in the leisure, travel, and tourism industry. She emigrated to the UK 20 years ago after her husband died. She lost everything she owned including her manufacturing business. Skilled in Business Planning, Coaching, Sales, and Team Building; she is a seasoned business development professional with an HND in Business from the City of Bristol College. Lilian is also a Board member and Trustee of a Bristol-based Homeless Charity. Through her experience, Lilian has developed an eminent passion to help others realize their God-given potential, be it in business or personal lives. She is blessed with three grown-up children, two girls, and one boy, as well as two grandchildren. The two younger children are both married to wonderful partners.

Contact Information

Facebook: https://www.facebook.com/liliantmusa
Instagram: https://instagram.com/lifestylewithlilian
Website: http://funandfreedom.net

CHAPTER 34

PRAY HARD WORK HARD: A ROUTE FOR ACHIEVING SUCCESS AND HAPPINESS IN LIFE

By Luis Guerra

I am the oldest of four children; born and raised in Venezuela. My father is the main inspiration for all my efforts aimed towards achieving personal excellence in life. He was a two-time cabinet member under two different Venezuelan governments, and he obtained two Masters Degrees in Law from the University of Rome and New York, as well as attaining his Ph.D. from Harvard University. How can one not be inspired by someone like that?

My father is the oldest of seven children, and he was seventeen when his father died. Being the oldest, he had to assume the role as head of the family and provide for six children. They were a lower-middle-income class Venezuelan family with no excess of economic resources. I didn't have the chance to know my grandpa, but my father told me he was a hard-working man in the construction business. My grandmother was a saint by nature who lived a calm and pure life and died at the age of ninety- three of natural causes.

At seventy-seven years of age, my Dad continues to challenge himself by continuously exploring new professional projects and goals, and in the last five years, he authored four books on Constitutional Law. When I say to him, "Dad, I think it's time for you to slow down," he always provides the same answer, "I just won't be only walking a dog around the neighborhood and sustain my living standards by rental income out of my properties."

My mother married my father when she was only eighteen years old. He took her to Italy when he did his first Master's degree in Law, and she had the great opportunity to learn Italian. She has a natural ability to learn different languages. Maybe it's because she has an ear for music and rhythm. Every time we go to an Italian restaurant, she speaks fluent Italian with the owner and waitresses. It is admirable. My mom is my inspiration for the steadfast belief in prayer. The moment you meet her, you immediately notice she is a person with God at the bottom of her heart who has a perceptible love for life.

Mom is the oldest of six children and was raised by the best grandparents I could ever have. I don't remember my grandfather being depressed or down about anything in life. My grandmother, even though she had a bitter temperament, was a world-record prayer. Yes, it's the truth. During my teens, I remember her almost falling asleep on her rocking chair every night trying to finish reading all her prayers (more than ten, easily) and praying the Rosary.

I am the father of three children or the beneficiary of three miracles. Yes, for those that don't believe in miracles, being able to procreate through God's will is a miracle. There's no doubt about it. Two beautiful daughters and a son are my miracles. My close friends sometimes like to call me the United Nations. You want to know why? I left my home country, Venezuela, in 2008, because of my job. I was transferred to Santiago de Chile. My oldest daughter was only 11 months old at the time. We lived in Chile for nearly five years and our second daughter was born there. I was then transferred to Miami-USA, where my son was born.

As you can see, we're the perfect example of a family that practices globalization and unites nations. I have two master's degrees. One in International Economics and Finance from Brandeis University and an Executive MBA from Universidad Adolfo Ibanez, which I completed while working in Chile.

I married a beautiful woman. My wife is also one of my main inspirations for hard work. I met her while she was an intern working for me. Isn't that funny? Long story short, we ended up getting married after dating for about two years (of course, after she finished her internship and went to work for another company). We are the parents of three blessings; our three children. My wife did her Master's degree in Finance, not only while on the job but when she was pregnant with our first daughter. And today, she continues to have a full-time job and puts all her efforts in as a mother and wife while always having that million-dollar smile that made me fall in love with her seventeen years ago.

So, what is all this Pray Hard Work Hard philosophy about? It all started during a seminar about "Virtuous Leadership: An Agenda for Personal Excellence." I realized then the tremendous power and value that God can imprint on our lives if we put into practice one of God's most precious gifts to humankind, The Cardinal Virtues. Whether you're a firefighter, head of government, a department secretary, successful businessman, famous sports player, rock star, housewife or nanny, you can exercise leadership if you put the Cardinal Virtues into practice: Humility, Magnanimity, Prudence, Courage, Self-Control, and Justice. Humility and Magnanimity set the foundation for the other four. To practice the virtue of Humility, you need to have the ambition to serve others. To practice Magnanimity, you need to have the ambition to conduct all your efforts towards achieving great things in life. I will get into each of the other four in more detail as we move through the chapter.

The Latin phrase "Sine Me nihil potestis facere" means "Without Me, you cannot do anything by yourself." It was frequently used by Saint Jose Maria Escriva, founder of the Roman-Catholic prelature Opus Dei (Work of God), whose mission statement is to help people become saints through professional work and in the ordinary life events (being a good father, husband, friend, brother or sister, co-worker, employee, etc.). We don't have to do extraordinary things to become saints. When learning about this Latin phrase, I began to look at the way I lived my ordinary and professional life in a completely different way. In the phrase, the word "Me" refers to God and invites anyone to remain humble, no matter the position or power you have in society. It automatically prevents arrogance and reminds us that we are in this world for a limited period. It helps you to detach from material things and not only strive for financial success but also to help others. Finally, it invites you to develop a close friendship with God by praying every day.

I allocate short periods throughout the day to pray. It can be calling God to give me strength and will to finish my work in the best way possible, or it can be praying Our Father or the Hail Mary. When I arrive at the office each morning, I imagine myself in a field where I need to chase God all day long to serve Him, my clients, my colleagues, or anybody. In soccer terms, it's like putting all my energy into running around the soccer field chasing God as if He was the soccer ball and trying to score as many goals as I can. There might be days where I don't run as fast as I would love to, but I always run. I don't stop running. My Monday mornings have become a Friday morning where all of us are thrilled and eager to start enjoying the weekend with our family and friends.

Virtuous leaders put all their effort into achieving personal excellence in everything they do. They are continually searching for new challenges that lead to serving others as God (Jesus Christ) always does. Put in another way, invite Jesus Christ to become part of your working team of executives, managers, analysts, administrative assistants, etc, and I guarantee that you will make sure you do your job the best you can to serve Him. You will immediately avoid mediocracy; you will never give up no matter the obstacles, pitfalls, and challenges you face in your daily life. You will always remember the suffering God endured on the cross to redeem our sins, and you will start to act like an eagle and not like a chicken. You will suddenly become and be seen as a natural leader and inspiration for others around you.

Let me share an example of what I mean when I say invite Jesus Christ to be part of your working team and to start acting like an eagle and stop acting like a chicken. I used to have a pretty tough and arrogant client. For those of you who work in sales as relationship managers, the situation will sound familiar. You could have the same situation with a co-worker or even with your supervisor. But, going back to my story, I tried to offer this client the best service possible, and he was never 100% satisfied.

Additionally, if something went wrong, he would humiliate not only you but your team members too and make us feel like cockroaches. We both agreed on having bi-weekly touch base calls, and when the date was approaching, I started to feel nervous, uncomfortable, and anxious. Once I began to establish a close relationship with God and prayed before each of those calls, I would tell myself I had to put all my sacrifice into this to serve Him as He did it for me while on the cross. The situation changed dramatically. I stopped dragging my feet when it came to making the call, and even the conversations started to turn in the right direction. My client started to follow me instead of me following him. I began to practice the virtue of self-control, which now leads me to explain what it really means to be self-controlled.

Everything in life, including self-control and leadership, is learned. Nobody is born with it. You need to learn to control your temperance, master your passions, emotions, feelings and not let them master you. In my client's case, what do you think I wanted to do with him? I wanted to hang up the phone, finish the conversation at once and insult him with any bad word that could come to mind. Self-control goes hand-in-hand with the virtue of humility. By being humble and reminding myself that I was to serve him, I was eventually able to establish a good relationship with him — an association governed by respect and credibility. I didn't take it personally. I didn't feel rejected by him.

In my daily work life, I encounter stressful situations. Important decisions need to be made, and I am accountable for any mistakes. If a deal goes wrong because of my fault, I will get hit. There are no excuses for blaming others. This is where I practice the Cardinal Virtue of Prudence. Having prudence is having the ability to make the right decisions.

Ensure you are deliberate and gather all relevant information, judge the information, and consider the different opinions. Finally, decide which is the best route to follow according to your perception. When you are deliberate, you are considering all the facts, the reality, whereas the decision-making has to do with will and action.

One of my favorite Cardinal Virtues is Courage. Why? Because when you practice it, you are putting yourself in a situation where you always need to stick to your moral values. As we know, in life, we're often faced with temptation. Whether it's as simple as controlling your food or alcohol intake, or making a tough business decision for the good of your employees, God will knock at your heart and soul and will tell you, "Hey my dear friend, stay on course, and don't let them influence you in a bad way". Instead, always act like an eagle and not like a chicken. Each of us has the responsibility to keep our ears wide open to listen to God's words and take the appropriate action. We need to have the courage to tell people in a good way when they're wrong. Try it, and you'll feel 100% fulfilled.

Finally, I'd like to explain the Cardinal Virtue of Justice. As Alexandre Havard defines, "It is the habit of giving others their due, not merely now and then, but always." A just person is always concerned about doing good while he or she walks through their life. We have a unique opportunity to do good at work.

Making the time to help a co-worker, servicing our clients with the right attitude, congratulating an employee for a job well done, and listening enthusiastically to a family member after a long day at work, are opportunities that God puts in front of us to practice the virtue of Justice.

I hope you all have found this chapter useful to improve work performance, become better citizens, and help you develop a real and close relationship with God. I invite each one of you to start making your Mondays a Friday where we set our clocks to countdown from ten to zero and once at zero, run to our houses to start enjoying the weekend with our family and friends. We live only once!

God Bless you all!

Biography

Luis Guerra has more than 15 years of experience as a relationship manager in the banking and technology payments industry. He has worked in more than ten markets across Latin America and the Caribbean. He holds a Master of Arts in International Economics and Finance from Brandeis University and an Executive MBA from Universidad Adolfo Ibanez. Luis is an active Catholic, known for his perseverance in the workspace.

Contact Information

Facebook: https://www.facebook.com/luis.e.guerra.9
Instagram: https://www.instagram.com/luiseguerra72

Chapter 35

YOU MIGHT SCREAM, YOU MIGHT CRY, BUT GIVING UP IS NOT AN OPTION

By Magga Sigga

Hello Dear Friend,

I sincerely hope that I am writing to you at a convenient time. I am so happy to reach out to you because I have some news I'd like to share.

If you haven't already guessed, I'm terrible at writing and reading books, but that won't stop me from expressing what I wish to say. I'm terrified of stepping so far out of my comfort zone, and my heart feels like it's going to burst out of my chest because I am so afraid.

Well, I'll give you the news. I am starting to write the first chapter of my book.

No-one would have guessed, not you, not me, or anyone that I know, that one day I would be doing this.

And that is the beauty of it all; given that, if you remember, I am so stubborn. The first thing is I don't often write in English. I read it well, and I have found new ways to do so as time goes on, but this has taken so much more time than I thought. Every sentence is a challenge, but I hope that my message remains clear.

I think back to my preschool teacher. He spent three years trying to teach me how to read and write. For most of the time, this appeared a near-impossible task, until one day he asked me, "Are you so stubborn that you have decided you simply cannot read or write?"

I sat there, my eyes filled with frustrated tears. I could not understand this. I had no idea how this is going to be possible because the letters basically seemed to drift right off the page, and I had no idea how to put them back, let alone the order in which they should be placed.

Then he told me that I could do this if I truly wanted to. I sat there with a huge question mark written across my face,

"How in the world am I going to do this?"

Well, I found a way. I made the decision that I could read, and I would spend countless hours mastering this essential skill. At the age of 10, I was finally able to write my own name. And that was my first victory.

However, despite these gains, I soon decided that school wasn't for me and that I would run away from home. I didn't actually run away, I just talked to my mama and said I'm not doing the formal education thing. I'm just not cut out for it. I was confident that I could find work, and I did, I started working at a fish factory.

Even then I was confident that I would be successful if I worked hard enough, and so I did.

At 23 years of age, I made another decision that would change my life. I decided to put the money aside, quit working all my different jobs, and go back to school. I had been in school for six weeks before I went to the headmaster and admitted my problem. I told him that I had to leave because I was so stupid that I couldn't read and write. Just like my preschool teacher, he didn't believe me. Once again, I had a teacher who had faith in me. However, this one asked me to take a few tests for my reading skills, and I found out that I was dyslexic. I had struggled for so long, and I finally knew why. Knowing this, my headmaster continued to teach me how to read and write while catering to the challenges caused by my dyslexia. I was finally able to read and get the grades I was capable of achieving.

This was true self-esteem.

The most difficult part of my dyslexia is miss-spelling words. It was so easy for other people to notice, and, for a time, led to people bullying and underestimating me. Of course, I didn't like that, but I managed to not to give in to hate and anger and worked hard to improve myself despite the criticism.

I know everyone is facing something challenging, and I know everyone has their own problems, and most people just need some help to feel confident in themselves. I soon decided that I wasn't going to be bitter. Growing up with these issues, I learned something I believe had helped me greatly. That's something I want to pass on to you. I bet there is something on your mind and I guess that you might be looking for a way forward.

The first thing I want to tell you, my dear friends, is that you are capable and you have something in your heart that will allow you to overcome these challenges. I know for sure that if I had known about my dyslexia earlier, I would have been able to receive suitable help for my reading difficulties. I know that then my life would be much different today.

I'm not willing to waste my time on regrets. Instead, I would recommend you actively explore the fear and see what is lurking there.

It's okay to cry, it's okay to scream, but it's never okay to give up.

I will now take you to the year 2010.

I've now started a family. I have my daughter; she is my youngest. I have two boys: the oldest is 30, and the youngest is 20, and they have both grown into amazing men.

My daughter was born on the 24th week of the pregnancy. She was quite small, only 31.5 cm and 530 g (12 inches, 1.2 lbs). We spent four months in the ICU, not knowing how things would turn out.

As you can imagine, this was a very stressful time for my entire family, and then, finally, when she got to come home, it started to be a very stressful time for me personally. I thought it would be a good idea to simply give up on sleep entirely so that I can take care of my daughter. Let me tell you; it's never a good idea. But when kids are used to waking up every two hours, it is quite difficult to stop doing it.

So instead of sleeping through the night, I just stayed awake. After about a year and a half of this I was so tired and feeling completely run down and exhausted; in a state of near total burn-out.

The time that I was taking care of my daughter I wasn't taking care of myself. I put on a lot of weight and my health suffered.

I also struggled to take financial care of my family, but I was in luck. I started in the network marketing business. In the industry, there is immense pressure for constant self-improvement and development. And that was exactly what I did.

You might have noticed that I'm a fighter, I don't give up easily. I started walking, swimming, and paying attention to my diet. I started attending a health care institution to work on myself. I noticed that I had developed a negative mindset. It was blocking my career progress, and it was diminishing my energy. I was no longer a positive person. So I started listening to podcasts that helped fix what was broken: to start building myself up to the stubborn fighter I used to be. I don't know if I was actually walking because I needed to walk or if I needed that physical discipline to change the way I was thinking and avoid negative, cyclical thoughts.

After so many years, I made another life-changing decision. I would change the world around me instead of trying to change who I was. That is what I have done. I choose what I'm listening to. I choose the people I spend time with. There are so many quality podcasts and YouTube channels and everything out of there, so many people spreading these great positive messages that it could be very difficult to choose the best one.

I recently had a talk with my cousin. We discussed living in fear, and I was explaining to her that you don't have to drive all around the country just to have the courage to go to the grocery store, you just have to take a little step every single day and go from there. You will grow and eventually you will be at the place that you have always dreamed of being.

I then decided that I didn't want to be afraid of heights anymore and that, despite my vertigo, I will go up the mountain, literally and metaphorically. That took me about four years! I desperately needed that feeling winning once more - of succeeding at something that made me feel great. I needed to know that my inner warrior was still there. I needed to rebel, so I decided to welcome the fear.

The trail started slowly, and soon we were halfway up the mountain. I sat down as I thought it would now be a good time to have a stress-busting cigarette, but I had given up smoking three years ago. That wasn't an option. I sat down and cried my eyes out as I was so afraid of becoming lost.

And I thought of the rescue team not being able to find me.

But I didn't want to go down; I wanted to go up. I knew that if I wanted to save someone I wanted to go up. I trained as an EMT basic for a long time, so I knew that saving someone else would get me there.

And so I did. I finally stood at the top of the mountain with the feeling that I was a winner coursing through my veins.

I knew that I had changed my inner direction. I knew that I had created the feeling of victory inside my heart once more. I knew that I wasn't afraid anymore and that on the other side of fear is freedom.

My dear friend, I am going to leave you with the words 'take care.'

And to me that means you are special, you are unique, and you have something no one else has.

And my dear friends, you are capable.

BIOGRAPHY

Magga Sigga is an Entrepreneur, ACC-ICF Life-Coach and an Influencer. Her strength is her inner power. She believes in people's greatness and helps them reach their goals in life. She is brave and ready to go where others do not dare.

Contact Information

Facebook: https://www.facebook.com/margret.jons
Twitter: @MARSIR Jons
Instagram: margret.jons

Chapter 36

I AM NOTHING. YET, I HAVE EVERYTHING

By Maiko Johanson

I am so deeply honored to share my humble thoughts in this chapter. In this eye-opening journey, let these wonderful people be your guides on the way to your unlimited success.

As we enter this life, naked and unaware of what lies beyond, we have already decided to be successful because we won the first race to be born.

As we grow, we are full of wonder and excitement about learning something new every day.

Our self-image is, "I am enough," "I am successful in everything I do," "I am awesome," "life is wonderful."

What we don't know is the fact that we observe the environment we are in, and it will form our way of thinking and acting. This first part of our personality, until the age of six or so, will remain with us. The most significant part of our belief system is developed by the example of our parents, siblings, attitudes, thought patterns and the immediate environment in which we live.

Then, as we develop an acceptable way of independent thinking, we are sent to an educational system where everything changes. It is the beginning of a careful molding of our minds and a new belief system about how life should go and should be lived. We dream, and we want to be somebody else; we choose role models, and we start acting like them, thinking it's cool and that is our identity, that might be a part of our essence, and we get lucky to become who we were meant to be. But, that's not the way it actually works out for the majority of people.

We start to lose the mindset that "I am more than enough." We grow, learn, get a job, etc.

We seek; we dream; we experience the magic and the ugliness of life.

First, all is well. We work hard for a better future; we hear stories about success, fancy things, different possibilities and lifestyles we want for our lives as well, but nothing changes. We don't feel content; we start to question things; we try to make ourselves feel better by consuming alcohol, drugs and junk food to give us little relief or to numb us down. Years go by, and we are stuck in the system that sold us an idea that there is freedom in entrepreneurship and that is possible for us, but most of us are blind to see that we are now modern-day slaves.

We have developed negative self-talk in our heads about us, and we are troubled in our heads how others see us. Questions like "Am I enough to do this" and "Am I capable for this and that," will take over, and we find ourselves lost in our own lives. We still have dreams about a better future, but we don't realize the negative ball of energy that is now growing bigger.

We start to be a victim and blame others; we start to talk about people behind their backs. Life sucks, and we need to escape.

We don't realize the power of thought and feeling because nobody teaches us that in school.

We don't know the laws of the universe and the power behind them. We are at a breaking point in our lives where usually something happens. This point in our lives can make us or break us. If we are shaken up properly, we might gain some new energy for the understanding that we need to change our lives, our selves, and that we have the power to do so.

I broke my back six times before I needed to go to surgery. It changed my view of life. I had to go to Peru into the Amazon jungle and take part in a one-week Ayahuasca retreat to lose the pain I had been carrying with me since my childhood. I learned a lot, and it made another change in my personality. I felt free, but I still lacked the confidence to step up another level in my actions. I got malaria and almost died before I woke up, to realize that I needed to love more deeply the family and closest friends I have.

I now understand deeply that I have only one life, and I need to be true to my calling. We don't have to go through so many painful and scary experiences to realize we are the architect of our life. Maybe we accidentally stumble on some motivational video or a book that changes our view of life, and we take action to change our lives because the old ways are simply not getting us anywhere. From this realization of an awakened mind, we pray for a better future and, because we had a rough path, we feel hope, and that changes us to feel better and attract better thoughts.

Like attracts like is a combination of words we grow up with, but we do not give it any real attention until we are pushed towards it. Here I, talk to the people who understand my thoughts or who want to understand. I talk to you, someone who is looking for a change, and that very reason is why you are reading this book. You want and need changes in your life, and you are developing your thinking to the point where you know that you don't know about things, but you need to know more for the change to come. This place in one's thoughts is magical, because you have changed your vibration just by realizing something, and that something gives you power.

A person creates their life just by thought. Whether or not you believe it does not matter because it is the truth, and if you just take the time to think deeply about it, you will realize that. Like attracts like, so your thoughts will attract like-minded thoughts, and that process will grow.

You should take time to think about your childhood and the dreams you had in the past, to realize that a big part of them have come to manifest already in your life. You just have been blind to see it; you have been like a zombie just staggering through life. We as human beings are all sensitive to the energies around us. We all say things like, "I feel this way," or "I sense that something is going to happen." Think more deeply about what you feel or sense. This is something we cannot see in the physical world, but we can feel it and sense it.

These thoughts will open up a new world, and that world is full of wonder and magic just like when you were a child. It is hard to comprehend at first, but I promise you that your life will change as you let yourself go into the world of thought.

We all have the power to feel, sense and think. If we think about what it means, it all comes back down to energy, vibration or high frequency. They are the same thing. Choose a word that resonates with you and go from there. Feeling and sensing is something we all know but we cannot see, so we call it energy. Thoughts are in our heads. We can hear them but cannot see, so they are energy?

Earl Nightingale said, "We become what we think about most of the time." Think about that; reflect on that; let it sink in. The people that sing think about it most of their time. People who do sports think about it most of the time. The person who thinks about writing becomes a writer. The person who wants to be an artist becomes one. The person who is crazy enough to think that he wants to change the world thinks about that most of the time and eventually is the person who does it. Nobody comes to make them who they want to be or what they want in their life; there is no savior. You are your own savior; you are the change; you have the power to change things in your life, and it all starts by thinking.

It is something so simple, and that is why it's hard to grasp at first, but as you start to play with that idea, you will notice the changes in your thoughts. You don't have to know how to do the change - you just have to think about it and feel good about it; this is all you need to do. As you think, you will attract more like-minded thoughts. Like-minded thoughts will attract like-minded people. We all have experienced and heard, "I felt so drawn towards that person," and "We had such good chemistry."

Like attracts like; it is energy! Like-minded people together form a mastermind as it is taught by Napoleon Hill, and from that, things start to change. I truly believe that, because I have known it in me, I have sensed it in me. I did not have the intellectual skills to explain it, but I knew this was something to learn about. I started reading all the self-development books I could get my hands on, and I started to look into the science by going through books to explain all of that to me in a little bit more detail.

The science behind everything does not matter; what matters is what you want. Think about your thoughts; start to be the observer of your mind; start to write things down to get clarity about your thoughts. You become self-aware; that will grant you a gift of patience and understanding of how unaware you have been before. You start to see the negative thought patterns, and you start to know you can reprogram your thoughts into positive ones.

This book is filled with golden nuggets of wisdom that will help you to make the change in your life if you truly want it! The fact that you are reading this book is a powerful step toward your future, and I salute you for that. It does not matter how far you have gone in your personal life or how successful you are in your business. We all have self-doubt at some level; we all are afraid of something. I am here to tell you that you will be alright; everything will be alright; you just have to believe in yourself! I believe in you! You are enough! You are a beautiful human being! We all have things we are not happy with about ourselves, but that is what makes us humans, that makes us unique, that makes us perfect as we are!

The best advice I can give you is to "develop self-awareness." You can do this by turning off the tv and just go for a walk, or simply sit in silence and marinate in your thoughts within yourself and listen. Be mindful about what is going on. Just observe and learn. It is quite hard to do at first, but you will get better at it! Develop your intellect by reading books; it will open up understanding about your own psychology. Eat good organic food; take care of your body. Meditate, and the biggest gifts you can offer yourself are compassion, patience, forgiveness, and self-love. It will make your inner self feel better and, from that, your whole perspective of life will reflect back to you in your reality.

If you want to change things in your life, change things in your life! You have that power!

If I could do it, then I am more than certain that you can do it, too.

I wish and pray for self-awareness, self-love, compassion, forgiveness, and patience to all the people in the world.

Biography

Maiko Johanson believes that everything in life will fall into place without labels.

He is a seeker, writer, son, brother, uncle, a friend, a man, and a world traveler. He believes that he is nothing, yet he has everything.

Contact Information

Facebook: https://www.facebook.com/Maiko.Johanson
YouTube: https://www.youtube.com/channel/UCTO5_OJ_64m2X6_ZYfiHiIA?view_as=subscriber

Chapter 37

LACK OF FINANCIAL LITERACY IN INNER CITIES

By Marquis Staton

When I was 18 years old, I was told that if I want to move ahead in life, I must attend college. So, I started applying to schools, not knowing how I was going to pay for it. After going through the process, I discovered there were government loans to cover my school expenses. Four years later, I finished school, hoping to get a great job to pay back the student loans. Unfortunately, I accrued $40k in debt.

I then started scrambling to find a job. I secured low wage work but was unable to pay back my student loans. I now had to be patient. My payments were on hold. This measure helped me to worry less about paying the debt; however, the interest kept accumulating on the loan at a rate of 6% APR.

Additionally, I bought a brand-new car. Since my credit was weak, I was paying nearly 20% APR on a $20,000 loan. I was stressed and felt set up by society to remain in debt. I continued to work low-paying jobs over the next six years, working double shifts up to 16 hours a day, 4 to 5 days a week just to try to make ends meet. After a couple of years of this endless cycle, I burned out. One day, I remember being on the bus when I blacked out from exhaustion. I missed my stop and ended up in another town. This mishap was my wakeup call. After this incident, I began to analyze my life and knew I had to make some serious changes. I researched online how to alleviate debt and live a more stress-free, productive life. The first thing I did was to start reading positive motivational quotes. This affirmation shifted my mindset tremendously. Next, I changed my spending habits and started to save money in the bank. Next, I stopped working so many hours by working part-time at one of my two jobs. Finally, I sold my car and bought a cheaper one that I could afford.

After making these changes, everything started to turn around for me. In fact, after working six years of low-paying jobs, I got an opportunity to work in my field of study that paid double of what I was earning. It was a sales job for a lawn care company, and they offered benefits and stocks. I was intrigued by the offer and began to work there.

Unfortunately for me, this job was seasonal. After nine months of working as a sales rep and sales technician, it was over. I can remember it like it was yesterday. I was called into the general manager's office. He told me that this was my last week. I was getting laid off after less than a year. The next thing I knew, I was in the unemployment line.

Being a seasonal employee, there were no guarantees of being called back and it was nearing the end of the season. I began to ponder how I would survive and how long I would have to wait for the unemployment check.

After waiting for one month, I got my whopping check of $133. I thought to myself, how could I survive off this each week for the next six months? This event correlates to when I hit rock bottom and I needed to do some deep soul searching.

During this time, I was frantically looking for different opportunities to make money. By the end of the six months, I received my last unemployment check. Around the same time, I came across the option of becoming an Uber driver. I started the venture in May 2015 and made the same amount of money in half the time compared to when I was working as a service technician. The second accolade was the freedom to create my own schedule. As I drove to various parts of the state, I noticed the difference in how people used money. For example, in urban cities, people would purchase name brand apparel but would live in rough areas. In the suburbs, I noticed people wearing essential, no-name brand clothing but had nice properties. I wondered why inner-city people focused on brands and not their living situation. After doing some research, I realized the majority of inner-city people lack financial literacy. I realized that financial literacy is the key to success and wealth in life. I am now on the path to becoming financially free.

A lack of financial literacy affects all ages, especially inner-city communities. The lack of financial literacy causes many people to become victims of predatory lending, subprime mortgages, fraud, and high-interest rates borrowing, which generally results in bad credit, bankruptcy, or even foreclosure.

The lack of financial literacy can lead to enormous amounts of debt through poor financial decisions.

According to the Financial Industry Regulatory Authority, 63% of Americans lack financial literacy, 44% of Americans do not have enough money to cover a $400 emergency, 43% of student loan borrowers cannot make payments, 38% of U.S. households have credit card debt, and a massive 33% of American adults have no money saved for retirement. This is because they don't know how to reconcile accounts, plan ahead to pay bills timely, pay off debt quicker, or plan for the future. And, unfortunately, they perpetuate the debt and dig themselves into a deeper financial hole. A lot of people do invest a significant amount of time, money, and effort on getting a job, but pay little to no attention to maintaining the money they make once they get that job. When some individuals get their check, they blow it on partying and shopping sprees within a few days, and then when its time to pay bills, there is no money left to cover expenses.

It is imperative to understand how crucial it is to have an emergency fund because it could lower the amount of credit card debt we see in this country and reduce homelessness.

According to College Board's *Trends in College Pricing*, tuition at public institutions has soared over 213% in the last 30 years. Roughly 10 million of the 22 million Americans with federal student loans are either behind on payments or were allowed to postpone payments due to economic hardship.

After graduation, students should have a better understanding of repayment plans so they can make educated decisions when choosing their degree.

With 38% of Americans in credit card debt, it's evident that most people are not aware of the enormous amount of interest they are paying and that there are multiple strategies to reduce the interest.

Finally, if 33% of American adults have $0 saved for retirement, then citizens need to understand how much money they will need and how compound interest works, so they can start saving earlier. When the numbers are broken down, it's apparent that hundreds of thousands of dollars are lost by waiting, so starting to save later in life does not make much sense.

Financial literacy refers to the education and understanding of multiple financial areas, including managing personal finance and investing. Financial literacy improves the ability to manage personal money matters efficiently and make sound financial decisions regarding insurance, real estate, college tuition, budgeting, retirement, and tax planning.

The lack of financial literacy will most likely lead to making poor financial decisions that can negatively impact the financial well-being of an individual. In fact, the federal government provides resources for people who want to learn more about financial literacy. You can find these resources through the Financial Literacy and Education Commission.

Financial literacy enables individuals to become self-sufficient and obtain financial stability. People who understand financial literacy will know if a purchase is an asset or a liability, and if it's necessary and affordable.

Financial literacy shows the behaviors and attitudes a person has about money and how it is applied to one's daily life. Financial literacy reveals an individual's ability to make economic decisions and develop a financial road map to plot out earnings, expenses, and debt. Small businesses are affected by financial literacy because they contribute to economic growth and stability.

Ways to achieve financial literacy include learning how to create a budget, track spending, apply techniques to minimize debt, and effectively plan for retirement. These skills can also be acquired through counseling with a financial expert. Education involves understanding how money works, creating and achieving financial goals, and managing internal and external financial challenges.

The first factor in financial literacy is having a savings and checking account, and having an emergency fund that covers 12 months expenses. Second is investing in the stock market. Third is obtaining credit and paying bills every month for a good credit rating. The main issue in the inner-city communities is that people do not understand how to leverage or manage credit. One step people can take is to use a credit card for small everyday expenses like grocery shopping, gas, or lunch. If they can afford their expenses and analyze their weekly spending habits versus their income, everything can be balanced. The problem I see with the lack of financial literacy is that people end up in a deep financial hole from which they can't escape.

On top of that, the lower the creditworthiness is low, the higher the fees. For example, if someone buys a car for $20,000 and has good credit, they pay a rate of 2%. Thus, the new loan is $20,400. A person with bad credit can pay at a rate of 20% resulting in a $24,000 loan, an extra $3600 for the same car.

Investing in the stock market is key to creating a passive income and having money for the future. It is vital to save $5 a day and invest it in the stock market when the price of the stock is low. Imagine those people who invested in companies like Apple or Amazon when they first hit the market at $5 a share; they are probably very financially comfortable now. Another epidemic is student loans. Student loans have decimated the minority community in overwhelming debt and set this country back financially for years to come. It is important not to take out loans for college. Investigate scholarships or grants through financial aid to cover school expenses, instead of trying to finance unaffordable courses. Financial literacy should be a school course requirement starting at elementary school. This early advantage will help individuals avoid debt.

Biography

Marquis Staton likes to educate inner-city communities on the importance of financial literacy and empower them with a positive outlook on life. When not absorbed with his day-to-day activities, Marquis loves cooking, discussing business ideas with friends, biking, playing basketball, and spends far too much time watching NBA TV. He lives in the United States with his family and friends.

Contact Information

Facebook: https://www.facebook.com/mastaton1
Instagram: https://www.instagram.com/mastaton1/

Chapter 38

THE 5 PRINCIPLES OF NETWORKING

By Nicholas Arbutina

While contemplating the opening chapter for this book, I wanted to focus on a topic that would benefit anyone in a networking company anywhere in the world so I can add value in helping them build a successful business. In other words, I want to share a strategy based on principles that have stood the test of time. Many of the tactics may change with technology, social media, etc., but the real fundamentals of this business remain as true today as they did 50 years ago.

So, after digging deep and reviewing what I learned, there is one teaching in particular, that I want to share. My mentor gave me advice that has added tremendous value to our business and team. It is based on the 5 Principles of Networking, or what I like to call, the 5 P's. I am going to illustrate how these principles relate to my business, health and wellness, but can be applied to any business model in the networking industry.

The 5 Principles are: People, Purpose, Process, Products, and Perseverance. As mentioned, I will detail how these principles apply to my business, which can be prioritized differently according to your needs and your business. Consider how these principles affect your business and the products or services that you offer. For example, if Products are more important than your business Process, then switch them around. Use these 5 Principles to guide your leaders most effectively and efficiently as possible.

PEOPLE - People First is core value #1, so I will focus on that first. Without people, you have no business. Let me say that again, WITHOUT PEOPLE YOU HAVE NO BUSINESS. People are the number one asset, whether they are your customers, discount buyers, or team builders; people make up the entire business. So, if you don't like people, I hate to tell you that you probably shouldn't be in this business.

But I say that with mixed feelings because truthfully when I started my business, I was an overworked, traditional business owner who was owned by his business. I was so frustrated with customers and employees that I felt that I no longer liked people. But I knew deep down that I loved people and had allowed society and my emotions to get the better of me. I knew I had to make a change, or it would cost me everything in the long run.

So, I made people my priority and started to love working with and for people. Whether it was helping them achieve physical, emotional, financial, relationship, spiritual, or mental goals, I wanted to help people DO LIFE BETTER. If I could give credit to one person who helped change it for me, it was a friend that I will call Stephanie. She was a stressed out, overweight, middle-aged woman who had lost her love of life. I did not know Stephanie until she joined my team and I watched her transform into an amazing woman, mom, and leader. Through her journey, she lost over 140 lbs and became a better mom, wife, and business partner. She even won several international level transformation bikini contests. Had it not been for the changes I helped her with and the potential I could see in Stephanie, I may still be stuck in my "business owning me mentality." Thank you, Stephanie!

PURPOSE - Purpose is essentially as important as people, because if you don't have a STRONGER THAN OAK "WHY" then you probably won't succeed in this business either. Your WHY must be what pushes you through the tough times because there will be tough times. As every thought leader on the planet will tell you: "Your Why has to make you Cry." I wholeheartedly believe that because you will encounter adversity. You will lose friends, possibly family; you will be called crazy, you will be ridiculed and even laughed at. So, find your purpose and use it to fight through the tough times.

Truthfully, you should not have to think about your WHY. It should be a feeling inside you that makes you want to RULE THE WORLD or achieve greatness. We all have greatness in our God-given potential. You need to discover how to unleash that greatness, and it all starts with your purpose.

And don't worry if your WHY changes. It will most likely evolve because as you grow and develop, so will your priorities, goals, and outlook on life. Personally, my WHY has constantly evolved as I have evolved. When I first started my business, my WHY was to regain my health, so I could see my girls grow up. Then, when I accomplished that, it evolved into being more involved in their lives and then wanting to retire myself from my business. As I achieved my original purpose from the networking business, I continued to grow bigger WHYs. Through this evolution, something amazing begins to develop. You realize that when you started this journey, you were most likely shooting for SUCCESS, but as you achieve more WHYs and serving a purpose, you begin to become SIGNIFICANT. And once you've ACHIEVED SIGNIFICANCE, SUCCESS WILL NEVER BE ENOUGH! As I sit here writing this book, I am accomplishing my evolving WHY.

PROCESS – This principle will vary depending on your company, the type of business, and the products or services, or both. The Process refers to how your company does business. Most of your process will be about how your corporate staff or accomplished leaders promote your business. This will be through different tools such as videos, graphics, or comparison charts – whatever materials your company has put together for you to use from the back office, as well as for front-facing services that include one-on-one, in-home parties, meetings, or hotel rooms.

The great thing about the process is that there is no one way to go about promoting your business, as it helps to have a diversified toolbox at your disposal. Sometimes, a one-on-one with a close friend is ideal, at other times, a hotel meeting could be more suitable and sociable for when the CEO is in town. No matter what your company's preferred method, make sure you show up and commit to the process. There is an old saying that I like on both ends of the spectrum: "Sometimes you need the meeting, while other times the meeting needs you."

For example, we are pioneering a movement with the world's first ever customized vitamin platform. So, the validity of our company and our core product is based on a free online health assessment. To keep this simple, our mainstream PROCESS is to JUST TAKE THE ASSESSMENT or #JTTA. Our whole business is based around our assessment. Not only does the assessment recommend a vitamin program based on 3rd party, independent, peer-reviewed clinical studies, but it also recommends our lifestyle products (we'll discuss products in the 4th P) On a lighter note, while coming up with our PROCESS, one of our leader's said let's make it #JTTFA, and everyone looked at him like WHAT? He said, "What's wrong with JUST TAKE THE FREE ASSESSMENT!" Just commit to your company's process because there is an objective behind it. It works!

PRODUCTS - There is a reason for leaving Products close to the end. Without products, most companies would not be in business because Products (or services) are the backbone of almost every business. Products are of paramount importance, and every company has them, so in networking, you must believe that your products are the BEST.

Your firm BELIEF in your products will keep you going when you start questioning your sanity. And you will question your sanity, or sometimes you may question network marketing, your company, your upline, your downline, or anyone, and everyone. So, make sure that you are passionate about your products. Make sure that you are a product of the product. You don't have to be the product expert but you will need to know how each of your products work, and there is no better way than using them yourself.

To add value for people, accurately assess the client's needs to determine which product you will recommend that will help and serve its purpose. But, how do you do that? Ask questions. Remember, networking is a social business, and you don't just want to sell products transactionally, you want to fill a need transformationally. In other words, you don't just want to sell for the sake of selling by getting someone to spend their hard earned money; you want to help them DO LIFE BETTER in an area where your products can benefit them.

PERSEVERANCE - This is the big one and why it is saved for last. Without perseverance, you could have the other 4 p's completely mastered and yet you would not survive in network marketing. Perseverance is what will keep you motivated after your tenth consecutive NO, or after your mother tells you you're crazy, or your oldest friend laughs at you and says you have joined a cult.

Perseverance is what will keep you from doing the absolute no-no in network marketing, and in life: QUITTING.

"Just Don't Quit" are the words I always remember from the late, great Mark Yarnell. No matter what you do, JUST DON'T QUIT! Whether you are part-time or full-time, quitting is a sure way to fail. If doing it part-time, it will take many more years to succeed, but if you consistently do something to move your business forward every day, you will see growth.

Believe me. I speak from experience. There were many times I considered quitting, the times when I lost my best associate and their entire leg, or when the new "Rock Star" never sponsored a single person, or when a leader stole a prospect. If you don't quit, you will most likely experience all these situations and more. The only constant is the belief in YOURSELF!

Your belief in yourself is what will keep you from quitting. As you continue to grow, hopefully from as many books like this that you read, you can also develop into a leader. As the foremost authority on leadership, John Maxwell, says in the Law of Victory "Quitting is Unthinkable!" That must be your mindset from the beginning. I think what helped me fight through those tough times is having a clear vision of the BIG PICTURE – your ultimate goal. Set your sights, as lofty as they may be, on where you want to be in 5 or 10 years, and just don't quit. At the beginning of your business, (and I know it sounds hard to believe, especially if you've struggled), but persevering and remaining consistent will power you through the hard times to see that light at the end of the tunnel.

Next, I will illustrate how to tie all five principles together. Stephen Covey describes Habit 7 in The Seven Habits of Highly Effective People as Sharpen the Saw, or, sharpen twice and cut once. This is the basic habit of honing your skills. Learn to master each of the five principles: Get to know and love PEOPLE, find your WHY and never lose sight of it. Learn your company's PROCESS and share it with unwavering passion and faith. Become a PRODUCT of the product and represent your company with pride, and PERSEVERE through the good and the bad.

I hope you can see how these five principles will help you succeed in any networking business. While each principle plays a vital role in the success of your business, an understanding of how they all come together is of utmost importance. You really can't have one without the other four. You could probably succeed with only one or two of the principles for a short period, but to sustain growth over an extended period, you will ultimately need to apply all five of these principles. Isn't that why we are all in this business? To have long term success growing an enormous team by applying certain principles over a long period. But if there was one piece of advice, I want to pass on that helped me through the hard times is "JUST DON'T QUIT."

Biography

As a contractor who wanted more out of life, Nicholas Arbutina has transformed his life into one of significance. Through personal growth, he has a passion for helping people DO LIFE BETTER. But his greatest accomplishment is the legacy that he is leaving for his children.

Contact Information

Facebook: https://www.facebook.com/nick.arbutina.7
LinkedIn: https://www.linkedin.com/in/nickarbutina/
YouTube: https://www.youtube.com/channel/UCfqmXRPmO80VP-CJwSsV86g
Twitter: https://twitter.com/ArbutinaNick
Instagram: https://www.instagram.com/nickarbutina/

Chapter 39

BELIEVE YOU CAN

By Peter Muzik

Recently, I stumbled upon a letter that I wrote ten years ago, which I sent to my family and friends. The letter covered the previous five years when I was in financial difficulty and friends lent me money that I hadn't yet paid back. I intended to apologize, ask them for forgiveness and tell them that I would change. Reading this letter again was devastating and depressing. I had to acknowledge that I messed up. Fifteen years later, I was back to square one; still broke, heavily in debt and far behind my promises to my wife, daughter, and friends.

Instantly, I thought of Albert Einstein's definition of insanity – repeating the same things over and over yet expecting a different outcome, which is exactly what I had been doing for over a decade. This was the moment of truth. I had to stop doing what I was doing.

I had success in my previous job. I was a high earner climbing the corporate ladder. Life was good. In 2003, I decided to take a sabbatical during which time my daughter was born. I was solicited by friends, who were all business owners, to do business. I decided to give it a try and became self-employed. I tried various areas such as real estate, venture capital, high yield "private placements," and day trading. All opportunities came up by coincidence, and all ended in failure.

The consequence was our financial situation deteriorated quickly. I was broke. Creditors wanted to beat me up, friends who had lent me money turned their backs on me, and others put pressure on my wife. Without the help of my wife and family, I would not have been able to survive. I was struggling from month-to-month and couldn't make ends meet.

In combination with my financial situation, I was changing as a person, going from bad to worse. I have not been able to keep my word and commitments to many people including my family. My integrity and reliability fell by the wayside.

Furthermore, my marriage was under more and more pressure. The financial situation overshadowed our daily lives. My wife resented having to be the breadwinner for so many years and even considered leaving me. Eventually, it was I who left after I started having an affair. After a long rollercoaster ride, my wife and I found each other again, but the healing process was not yet complete. Too much had happened.

Finally, I decided to go back to my "roots" – the Internet - and started creating websites and online shops, but I knew that my current business wouldn't get me off the ground and provide me with the lifestyle I wanted to live. I felt trapped.

I knew there had to be a real business opportunity that could save me. The search began, and I found it in Network Marketing. Like in any business, success didn't come overnight. You need to develop the skills and take committed actions to succeed. Because of Network Marketing, I got into the area of self-development and began studying topics like motivation, leadership, and entrepreneurship. During that learning process, I had continued setbacks and had to start from scratch many times.

I was getting angry with myself as I didn't draw the line and stop doing whatever was causing the poor results. I had to face reality and take full responsibility.

So why didn´t I stop immediately after the first failure? Well, I love running, especially marathons, and I am not one to give up after 5 miles. Besides, all business opportunities seemed reliable and legitimate. More importantly, my unshakeable belief that I am safe and that everything will turn out right is because of my faith in God.

I was 55 years old, married, a father to a fifteen-year-old daughter, self-employed, and living in Zurich, Switzerland.

I refused to let those fifteen years and the people I offended, determine the rest of mine and my family's life. I was determined to find the reasons why I had failed and then make the necessary changes to achieve massive success. Giving up was not an option.

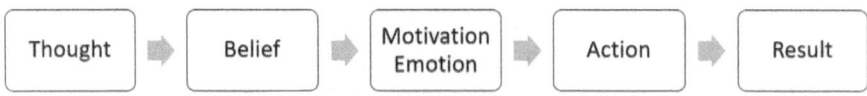

Shad Helmstetter and Napoleon Hill helped me to find the reasons that led to my failures. In my understanding and interpretation, what they say is that our thoughts ultimately create our reality. When I heard and read it, I started to understand and internalize it.

Our results come from our actions, and actions are based on our motivation or emotions. These are determined by our beliefs, which are created by our thoughts, and how we think about ourselves and others. Our thoughts are the internal programs that operate our subconscious.

How could I benefit from this knowledge? I needed to find an area in which I was successful so I could learn from there and apply my knowledge to the financial and business area in which I failed.

I have been running almost my whole life and one day I decided to run marathons. I completed Chicago and Berlin so far. I registered for other marathons, but injuries and obstacles made it impossible to participate.

The process started with the results first. I analyzed the results and then worked backward to analyze each step in the process. These were my observations:

Result:

I finished two marathons, and my best time was 3 hours, 28 minutes (age 45).

Action:

First, I made the decision and registered. Second, I planned the entire preparation process, starting with my desired finishing time, followed by the required monthly, weekly, and daily activities. Third, I executed the plan.

Motivation/Emotion:

I stayed focused, was disciplined and consistent with my daily routine. I knew there was no shortcut, no instant gratification. I had to do the work. More than once, I needed to overcome my inner temptations, but my WHY was big enough, and I knew that the moment of truth was on racing day. I wanted to triumph.

Belief:

I was confident and certain.

Thought(s):
My thoughts were clear and straight-forward. I can do it and I will.

Afterwards, I examined the financial and business area in which I messed up. My observations were the following:

Result:
Poor results. I was unable to make ends meet for a very long time.

Action:
I didn't put in the work needed wholeheartedly. I occupied myself with planning and analyzing instead of focusing on revenue-producing activities such as calling prospects, getting new clients and having meetings. I did not commit to work on my Internet business or on the Network Marketing business. I meandered between the two.

Motivation/Emotion:
I was frustrated with my Internet business and without any motivation.

Belief:
I believed that most customers wanted premium services for a shoestring budget without appreciating the service I was providing. I knew my business was about to end.

Thought:
I knew I was in the wrong business model with no chance to get ahead in my finances and lifestyle. Without a shadow of a doubt, I knew that my future was in Network Marketing. All I had to do was get involved entirely and work my butt off.

The before/after comparison revealed that the single component that made all the difference was clarity. Clear thoughts lead to success. Ambiguity turned into indecisiveness and procrastination ending in massive disappointment.

As an industrial engineer, I love systems and processes. I needed a framework to stick to and follow through until I accomplished my goals. In my previous jobs and due to my studies in self-development, I compiled a simple framework that worked just fine for me.

I called it MPBP (My Personal Becoming Process). I could use it in any area of my life that I wanted to improve. The graphic illustrates the single steps involved:

Assessment:
If you want to change in a specific area, you need to understand your current situation. You might use Darren Hardy's "Life Assessment" questionnaires to get started. I did a re-assessment in the financial and business corner of my life using Shad Helmstetter's and Napoleon Hill's ideas and analyzed it as described above.

Goals:
What do you want to accomplish in life? In this section, design your life as you want it to be.

The most difficult part for me was to be truthful to myself. What did I really want, not what my wife or daughter wanted? To get answers, I needed time to be alone in a quiet place and listen to my inner voice. When I listened to my heart and soul, I gained clarity. I still wanted to be free and to live a life of abundance, contribution, and fulfillment - a meaningful life. I want to leave my mark on the planet.

My future was Network Marketing, and I wanted to hit the highest company rank within six months. I had to burn all bridges with my current Internet business within a narrow timeframe. I had to be all in, without any excuses for not doing it.

Essentials:

The essentials were the internal work I had to do to achieve my goals. As Jim Rohn said: "Success is something you attract by the person you become." I had to ask myself what kind of person I needed to become and with what attributes and character traits to accomplish my goals. The essentials also indicated that I had to work on my habits. Start new habits and expand existing habits that were contributing towards my goals and stop the poor habits sabotaging my ambitions.

Action plan:

Like planning a marathon, I started with the end result in mind. First, I decided to go all-in within Network Marketing. Second, I would hit the highest rank in the company within six months. Third, I would shut down my Internet business within two months. Fourth, it was imperative that all my actions could be broken down into my Daily Methods of Operation.

DMO (Daily Method of Operation):

Mentor and friend, Randy Schroeder said, "Daily Disciplines Done Daily Build Character" - DDDDBC. What you do on a daily basis becomes a habit in time. When it becomes a habit, your subconscious mind will absorb it. Doing your daily activities over time transforms you into a new person with new character traits. DMO in a nutshell: do – review – adjust – do.

Results:

I knew I had to be patient with my results. I knew that if I focused on my DMO, the results would be predictable, and no guesswork was needed. When this book is published, I will be on my journey to reaching the highest promotion level as an independent sales representative in the company.

Once I had clarity, and my systems and processes were in place, everything started to get easier. Instantly, I had that swag. I was more relaxed and happy. This new positive energy was perceivable to everyone. My pain and stress faded and my self-esteem grew. Our family life began to flourish with more fun, laughter, happiness, and appreciation of what we already had.

Looking back, I am amazed at how many times I hit rock bottom. I disappointed so many people, I distanced myself from former friends, my character changed, my marriage nearly ended, and I was close to giving up on my dreams. I believe that everything happened for me for a reason. I truly believe that getting crushed several times was unavoidable to becoming a better, caring human being with more empathy for others, being a better husband, father, friend, mentor, and an exceptional leader.

The process of running a marathon showed me that I could achieve anything. So, put on your sneakers and run for your dreams.

Biography

Peter Muzik graduated as an industrial engineer in Germany and has been an entrepreneur in Switzerland for over a decade. He is known for never giving up, turning difficulties into positive results, and leadership. His mission is to lift people up regardless of their current situation and make an impact on their lives by helping them achieve their goals. He currently lives in Zurich, Switzerland, with his wife and daughter.

Contact Information

Website: https://www.petermuzik.com
Facebook: https://www.facebook.com/petermuzik.online
Instagram: https://www.instagram.com/petermuzik/

Chapter 40

ROADBLOCKS IN LIFE COME FROM OUR MINDSET

By Robert Bucko

I was born in 1984 in a small town called Snina in the eastern part of Slovakia, which is one of the poorest areas of my country. My parents worked hard to get my brother and me to University. Their mindset (and many other people's during the time) was to go to school, get the best grades, get to University, get a "stable" job (meaning they cannot fire you) to get a "secure" income. The reason my parents taught me to get a University degree and a well-paying job was because of my health conditions. My parents were always giving me all the support I needed over time. Even when I did not realize it, they were still there for me, and I am exceedingly thankful for my family. When I was a year old, doctors diagnosed me with a joint disease called "Magnus Perthes," which means my hip joints are not developed, and I will walk in pain. So when I was two years old, I was sent to a clinic for 14 months where it was forbidden for me to walk.

After the time in the clinic, I had to learn how to walk again. When I was ten years old, I had an operation where the doctors had to break my right hip joint, turn it around and fix it with a steel plate and four screws for it to heal. I remember the Head of the orthopedic department saying, "We will have to replace your joint for a titanium one by the time you are 25 years old." I lived with that statement for a long time.

I could not play any sports for my entire childhood. That is my background, and all those aspects shaped my life. I was one of the best students at school and got into University, where I studied programming and information technologies, which is one of the best-paying professions, even today.

I was also doing research in the field of applied informatics during my Ph.D. studies and also made some professional publications on the topic. I got so many great deals and job offers, but somehow, I knew that it would not fulfill my calling. I wanted to discover how I can use my skills and my expertise to serve others better. That was when I started my first company, before I even finished my university studies. It was a language school where we taught people new languages to get better jobs, positions or even start a new career abroad. Education was always the key element in my life, but very soon I realized formal education is not enough. I needed to get new skills to help more people faster, better and more efficiently.

When I was 28 years old, I was expecting to go in for the surgery to replace my hip joint for the titanium one. When I came for the last checkup, the doctor told me that I did not need the replacement, and I can come in for the next checkup only if I have some pain in my legs. I will be 34 this year, and I feel completely well. I also run and play sports on a daily basis without limitations.

You can read my story "How I was healed by God" on my blog www.robertbucko.com/blog.

After some time, I realized that all the roadblocks experienced in life come from our mindset.

I graduated from one of the most difficult Universities in my country, but that did not give me what I was expecting. The opportunity to go further with an education came with my education company. I am not saying that a University degree is not valuable, it was valuable in my case. I just want to emphasize the power of personal growth.

I have invested thousands of Euros into my own personal training. I realize that growth happens only if you are <u>constantly</u> learning. Persistence is the key to overcome any roadblocks.

People in my country still value a University education very highly. I was taught that the only way to success is to work hard for 12-16 hours a day and work for "someone" else. It all depends on who you know and if you have good connections in the right places. And because we still have such thinking, University education is still a big deal in my country.

My goal is to reprogram such thinking and teach people to reclaim responsibility from "the government, the boss, wife, husband, kids, young age, old age, etc." That is why I started an education program for young people called "Program Leader." In this program, we teach students the English language, as English opens up doors to the world, and also personal development strategies, techniques, and methods of how they can change their thinking, how to become a leader in their community, how to work on your dreams, and overcome fears that limit us.

One of my great role models taught me to build up the value of your mind. That means, no matter what the circumstances are, try to increase the value of your mind. Anything might happen to you as a person, or to your business, your career, your partnership, but no one can take away what you have learned, no one can delete your expertise, the unique perspective you have obtained from your experiences. That is the value you can bring to others, or in other words, to serve others.

My life taught me to be grateful for every minute you have in this life. I am so thankful for what God has done in my life. It is not possible to describe it in words, I am thankful for my wife, and I have just become a daddy last week of two beautiful princesses. We are full of joy, appreciation, gratefulness, and blessings. It changed the game in my life. I encourage you to stay on your track and lead yourself as the captain of the boat.

But it does not happen overnight. The single most important key to achieving success is to know crystal clear what "SUCCESS" means to YOU and then make a roadmap on how to get there. The amazing thing about that road is the never-ending process. When you get to the TOP, you will get another perspective that excites you even more.

I believe there are proven ways on how to achieve anything in your life. It requires a certain level of leadership. My first lesson on leadership was to learn how to lead myself. If you master that, you are 80% done. I would love to share my strategies and tools on how I get better every day and what keeps me on track to constantly give my better self to the world.

There are 2 KEY QUESTIONS to make your dreams come alive.
1. Knowing where I am

2. Knowing where I want to go, which includes knowing what I want to do and also knowing who I want to be (this one is the most important). Let's take a closer look at what I mean by these keys.

1. Knowing where I am. I make sure to have a good mirror. It is essential to know where I am in life, with my finances, with my relationships, with my health, and wealth as it applies to all the other areas of life. I discovered that for many people it is difficult to answer this question, "Where are you at the moment?" I do not mean physically, but where are you as a human being, as a person in terms of fulfilling your calling? Some great questions helped me understand where I was in my own life and it was a great impulse to establish new goals and habits that helped me to reach what I wanted with less stress, less time, and fewer resources.

Try this exercise. Complete the sentences below. Write down the first thing that comes to your mind.
Life is...
Success is...
Love is...
Passion is...
Happiness is...
Joy is...
The reasons WHY I am/I am NOT/successful are...
The reasons WHY I am/I am NOT/happy are...
My biggest fears are...
The most beautiful thing about my life is...
The worst thing in my life is...

These questions give you a significant reflection, which could lead to starting a change (or a small shift) you need to do, or you are about to do. I answer them from time to time to make my vision clear. If you are honest with yourself, it is a great reflection and amazing tool to start something new or improve the way you are currently on. The great thing about this is that even if you answered these questions yesterday, today is a new day and you are not the same as you were yesterday. So much is happening in our everyday life, we learn, we reach, we love, we discover, we develop, and so on. This exercise is never the same, and it gives you the reflection of where you are at the moment.

2. Knowing/discovering:
a) where I want to go:

I always make sure to write down all of my goals. There are three stages in writing my goals list. I will not go into details on how to visualize or write down your specific goal using any well-known strategy (S.M.A.R.T. goals etc.), but I will explain the process of making such a list and how it will influence your mindset and decision making.

The First stage is: I write down all the goals which occupied my mind the most, therefore most of them are "urgent goals" such as: repair the roof, get a bigger car for my two kids where you can put a pushchair and suitcase in as well, change the flat for a bigger one, and the list continues... Interesting things happen when you do not STOP writing your goals and finish your list of urgent goals.

The second stage starts right after you will start thinking about the things you want to do, you want to achieve, you desire or dream about. Examples: go for a 2-month vacation with your family, travel around the world, see the most amazing places, buy the most amazing car, move to a better place, and so on. You will start changing things for experiences or improvements to your lifestyle! Something that will create amazing memories that you are able to collect and enjoy.

The third stage is about WHO you want to become, who you want to meet with, what significant project you want to work on, how you want to improve other people's lives, etc. One of the exercises I would recommend is to write down 101 goals. Why 101? First of all, it is more than 100. If you tell yourself to write down 100 goals, most people will end up with 60, 70 or 80; they will barely reach 90. When you tell yourself to write down 101, it is a specific number, so you will go through the process of all the stages just as described above, that is WHY 101. Writing those goals will be challenging, but make sure you enjoy the entire process, it is not a race, you have the time, and it is one of the biggest investments you could give yourself.

b) what I want to do

This question opens up the "HOW" method. How are you going to fulfill your calling? What strategy or method do you have to follow to get the results you want. There is one very simple, but useful farmer proverb in my country.

"If you want to have the same harvest as the best farmer in your village, go and ask him how he did it. Then just follow his instructions."

There are many great and proven strategies and business models in today's world to follow. There are so many great leaders in a particular industry who you can follow and use the same strategies, methods or instruction to get the results you want. That is why I want to partner with Matt Morris. I think he is a great leader with extraordinary results. I am super excited to be a co-author with Matt and learn those strategies from the TOP leaders in the industry. As the proverb said: "Just follow the instructions."

c) Who I want to be (this one is the most important)

We have been created by the Creator in His image, that means: we are called to CREATE as well. That is why we, as human beings, are called creatures (creatures = those who create). It is that simple. How would you feel if you could create anything with no limits? Just imagine that. Make a clear picture in your mind of how exactly your life would look like if you had the power to create anything? How would you feel if you knew your specific calling, your purpose, why you have been installed into the current space and time? I can tell you there is no OTHER person exactly the same as YOU! Never was and never will be. You are UNIQUE, and this uniqueness is the way you see things in the world, in other people, your experiences, skills, and background are so valuable that someone is willing to pay a high price to get to know your view, your advice, and your point. The truth is, you have the power. Just STEP UP and BE who you are called to be! If you know who you are and the price of yourself, you become unstoppable.

These areas are essential to understanding who we are, why we are here, and what we are called to do. If you are not clear in any of those questions, it will make you go around searching and looking for new opportunities, new doors to open, from one training to another and so on. On the other hand, if you have a crystal-clear vision of those areas, you will make decisions or take actions, and it will get you to the mode of certainty, and you will be aware of the value you carry or present.

I used these exact strategies to build my companies. I made exact plans to achieve them. And you can too!

Biography

Robert Bucko found his passion for serving others. He helps people find their talents and strengths. He is the co-founder of the Institute of Education that provides leadership programs for people to change their mindset from fear to courage and victory.

Contact Information

Facebook: https://www.facebook.com/robert.bucko.9
LinkedIn: https://www.linkedin.com/in/robertbucko/
YouTube Channel:
https://www.youtube.com/channel/UCaYHj1mABKAhFG4cYF9cpew?view_as=subscriber
Twitter: @BuckoRobert
Instagram: https://www.instagram.com/robertbucko/
Website: https://www.robertbucko.com/
Blog: https://www.robertbucko.com/blog

Chapter 41

THE STREAM

By Sabrina Henne

I was lying in The Stream, in front of my beautiful Victorian dream home, when I woke up with sand scattered all over my face. I realized I passed out in The Stream. "How did this happen?" "How am I still alive?" Then, I remembered what happened the hour before.

UPS was going to deliver packages for my business, but I didn't want the delivery truck to go over my dirt road because The Stream below was clogged up with leaves, making the road vulnerable to collapse. As I looked out of the beautiful bay window of my dream house, I ran as fast as I could downstairs, outside to catch the UPS truck, but he drove over the road anyway and the road survived. But it may not survive next time, so I went down to The Stream and got in to unclog the leaves. They were everywhere. I started thinking about the past year and how difficult it was for me.

My intentions started out well. One of my real estate savvy friends encouraged me to buy properties. Yes, it was something I always wanted to do, so that's what I did. I purchased the Victorian dream house I always wanted. I rented out my starter home to a nice man on Section 8. This is a no brainer, I thought to myself. If I keep this up, I am going to be FREAKY RICH. Anyway, as I continued to change on my journey to success, people started to notice. Then, my ex-boyfriend wanted to sue me for custody of our daughter. Undercover haters seemed to emerge.

Family members turned on me and supported my ex-boyfriend in his custody efforts. I was a single mom doing the best I could for my daughter. I had my daughter in a private Christian school, and she loved the home in which we lived. Every time I blinked, I needed another $5,000 for lawyer fees to continue the fight of my life for my precious daughter. I was then laid off from my job because the real estate market was in a downfall and my renters stopped paying rent. They had also lied to me as they were not on Section 8. So, I had to hire another lawyer to evict them because my renters knew the legal system better than I did. They knew all the loopholes that would keep them longer in my house without having to pay me — another $1,500 for lawyers to evict my tenants. Then, I lost 95% of my stock portfolio, and I started to fall behind on my bills. I went from having just about everything I wanted to "How do I do this now?"

While at The Stream, I thought about all these things. My body probably went into stress overload, and I passed out. My daughter was the most important thing in my life. I could lose everything but not my baby. I had to develop a warrior mentality. I sobbed and cried. I had an awakening experience. It was the first time in my life, I felt broken, but I realized I didn't know enough. "I thought I was ready to be an entrepreneur?" Nightingale Conant tested me several times and said I think like the 3%. I thought about all of the beautiful self-development books I read over the years. They came alive at The Stream. One of the books was Robert G. Allen's "Multiple Streams of Income." I realized I was unclogging one stream at a time. To me, The

Stream represented my life. It was clogged up with limited cash flow, shitty people, massive stress and greedy attorneys. I'm supposed to have many streams of income, I thought to myself. I failed. I'm a failure. But then once again something amazing happened to me.

The Universe showed me how many of my amazing mentors failed. Did Walt Disney, Thomas Edison, Robert Kiyosaki, The Wright Brothers, Donald Trump, and Abraham Lincoln ever fail? I realized I was outside of my comfort zone and in a learning process. There is a big difference between working in a safe secure cubicle and making your dreams a reality. Even though my credit report did not reflect my intelligence, I became smarter. Failure is one of the roads to success. But when you are in a low state, you will know who loves you and who thrives off your mishaps.

How did I turn my life around? I left The Stream that day. The next time I went to court, I represented myself. I told the attorneys and the judge that nobody was going to take my baby away from me, and I was clearly the better parent. That was the day I was awarded custody. I then sold my rental house in 15 days and made enough money to sustain me while getting back on track.

Through all of my beautiful highs and lows of being an entrepreneur, I developed a system that keeps me on track. We are all vulnerable to whatever life dishes out, so I want to share my daily action plan to help change your life.

1. Health and Fitness: The best thing you can do for your life is to dedicate at least one hour per day for health and fitness. This won't only increase your cash flow while minimizing costs on doctor visits and medication; it also reduces stress, increases your energy and mental clarity. If you are always tired, improving your health improves energy levels, increases happiness and boosts confidence. Confidence transforms into opportunity. Make sure you do different exercises to avoid boredom or consider a personal trainer.
2. TELL YOURSELF WHAT YOU WANT: Everyone has a dream. I believe God designed you with a beautiful purpose. Are you going to search within and extract your dreams? It could be something you wanted to do as a child, but you were always too afraid to work on it or never spent enough time to develop your dream. It takes courage to go after what you want. It can be scary because you are forcing yourself to step out of your comfort zone and go to a place you have never gone before. You might think you'll fail outside your comfort zone but think of a baby trying to walk. As soon as you fall, get back up and try again. You might get a boo-boo and cry, but it will be ok.

   You are no copy. God created you perfectly. What are the perfect things in your life? "Perfect love casts out fear." When both my daughters were born, they were perfect to me. So, tap into the amazing gifts and talents you have and share them with the world. "Who are you?" Search the core of who you are. Usually, only a select few know the real you and what you are about, because they were interested in you enough to find out everything about you. Be your authentic self, not the person your parents or spouse want you to be, and don't just do it for the money. What are your dreams? There are dream killers everywhere who will try lower your expectations of what you want. You don't share your dreams with everyone. Only the people who support your dreams and who assist you can help make your dreams a

reality. Make sure you are not your own dream killer. Make sure all of your thoughts are positive.
3. Daily Goals: Accomplish six goals every day that takes you in the direction of your dreams or to the next level. A true entrepreneur chooses not to settle for the cubicle. If you are not building your dreams, you are building someone else's. I use Brendon Burchard's High Performance Planner. Writing down your goals is an effective way of imprinting them in your subconscious. If you don't finish a goal in one day, simply move it to the next day. Fight every day to achieve your goals because your brain will try to talk you out of accomplishing them. You must have clarity, focus, determination, and persistence. You may need cash to achieve some goals. Goals that stretch you and scare you will make you grow. So, to achieve your goal, write it down, and make it visible where you see it every day. When you accomplish the goal, erase it.
4. Decision: The biggest secret for me is making a sound decision and sticking to it. I have been practicing this in my life, and it's been very rewarding. When you make a clear decision, you are eliminating procrastination. With a decision, you have creative awareness on how to make it all happen and achieve your goals.
5. Awareness: Awareness is key to being ready for the opportunity. I was amazed at how many opportunities I presented to friends and family that they would pass up. It's okay if something is not for someone. Focus on yourself, your goals and what you want. You don't have time to transform people because you need to transform yourself first. When people see changes, they will ask what you are doing. Don't be a chaser. Let them chase you. Know what opportunity looks like, and never be the smartest person in the room.
6. Focus: Get a mirror and look at yourself. Tell yourself what you want and what you expect from yourself daily.
7. Determination: Don't get discouraged if things don't work immediately. Sometimes, plans will change, and you might go in a different direction. It's just part of the game. The more you practice, the better you get at knowing what to do next. Become relentless, go to the next level and don't sweat the small stuff. Focus on the Now, because it is all you have. When you get ahead of your goals and live in the future, you will experience anxiety. Implement well-organized action.

As soon as you accomplish a goal, go to the next one. Keep doing it. In 90 days, if you stay focused, you will see results.

Biography

Sabrina Henne was born in California but lived in the Carolinas for over 30 years. She resides in South Carolina with her amazing daughters. A graduate of High Point University, High Point, NC, Sabrina holds a Bachelor of Science Degree in Business

Administration with a concentration in Marketing. Her background includes real estate, technical recruiting, telecommunications, and banking. Sabrina is passionate about protecting the environment and the rights of animals. She enjoys international travel, fashion designing, and fitness. She also collects autographs from celebrities and politicians.

Contact Information

Website: http://www.sabrinahenne.com
Facebook: https://www.facebook.com/SABRINAHENNEREALTOR/

Chapter 42

SUCCESS STARTS AND ENDS WITH SELF-LOVE

By Sean Reid

This chapter is a story about learning to love yourself and reveal who you are so you can catapult into a world of success. To be successful, you need sincere and trustworthy people around you. But, if you don't truly love who you are, how can you expect anyone to even like you? And, this is where my story begins.

For quite a long time, I hated the person I saw in the mirror. I tried very hard to change. I felt I needed to blend in more with those around me and stop being so 'different.' Unfortunately, in our world today, being different is not always seen as a good trait. And for me, that perception was no different. I was ridiculed by many people around me for simply being me. I was very outgoing with a big personality. For a while, I was not afraid to show it. But then, the fire in my personality began to fade to the point where it was nearly extinguished. I wanted so badly to be 'like everyone else.' I just wanted to be the normal guy. The guy who people didn't shun and a person who blended in with the crowd.

Looking in the mirror and hating the person staring back is one of the absolute worst feelings to have. And, what's more damaging is the capacity for self-hate to impede success in just about anything. Since I can remember, I always wanted to be an entrepreneur. I had a desire to do something more with my life and control my own success. But, that objective was put on the back burner for a while. When you don't love yourself, it's difficult for others to love you for who you are, let alone want to work or do business with you, or even get to know you.

I put my passions and desires aside because I didn't want to be different anymore. I didn't want to be mocked for being different. Truthfully, I just wanted the people around me to like me for who I was. But I felt I had to change for people to like me and become what they wanted me to be.

Trying to change *who you are* is one of the most difficult tasks in life because no matter how hard you try, the real 'you' is still there. The real 'you' is deep inside you, begging to be set free. And over time, the more I tried to change, the more I realized what it was doing to me.

I became a very angry and negative person. I projected my feelings of self-hate and anger onto the people closest to me. Typically, we all tend to project our feelings onto others, mostly when those feelings are negative. I hated seeing people around me be happy because I knew deep down I was not happy at all. And why should those around me be happy when I could not be? And for a while, my unhappy feelings became normal, and it became such a part of me that it started to shape who I was becoming as a person.

I mentioned earlier in the chapter how difficult it is trying to change yourself, but what I did not highlight was when you mix in self-hate to the equation, it becomes increasingly easier to change who you are. Unfortunately, the person you change into is usually very angry, depressed, and sad. I tried to hide the sadness and depression with a smile, or worse, angry outbursts. I could see those around me start pulling away and becoming more distant. Let's face it; no one wants to be around an angry, sad, and depressed person.

Fortunately, this story takes a positive turn ahead. A turn, I hope, will help at least one person realize a key aspect of being successful. I will never forget the day I saw who I became, and it scared the absolute shit out of me. Up until that point, I couldn't remember when I had actually looked in the mirror. But, when I caught a glimpse of myself in the mirror, the anger and sadness was written all over my face. I didn't recognize the person staring back at me.

That is when everything hit me harder than the house that fell on the wicked witch of the west. I spent so much time hating myself and being angry at the world that I lost sight of who I was, and even worse, I pushed away so many people. I realized that, for the most part, I was alone. When I was isolated with this sad and angry person, I knew this was not who I was supposed to be. That fire that was inside of me (the same fire that's inside of you) may have dimmed to barely a flicker, but it was still there, deep down and waiting to burn bright again.

I won't say it was easy learning to love who I was, because it wasn't. When you spend so much time hating yourself and trying to change, it becomes that much more difficult to learn to love who you are. But with commitment and hard work, you can achieve it. And, that is exactly what I did.

I realized the things that made me unique and different were what was needed to attract success. I then used my uniqueness to stand out in the crowd and get people to notice me. It was at that point when I learned to control how people perceived me. I regulated it by loving myself unapologetically. I did not give anyone the chance to bring me down because I was loving the person and nobody could break that. Once this mindset changed, success started coming to me instead of me chasing after success. I started doing so much better in my job at the time and also with my own business.

To be a successful entrepreneur, you need to be able to master the skill of attracting people. What I found is that it's much easier to attract someone when you love who you are. We are all unique and we all have something that makes us stand out in the crowd. That 'something' differentiates us and is a tool to get to know people personally, and only then can they begin to like and trust you.

My life changed tremendously through learning to love who I am. I can stand in front of hundreds, even thousands of people, and talk about how they too can live a wonderful life. I motivate them on how to grow their businesses beyond anything they ever imagined. And of course, I have tips and tricks, as well as products and services, to help with this transformation. But all of those "tools" are only useful once someone learns to use what they already have inside them. Once people truly learn to love themselves, then and only then, can any of the other tools and tips I teach them be useful.

My intention, by the end of this chapter, was to encourage you to look at yourself differently. Self-love is not an overnight process. It requires determination and constant willingness to stick to it even when things get tough. And I assure you, they will get tough. But, if you are able to stay on course and not give up, then you will truly shine in the toughest times, and it's when you learn things about yourself that you never knew before.

Everyone has a different definition of the word success. And each person's path to success is different. But, the one thing I can assure you is we all start off at the same point. Our journeys start with ourselves, and when we begin to love who we are, we can watch the journey of success begin!

Whenever you can, look at yourself in the mirror or your phone camera and use the affirmation below to commit changing for the best to enjoy lasting success.

"Self, I love you. I was put on this Earth with many attributes and features that make me different from everyone else. Attributes and features that I embrace wholeheartedly, regardless of what anyone says. I know what makes me different sets me apart. It will be what differentiates me on my path to success and what will bring me true happiness. I love who I am and who I am becoming, and that is something no one can ever take away from me."

I sincerely wish the readers the best of luck for their journey to self-love and success. You are the only you in this whole world. Take that and use that to change the world for the better. Because in the end, the only way to change the world is first to change how you see yourself. Love yourself harder than anyone else could love you and watch the doors and opportunities open! I am rooting for every single one of you. I cannot wait to see what you do with the life you are given.

Biography

Sean Reid has been helping entrepreneurs succeed in business and life for over five years. He has taught on stage in front of thousands of people and consulted individually about the keys to growing a sustainable business. He has enabled entrepreneurs from all around the country to learn how to double or even triple their business. Sean has studied not only the critical aspects of growing a successful business but also the mental preparation for standing out in the crowd.

Contact Information

Facebook: https://www.facebook.com/theseanreid1
Instagram: https://www.instagram.com/theseanreid/

Chapter 43

CHANGE YOUR FOCUS *FROM WHAT <u>IS NOT</u> IN YOUR CONTROL TO WHAT <u>IS IN</u> YOUR CONTROL*

<u>By Shameel Fazaldin</u>

She stopped to catch her breath. Looking to the left and to the right while filled with anxiety, she knew she couldn't just stand there. She started sprinting as fast as her legs could take her and as much as her insides could endure. Suddenly, she reached a riverbank; water gushing along, an impossible feat to cross. As she looked to her left, she saw a hunter aiming his .30-06 rifle at her. On her right, she noticed the grass ruffling and saw a lioness preparing to pounce on her weekly meal, showing her beaming eyes that sent out a shivering chill. To her back she saw a forest fire drawing closer and closer, sparing nothing in its path. She collapsed; tired, weak, and almost breathless, knowing there was nothing more she could do! Looking up to the skies, her eyes filled with tears, she murmured a small prayer: Oh Lord, I turn to you the All-Wise!

So, what happened to this beautiful and heavily pregnant Doe? With challenges on every side, how could she possibly survive? How many times have we felt so caged up in our lives that we think and question how we are still alive? Joy Page once said, "Instead of focusing on the circumstances that you cannot change – focus strongly and powerfully on the circumstances that you can."

The Doe was surrounded by deadly risks, each one different and more intense than the other. But what transpired in the next few seconds is what's important. The Doe looked up to the skies, closed her eyes, and decided to concentrate on the only action that was in her control, which was to give birth to a fantastic Fawn. While she focused all her energy on giving birth, at that instance, a tiny piece of the burning grass suddenly flew into the hunter's eye. He lost his focus and fired his rifle which had his last and final bullet. Just then, the lioness took a majestic leap, and the hunter's bullet missed the Doe and struck the lioness. At the same time, heavy rains started to pour from the skies that completely doused the forest fire. Minutes later, the Doe opened her eyes and saw the beautiful innocence of her baby staring back at her. It was her choice to focus on what was in her control, which proved to be her most significant achievement of all.

Be it in business, personal lives, intimate relationships, or friendships; we will always face situations that require us to choose where we need to focus our energies. Trying to be everywhere and do everything in the hope of creating our perfect world not only burdens our shoulders but no successful person has ever achieved it.

Ten years ago, I was blessed with my own bundle of joy: My son. He is the blessing of my life. As he started growing, my wife and I began noticing that his developmental milestones such as speech, walking, and eating solids were delayed.

Initially, this wasn't an issue as we had the support and love of family members reassuring us that he will blossom at his own pace when he is ready. However, after some time passed, we had an evaluation done and received the news that no parent can ever prepare themselves for, our son was diagnosed with mild autism. We started off in denial, which turned into anger directed at anyone stereotyping our son. Over time, we researched more, tried to gain a better understanding of our son, and worked on getting closer to his world. We knew we could not change his condition, but what we could change is the one thing we could control – our acceptance of his diagnosis. Once we accepted it, life became slightly easier as things fell into place. The right school, an adequate support system, the required developmental tools, and most importantly, just letting him be. Once we were able to change our focus to him and appreciate his amazing qualities, we were able to control situations much better. Not having our son operate as society "required" was fine with us, because we cannot control what people think, feel, or expect. We found peace and happiness by focusing on our own needs and addressing factors that were in our control.

When I set out on my Network Marketing journey, my excitement was sky-high. I made numerous calls to prospects, had many business meetings, and work was progressing. But over time, with more rejections, meeting cancellations, and unanswered calls, I became dejected and demotivated. I found myself blaming everything else because my focus had shifted. I felt my lack of earnings was a result of people not being open to the Network Marketing industry; people not having additional time, not being receptive to change, not being ready for hard work and everything else! It is so easy to fall into the mindset of blaming all factors around us for the lack of personal success. The real reason I was not earning money or growing my business was due to me not talking to more people. The only elements I could control were my actions. When we look inwardly, we can remove the shackles that prevent us from truly excelling at whatever we put our minds to.

What steps can we take to help change our focus? Through the many talks I've heard and countless articles on this subject, I selected to elaborate on an area that I call the 'ABC Rule". Change doesn't happen overnight, but the consistent effort and constant self-reminders can aide that change. The 3-step rule is as follows:

1. ACCEPTANCE

The faster we learn to accept that the problem is internal and not external, the quicker we can work towards achieving our goals. Acceptance should not be confused with succumbing to the pressures around us. It is about understanding where to focus our energies, as we can achieve our goals only when we choose to look at the positives.

A friend of mine, who was the CEO of a multinational company, instructed his commercial team to put in a tender for a buy-out of a 35-year-old company that would increase their profits ten-fold. A lot of work, time, and effort went into preparing and laying the groundwork for the tender. His company had the best tender by far, but a month after submitting the bid, the country broke out into civil-war, creating huge political risk. The company that was being acquired lost a lot of business that posed an economic risk. My friend couldn't understand why everything was going against him until he chose to accept the situation and decided to focus all his efforts on his existing business. With a few tweaks in the business plan and a great supportive team, he managed to quadruple the company's profits by focusing solely and growing his existing business.

2. BELIEF

Once you've accepted the need to change, believing in yourself and your abilities is vital. Many times we accept that we need to alter our thinking, but we lack conviction because past experiences have shaped self-made bottlenecks for growth.

Great sports athletes reach their peak of greatness not only through hours of training and failing but also through having a colossal amount of self-belief. None of these athletes let their past failures clog their minds. Never be a prisoner of your past. It was just a lesson, not a life sentence. Had he listened to his high school coach, the world would have never heard the name Michael Jordan. Had he yielded to the words of the first editor he met, we would have never known the Rocky Balboa movies. Had they listened to society and the media, history books would have never recorded the massive success of The Beatles. You create your life from what you constantly believe!

3. CHANGE

After accepting where we are, whether it's in a particular situation or a life phase, we will realize we've been focusing on the wrong thing, and we'll first need to believe that we can grow out of it and become better. After following these steps, change is inevitable, and we'll be able to taste success in achieving our goals, targets, and dreams.

A good friend of mine was in a toxic relationship for over 17 years. He had surrendered his mind to believe that this was his destiny. He was imprisoned by thinking that he could not seek change because of his two children, and he was the cause of all the suffering, fights, arguing, and his pitiful plight. "What you tolerate, you cannot change." He was tolerating his situation and circumstances because he was held captive by his own tolerance. The day he decided to reflect and accept that he needed to transform his life, he mustered up self-belief and took the step to call it quits on his long thorny road in life. The change in his destiny was waiting to set him free from his self-imposed manacles. He found his soulmate and today lives a very fulfilled life.

We've all come across the saying sometime in our lives that life is 10% what happens to us and 90% how we react. We cannot change how other people perceive us or what they think of us, but we can change how we react. Don't depend too much on anyone in this world because even our own shadow leaves us when we are in the dark. The simple answer is to change the focus! Just like the Doe, we need to focus on what IS in our control. Don't get distracted by other external factors that we cannot change or control.

Once upon a time, there was a learned master and his very devoted student walking to get to the top of a mountain in a bid to perfect the student's teachings. The walk was long, and nightfall was upon them. They were tired and hungry and needed a place to rest. They were lucky enough to see a tiny hut at the bottom of the mountain and decided to request shelter for the night. They were welcomed by an old man in rags who offered them a meal of milk and cheese. The student felt sorry for the family as he could see how poor they were. He asked them how they survived, and the old man said that they relied solely on one old cow for their daily provisions. Perturbed by this, the student asked his learned master how they could help them. As they set off on their journey early in the morning, the learned master instructed his devoted student to take the cow and lead it over the cliff. Shocked at this request, the student knew he had to comply as he had sworn to follow his master in everything! With tears in his eyes, he led the cow to the cliff and saw it go over.

After a whole year up on the mountain, the student was still not able to overcome the vision that he was the cause of the downfall of an already struggling family. The master seeing his student's disturbed state instructed him to go down the mountain and bring some more provisions to last them another year. As the student came down the mountain, his curiosity about the family got the better off him, and he decided to take a detour and go towards where the old hut was and ask about the family. As he came over the valley, he was surprised to see a lush garden, a beautiful mansion, and highly cultivated crops. He proceeded to go to the house and inquire about the old man. The old man who now looked healthy instantly recognized the student and welcomed him in. The student now completely aghast, asked the old man how all this happened. The old man shared that a year ago their only provision was an old cow. One day, the cow ventured too close to the cliff and fell over. Not being in their comfort zone, they knew they had to change. They learned new skills, and overtime were able to completely change their destiny. The young student immediately thought of his master and the wisdom behind his instructions.

As the famous Confucius once said, "What the superior man seeks is in himself; what the small man seeks is in others."

YOU are the only catalyst needed to propel YOUR life's chain reaction.

YOU are the only mineral required for YOUR life to blossom.

YOU are the only artist painting YOUR life's portrait.

YOU only live once! So, make it count.

Biography

Shameel Fazaldin is an ACCA-qualified Financial Analyst, Entrepreneur, Peak Performance Coach, and now an Author! With over 15 years of experience in finance and more than a decade's experience as an entrepreneur, his biggest asset is the ability to uplift anyone around him to see the 'greener side.'

Shameel develops people around him by empowering and encouraging them to succeed.

His Success mantra, "People don't buy what you do; they buy why you do it. And what you do simply proves what you believe."

His mission is not to earn a billion dollars but to touch a billion hearts!

Contact Information

Facebook: https://www.facebook.com/shameel.fazaldin
LinkedIn: https://www.linkedin.com/in/shameel-fazaldin-b1b6b51a

Chapter 44

PUSHING THROUGH

By SherRie M. Blango

I've worked in leadership and management for over 17 years. Ever since middle school, I wanted to be a supervisor. My father had his own business, but prior to that, he worked as a supervisor with his last employer. Even though he was a leader and an entrepreneur, we never had dinner table discussions about how we, as young adults, were going to make a living. It was always understood that once we finished high school and completed our studies in college, the expectation was that we would get a job, move out and "hold our own" by maintaining our own homes and anything we purchased or acquired.

As long as I was studying and living under my father's roof, I was not allowed to work. Now that is what I call old school and double standards because my brothers were allowed to work from the time they were 15 years old. Even though my father would never allow me to work, he always told me that I could do and be whatever I wanted, and he knew I would be good at whatever I chose to do.

Throughout my life, no matter what organization I joined, whether it was student government, the Beta Club, volleyball, softball, 4H, or organizations within my church, I played a lead role in some capacity or another. As a result of these experiences, I realized my life purpose was to lead.

The examples I saw in my father as a leader and an entrepreneur, coupled with my own experiences with leading in various capacities laid the foundation for what was to come later in my life. Now allow me to take you Beyond Success.

During my first job at the age of 20, I was like a kid in a candy store. I wanted to try everything and learn as much as I could. A few weeks in, I became adept at being the top producer. I quickly became a one-woman team where I was the only person performing the task because I produced enough work for two shifts. I was excited and working my butt off for the minimum wage of $3.35. Can you imagine making that now?

A year later, after getting married and having a baby, my second job comes into play, which made me realize how much I loved helping people and making an impact in their lives by inspiring them while helping them to accomplish their goals. As much as I loved what I was doing, I needed more than $3.35 an hour. Can you identify with the dilemma I was facing?

Moving on to job number three. You couldn't tell me anything, because I have acquired a job where I am now making a whopping $8 an hour. I learned as much as I could, worked 8 to 9 hours a day, six days a week doing the same thing day in and day out, mastered my skills, trained others, became one of the lead people in my department, and received accolades for my leadership, while moving on up. Then something new was introduced to the company, temporary employees. After being with this company for 10 to 11 years, the temp employees came in and were treated better than the full-time employees but worked less. My years of working at a high level of standard and producing the numbers and quality across the board were now in jeopardy. I had nothing against the temporary employees; it wasn't their fault.

We are now at a point where upper management needed to make a decision on what direction we would take in order to continue to grow as a company. Although it was their responsibility to cast the vision and we execute and carry out the plan, leadership wanted to micromanage and do both. I could see the writing on the wall and realized the department was heading for trouble. As one of the line leaders, I thought I was looking out for the company and voiced the team and my concerns, backed with documented proof. I was informed that I was not the manager who makes the decisions. After working a total of 12 years, I was now making $12 an hour. At this point, I was furious with all the unfairness, so I realized it was time to leave the company and move on.

The most interesting part about all of this is, I already knew my time there was coming to an end. I am a woman of faith, and I believe GOD speaks or lets us know in some way that things are about to change, but we tend to overstay our appointed time in one place. Once I realized my time to move on was approaching, I started looking for another JOB before I left the company. The one time in 15 years that I went to a job service, I saw a posting for a new company coming to town. I applied and got accepted for their training program.

I was working during the day and went to school at night. Before the class was completed, I got a job offer with a start date, which was fantastic, right? Not so. I accepted the offer, completed and signed all the paperwork, including insurance and 401K enrollments, and I was all set for the first shift, then BANG! A week before the start date, they called and apologetically stated the first shift positions were filled, and I was to report to the second shift instead. I said I would not and could not work the second shift as I was hired for the first shift, and if that now changed, then I would not be reporting to work on my hire date. So, that was a wrap, or I should say, another one bites the dust. This was the first time I began realizing my self-worth.

My next seven years were excellent. I left my previous company two weeks before I was supposed to start with the new company that I never started with, so that means I was now unemployed. This made my husband a little nervous but life continued. Saying I will not and could not work the second shift was the best thing I ever did. For the next seven years, I worked in the school system as a substitute school teacher and teacher's aide. The bells and whistles were all going off at once. It was like heaven opened up, and the angels were singing and welcoming me home. I loved teaching and making a positive impact in the lives of children and their parents.

Our baby girl had just gone into middle school, and my husband and I agreed I would stay on her schedule until she graduated from high school. After that, I would return to, as my husband and I called it, the "real work world" with no summers off. No disrespect to teachers, because what they do is hard, important, and necessary work, which they do not get paid enough to do. Those seven years taught me that everyone doesn't learn the same, and you can't talk to everyone the same way. The one thing that had the biggest impact on me was when I learned, once the students realized I cared about them and they actually mattered, their lives were impacted positively, and they would go the extra mile for themselves. What I didn't realize at the time was how it was preparing me for my next ten years of Heaven and Hell, in one place.

Although it was worth every penny, understand that I had taken a $25K annual pay cut, during the seven years of working in the school system. Ouch, Ouch, Ouch! As a result, my daughter and I developed a lasting close bond. The decision my husband and I made that developed the bond with our daughter, drives the choices she makes for her children today. It's incredible how we impact our children's lives, and it's never spoken of, but we can see it in their actions, whether negative or positive. Seven years later, my daughter graduated from high school and went to college while I prepared to move back into the "real work world" as agreed between my hubby and me.

I took the summer off and went back to work at the school and began looking for a full-time JOB, eek! Naturally, I applied for full-time positions in several school districts, and nothing happened. So, during this time, I distinctively remember praying to GOD, I want my tithe to be $50 a week, equating to $500 a week for me. Well, I went to my first ever job fair and saw schools and companies I had never heard of before. There was one company that was advertising to pay tuition for school. I didn't know what type of business it was, what their product was, or what kind of schooling they were offering tuition for. I just said sign me up, and that's precisely what they did. I was tested the same day and went through the hiring process and was employed at $12 to $14 an hour, 11 days after walking into the job fair. Being paid $12 to $14 an hour to go to school was the best thing since sliced bread, at least that's what I thought.

It was a ten-year journey in and out of Heaven and Hell in this same place. As usual, staying true to myself, my character, my integrity, and my work ethic, I dove all in, learning all I could, working 9 to 10 hours a day, 6 to 7 days a week for almost two years. Within that time, I gained two promotions. The first one was a lead position, and the second one was in management, which actually exceeded my goal to get a supervisor's JOB. The supervisor I knew I would be since middle school. Not only am I now supervising employees, but I am now managing teams. I finally made it! It was beautiful; it came with an excellent pay increase and the hidden strings that I could not see at the time.

In the next three years, I was so dedicated to the JOB that I didn't even take a vacation. Then I got an email saying I couldn't accrue any more vacation time because my vacation was maxed out. In other words, any time I accrued from that point on, the company would take it back. I said, "Oh no, I've worked too hard for them to take my time back." So, I went to London for ten days, went on a cruise for seven days, and took four 4-day vacations within nine months. This was the beginning of a mindset shift. I realized my body needed rest and time to rejuvenate. From that point on, I vacationed every year, but here is the funny but sad thing. I still worked 6 to 7 days a week, 9 to 10 hours a day, and I only took my vacation around the Thanksgiving Holiday, because we already had Thursday to Sunday off so that would automatically add three days around that time.

Initially, I thought it was a good idea because I only used three of my vacation days, but, in reality, it was the unseen strings attached. I felt guilty for taking seven of my vacation days off from work at one time. WOW! Can you identify with that? Are you taking your hard-earned and well-deserved vacation time off like you should?

According to my annual reviews, I did my job and did it reasonably well. I had no complaints. I stayed true to myself, which kept me knowing what my weaknesses (areas of opportunity) and strengths were before my manager brought them up. My reviews were good until a new regime of leadership came in.

I was the type of leader who led teams that took ownership and did so proudly. Remember what I said earlier, the seven years in the school system prepared me for the next ten years, and once the students realized I cared about them, their lives were impacted positively, and they would go the extra mile for themselves. The teams knew I cared about them, had their back, and they trusted me and moved mountains if they had to, because I was part of the team, and not just their manager. I've always believed a leader should lead by example. It was my job to execute the plan, and the execution of the plan came by pushing through uncontrolled circumstances. When you must depend on other supporting systems to complete your tasks, but you have no control over them, it does not provide you with an opportunity for real success, unless your supporting systems are set up for success. Almost no one was successful on a daily basis at that time. Because nobody was listening to the concerns, I could see another train wreck coming. A good leader can see past the present and prepare for the future.

Things were moving, but not fast enough. The new regime of leadership came in with the idea to make everything "cookie-cutter" and have everything look the same across the board. To top it off, they made other changes and reorganized everything at the same time which overloaded the system and the employees. When this was taking place, we could see the derailing was about to happen. You would have thought I learned years ago about bringing my concerns to the forefront. Well, I did it again, and no one listened until the train ran off the tracks. We had to then operate in recovery mode, which always baffled me, because I'm a firm believer in taking a few extra hours to get it right the first time, rather than having to go back and spend days doing it all over again.

Now, Hell began… By not bringing a solution to the problem, I was perceived as not caring, defiant, and anything I said was received as rude.

Now, the train derailed, and they blamed my performance. I'm not performing, I'm not planning, I'm not holding my people accountable, and the "I'm nots" kept coming. So, what do you think I did? I began to execute their plan; their way and it continuously sank. They moved me and brought in another manager since it was "my performance," while more train cars ran off the track and stayed off the track for months.

The new area team began to do great things; however, I was never recognized, and somehow it was still my performance on paper. Yet, I was told by others that I was doing a great job, but on paper, it was my performance, not meeting standards. By this time, I was making a six-figure income in the game. Obviously, I didn't know how to play the game well enough.

Others noticed how I was being treated. The one question I was often asked was, "How do you do it?" They would say, "You come in here every day with a smile on your face, staying long hours and coming in when others aren't, even after being treated the way you are." I would smile and say, "I don't work for them, and I do it for my team (employees) because they are the ones who truly carry out the plan."

After working for about a year under this scrutiny, yet still working hard, enough was enough. I began preparing my team for their next manager; I told them I wasn't going to be there much longer. Then it reached a point where I told my manager the same because I know what I've done and what I'm doing for this company, but to not be recognized by my departmental leaders was unacceptable. Then, that glorious day came when the company and I were no longer a fit with each other, and the separation took place. Only this time, what I went through made me really realize I was worth a whole lot more than what they paid me, and I would never work for another company that didn't recognize my value.

Working the average 9 to 5 job is not for me, and if I can't serve others, then it's definitely not for me.

My self-value, my self-worth, my annual pay increases, my promotions will never be in the hands of another human being on this earth from now until eternity.

Now I have more freedom, fun, and fulfillment doing what I love most, which is changing people's lives one life at a time. Sharing how you can acquire wealth, impact communities through economic growth advancement, sharing knowledge on how to leave a legacy for families, and have the incredible opportunity to be a part of global expansion projects.

My destiny since middle school has always been to be a leader, and I'm still leading. There are some things that can never be taken from you, no matter how hard others try. If you do what is right and from the heart, you will always win.

I've already pushed through this journey. Now it's my time to move Beyond Success.

If I can do it, so can you, so go and move beyond your Success!

Biography

SherRie M. Blango is a leader of leaders for the Tri-County (Berkley, Charleston, and Dorchester) chapter of Women of Purpose Fellowship Ministries (WOPFM) SC. It was 25 years ago that SherRie responded to her heartfelt passion to teach and minister to others the Word of God, impacting the whole person in mind, body, spirit, and soul. She encourages them to have an intimate relationship with God and teaches how to practically apply the Word in everyday life. Additionally, SherRie is a successful entrepreneur and an advocate for strong families as a devoted wife, mother, daughter and more.

Contact Information

Facebook: https://www.facebook.com/sherrie.blango

Chapter 45

RULE YOUR MIND, ROCK YOUR BEST LIFE

By Steph Shinabery

"Awareness is like the sun; when it shines on things, they are transformed." ~ Nhat Hanh

Dr. Victor Lord Oliver was my Zoology professor in college. He was an interesting guy. He showed us vinegar eels, which are actually nematodes (worms) in the vinegar and he then swallowed a dropper full from a pipette. Got to love a scientist. One of the things I remember him saying more accurately than the topic on the *stratification of epithelial tissue* is: "if you watch what you think, you won't have to watch what you say."

I contemplated this deeply, and it wasn't until years later when I understood that my thoughts create my results. My thoughts create my reality.

I had a life-changing event that forced me to evaluate my thinking patterns and learn to practice awareness of thought. Awareness is a gift because you miss so much when you go through life on autopilot. I am fascinated with the brain, the mind, neuroplasticity, habits, and the biology of thought as it relates to human potential.

Watch your thoughts; they become words. Watch your words; they become actions. Watch your actions; they become habits. Watch your habits; they become character. Watch your character; for it becomes your destiny. ~ Upanishads

---

"Scar tissue is stronger than regular tissue. Realize the strength, move on." ~ Henry Rollins

Kintsugi is a Japanese art form where broken or cracked ceramic vessels are repaired with gold instead of being discarded. Its flaws are strengthened, celebrated, accentuated, and honored instead of disguised. Human flaws give us character as well, and they can become our strengths and should be celebrated.

My brain is not normal. Many of my friends and most of my colleagues are not aware of this as I haven't shared it publicly, due to the stigma it carries. People still whisper about this sort of thing and pass judgments. Because of this attitude and mindset, people continue to suffer in silence. I know because I was afraid to seek help.

Those days were a dark hole of depression for me, feelings of despair, and impending doom was not uncommon. I felt at any moment, my world would crumble. I was wrecking my health, my relationships, and I felt empty inside. I looked in the mirror and could not recognize who was looking back. I was a shell of a body; just hanging on, swearing tomorrow would be different, tomorrow I would have the resolve I needed. That's a lonely place to be.

There was a period in my life when I realized my drinking was abnormal, but I was stumped. I couldn't figure out how I could have so much willpower in so many areas of my life, but absolutely no control over my drinking. I could endure pain and suffering when it came to pushing my body to its physical limits. I ran marathons and ultra-marathons. I pushed myself with round-the-clock adventure racing. Being tired, cold, and even lost, but still, I pressed on. I was disciplined in my studies and my work. But alcohol had me whipped. Despite understanding the harmful effects of this progressive and fatal disease if left untreated, I felt I was losing the battle. Fortunately, I had that moment when I said enough is enough, and I was able to get help.

Eventually, this disease will become known for what it is, a disorder of the brain, of altered cognition, instead of a character defect. We don't have to whisper about heart disease or diabetes, and we shouldn't have to whisper about addiction. With addiction, just as with any disease, once you understand that you have it, you need to take responsibility for the treatment of it. Fortunately, I was able to do that, and it turned my life around.

Scientists have now pinpointed the exact areas of the brain that are involved namely, the *nucleus accumbens* (reward circuit), *anterior cingulate cortex* (impulse control), *basal forebrain* and the *amygdala* to name a few. They accurately understand the areas of the brain affected and have been able to do experimental treatments for addiction with pulses of electromagnetic wave therapy to the pre-frontal cortex, and it worked! I like to use the scientific names as it seems hard to say you have a moral failing in your nucleus accumbens or to place judgment on your amygdala, but you can say that your anterior cingulate cortex failed you.

Due to the neuroplasticity of our brain, new neural networks can be formed. With abstinence, implementation of new practices and behavior modification, addiction can be treated. You change your brain with new thoughts and new habits, just as you can with anything in your life that you want to change.

"We are constantly invited to be who we are." ~ Henry David Thoreau

I believe if I would have understood that my thoughts create my reality, the importance of tuning into my intuition and using my emotions as a guide to being on the right track, my career would have been on a different trajectory.

When I went off to college, I thought I wanted to coach basketball and teach physical education. In my first physical education class, I quickly realized it wasn't for me.

I discovered art and science. I fell in love with creativity and spent hours in the studio. I loved putting marks on paper and giving thoughts and ideas a three-dimensional life. It still amazes me that our physical world was first "made up" in our heads. I wanted to find a way to earn a living as an artist. Mom was encouraging me to stick with the sciences. You know, something I could get a job in. It became my belief system that it was unlikely I could make a living as an artist.

I was majoring in biology and had a wild idea about becoming a marine biologist and swimming with sharks. That summer, I took a diving class so I could spend a semester at the ocean studying marine life. I couldn't descend past 10 feet as I was unable to equalize the pressure in my ears due to childhood scar tissue from ruptured eardrums. I marked marine biology off my list.

In my fourth year of college, I was still trying to figure out my path. If you were following this narrative on a visual timeline, this is the spot I would emphasize with a red sharpie: here is where I became a conformist. I bought into the conventional wisdom of having to pick a career with health insurance benefits, 401K. Work for forty years and then collect your retirement. That was my plan.

This would have been a good time for me to sit down and write; do some soul searching to examine what was holding me back. What do I want in my life? What do I love to do? What experiences do I want to have and what contributions do I want to make to the world? That's not what happened because, after four years of college, I felt I needed to hurry up and figure it out.

I applied and was accepted to nursing school. I graduated and first went to work in a Burn Unit, then a Trauma Unit. About a year into my nursing career, I knew I didn't love it. I stayed in the field for years, spending most of my time working in Intensive Care Units. Making changes can be uncomfortable. Comfort, or not being able to sit in discomfort, can be a killer of dreams.

While I didn't love my career as a nurse, life was still good. The schedule I worked afforded me opportunities to do some awesome things with my time, and I got in crazy good shape. I went back and finished that art degree in printmaking and sculpture. I have had my art displayed in shows, a sculpture garden, university, and in personal collections.

Shortly after finishing my art degree, I went back to graduate school for anesthesia. I was 42. I love the variety, and I love the mix of physiology, pharmacology, and compassion that I get to utilize every day. It took most of my adult life to get into a career where I was happy to jump up and go to work.

I'm still writing my story. My career is still evolving. I have a passion for helping others reach their highest potential. I love having a conversation with someone and seeing the light bulb go off when they have that AHA moment of "I can do this!" or "why not me" or "why not now." I have often heard people say they have always wanted to "x," or they felt there was something else they were meant to do. Yet, they ignored that voice and continued to settle for where they are because of fear or limiting beliefs. Be willing to get uncomfortable; it's where the magic happens.

Vishen Lakhiani is one of today's thought leaders. Through his company Mindvalley, he has a program called Conscious Engineering. He interviews other thought leaders and game changers from around the globe. One of the questions he asks all of them is, "what gets you out of bed in the morning?" I love that question. We should all strive to do work that makes us want to jump out of bed in the morning.

"The authentic self is the soul made visible." ~ Sarah Ban Breathnach

Listen to that voice inside, it knows. It is the universe nudging you to your greatness. There is always a next level in you. Lean into it and cultivate your passions as that is where you will decode your genius and find your gift to the world. Be authentic; celebrate your Kintsugi. When you show up authentic, it paves the way for others to do the same.

I believe if we gave people the tools they needed at an early age to maximize their human potential, we would see a happier, healthier, and more productive society. I believe we should introduce a 'success for living' toolbox to the school systems to teach kids the power of thought and teach them how to think. Socrates said, "To find yourself, think for yourself." You know, conscious engineering.

"In order to succeed, we must first believe that we can." ~ Nikos Kazantzakis

Success starts in the mind. Success is brought to life through persistent focus and action. It is bringing value to the lives of those around you. It is waking up with gratitude for what you do and knowing that you are having a positive impact on the world.

Rule your mind, or it will rule you. If you feel there is some passion or vocation calling you, there is. Go for it! Work on changing your inner dialogue if it is not serving you. Lean into the uncomfortable. Put these four A's on your radar: awareness, authenticity, attitude, and action.

You have infinite potential. It is never too late to open a new chapter in your life. You get to write your life story. Jim Rohn said, "you have two choices: you can make a living, or you can design a life."

I'll end with this quote from Paul Arden, who said, "You need to aim beyond what you are capable of. You need to develop a complete disregard for where your abilities end. Make your vision of where you want to be a reality. Nothing is impossible."

Biography

Steph Shinabery is a Certified Registered Nurse Anesthetist, business coach, and entrepreneur. She is helping people transform their business and lives through cultivating practices and habits that upgrade mindset, focus, clarity, energy, and systems for success. She works with network marketing professionals to leverage social media marketing to grow their business.

Contact Information

Facebook: https://www.facebook.com/steph.shinabery
LinkedIn: https://www.linkedin.com/in/steph-shinabery-966457176/
Twitter: https://twitter.com/pedalart
Instagram: https://www.instagram.com/stephshinabery/

Chapter 46

EVERY DAY ALL IN!

By Tabetha Tuck

Success can come in all shapes and sizes and can be viewed differently by different people. Some people think success looks like mansions, yachts, and big fancy cars. Many of these people have financial success yet they are miserable in their personal lives and have no time to enjoy the fruits of their success. Others may talk about success based on relationships or attitude, yet never have any money to do anything. I've experienced both and, with that in mind, let's process together further.

Money is not everything but, as they say, "it's right up there with oxygen." If we don't base our success on our finances, are there other ways to gauge it? Who's to say that just because we don't have financial liberty we're not successful? I'm going to be so bold as to say that you can have it all! In this chapter, I'll outline how I created my success and how I continue to do so, how I've passed this success on to my children and will continue to pass it on to my grandchildren's grandchildren.

Let me go back to the beginning. I was able to secure a fantastic sales job, which I turned into a career for myself right out of high school. After ten years with my company, though, I wanted more. I wanted a family. I'd always known that I wanted children. I had been in multiple failed relationships over the past decade. I was only willing to give it two more years to meet the man of my dreams as my biological clock was ticking. I told myself that if I didn't meet the man I was looking for, I would do artificial insemination and raise a child on my own. I was more than capable and made enough money. I decided to make a list of clear intentions about exactly what I wanted in my life partner and father of my children. I wrote clearly at the top of the list: "Prince Charming." Below, I listed all the qualities I wanted in a man. Not more than three months later I met him. I knew exactly what I wanted (a family). So, with courage, I asked him on the second date if he was interested in another child, as he already had a son from a previous relationship. He was willing and that was enough for me. We fell in love, moved in together, got engaged and shortly after got pregnant! When we went to our first doctor's appointment and got a due date, I was ecstatic! My dreams were coming true. I was going to have it all. I told all my closest family and friends my wonderful news. My heart was the happiest it had ever been, and I was glowing both inside and outside.

We arrived at our second doctor's appointment, excitedly awaiting the ultrasound to hear the heartbeat. The doctor informed us that they must have had calculated the due date incorrectly and I was not as far along as predicted. The doctor scheduled for us to come back the following week saying that we should hear a heartbeat then and, if we didn't, I might be having a miscarriage. We went home. I knew I had to put all the positive thinking into play. I visualized the sound of the heartbeat in my mind during our next appointment. But, at the back of my mind, I had doubt and fear - two powerful feelings. We found out a week later that I was having a miscarriage. It was possibly the most painful moment of my life.

Even though I was visualizing the sound of the heartbeat, the feelings of doubt and fear in the back of mind ultimately outweighed the visualization's effectiveness. I'm a vision board kind of gal. "To think is to create" is one of my favorite quotes. However, doubt and fear will overcome that other stuff every time. Now, to believe that *everything happens for a reason* was, let's say, more than tough for me to wrap my head around at this time. I thought I understood this concept, but three months later it became much clearer to me.

I was reassured when the doctors told me that we could start trying again, right away. So we did, and within three months I got pregnant and had my beautiful daughter. I was engaged to the most amazing man. I was blessed to be a stay-at-home mom. Life was great. My stepson called me mom. I had a boy and a girl. I always knew that I would have the option to be a career woman when the kids were both in school. For now, I had it all.

Who was I to judge why things happen? Had I not miscarried, I would not have had my amazing daughter. When problems arise – and they will – it's not on us to figure out why, or judge, or shame, or blame. We have to get up, brush ourselves off, and get in alignment with consistent action to get what we want. And trust me, we got right to business on baby-making. The day we think our dreams are going to be easy and handed to us is the day we fail. Also, because it's going to be hard, this is all the more reason to find the fun and focus on the positive. Baby making was a lot of fun!

Because of the personal growth I had done, and books I continued to read, I was sure I would be an amazing mother. Of course, I knew I would fall along the way but I understood that was part of creating greatness in myself and my children. I would do my absolute best to help program their core beliefs, support the hard-wiring in their brains from the beginning with "anything is possible" attitudes. It was my committed duty to teach our children because, as I understood it, 80-85% of our beliefs are created from 0-8 years of age. Anything after that age, in the road from core values to action, gets harder and harder to stick.

I know we can only change ourselves in life, but if I could have a positive effect on these little humans, I was ALL IN. My daughter is now almost five, and when I asked her last week if she wanted to quit school because the other kids were teasing her (I was exaggerating about quitting, of course, to make a point), her response was, "What's quit mom?" I replied, "It means to give up." Her response was the same, "What's give up mom?" Hearing that from my daughter is success for me. I asked her what she wanted to do about the girl at school who was teasing her and her response was, "I want to draw her a card and maybe she would want to be my friend." My hope is that we can create more "quitting is not an option" attitudes, no matter what doubtful thoughts others might encourage. If we create kindness as a response in our children, and then they pass this on to their children, imagine what the world could look like in the future.

My dream in high school was to be a child psychologist. I always knew that I wanted to help people but when I started college and saw the eight years of schooling needed to become a psychologist, the *fear* of not being good at school stole the dream right out from under me.

So when I say living every day ALL IN, I mean overcoming limiting beliefs all day, every day. I mean, pushing out the doubt and fear when it comes to decision making. The fear and doubt are going to come in, but, as they say, "feel the fear and do it anyway." When we shine bright, we give others the permission, courage, and faith to do the same. We've been given this gift of life, what we do with it is up to us. We're here for such a short time, "days are long, years are short." Tomorrow is not promised and there are no guarantees in life. But there's absolute success in making a conscious decision of living every day ALL IN.

Affirmations are wonderful but by themselves they are not enough. They have to be combined with consistent action. I was once told by a professional that the things you want in your affirmation should make you wiggle the most. The things you believe the least about yourself, those may be the qualities that launch your personal and professional life to the next level. Those are the things you should add to your affirmation. As an example, here are mine for 2019: " I am a humble leader, vibrating with passion and integrity, traveling the world, making a positive difference in human beings, living every moment of every day ALL IN." Honestly, when I first wrote this, it scared the crap out of me. But that's what makes it work. Playing small doesn't serve me, my kids, my purpose, or anyone on this planet.

Too many people on this earth walk around, bumping into each other like we were in a dark room, scared of what to say or of what we might bump into. Some snap at each other as if they were monsters instead of human beings. When we make the choice to see each other, we can be the chain reaction, the ripple, the first domino that can set forth the synergy of our human race.

Take a look at your life. Are you where you want to be? The answer will come from your gut, almost immediately. Visualize your funeral at this moment: Who's there? What are they saying about you? What are your accomplishments? If you think, even for a second, that you wish they were saying better or different things, STOP HESITATING. Go put that into action NOW.

When opportunity arises, seize the moment, and have the courage to take risks. Don't ask yourself, "Why me?" When you think this is for somebody else, or I can't do this, ask yourself instead, "why NOT me?" There's a well-known phrase: *"The quality of your life is determined by the quality of the question."*

No matter what I'm doing on a daily basis, I'm consistently checking in with myself and making sure that my end goal is in mind and my actions are in alignment. I know that I am capable of making a difference in my life and the lives of others around me. I'm not perfect, and I mess up. But, when I make bad decisions, I acknowledge them, learn from them, and communicate with the other party, what my part was and what I could have done differently. I watch relationships grow and blossom all around me because of these practices.

God gave us a gift: *potential*. It's our gift to God to live up to that potential. Listen to the nudges before the nudges turn into shoves and knock you on your ass. Listen to the whispers of truth not the roar of the giants. Giants only roar when we're moving forward in life. And the names of those giants are *fear* and *doubt*. It's not supposed to be easy. If it were easy we'd see more success around the globe.

Acknowledge that when the opportunities start flooding towards you, you've created them with all the work you've put in. Your dreams are finally coming true and it's because you've set clear intentions, created a vision to make a difference, and pushed through the giants. I fell in love with the universal laws a long time ago. I experienced the power of feelings and how they affected me and others. And that's something I will continue to share with human beings all over this planet until the day I die.

This is what I was born to do. By accepting my greatness, pushing through the hardships, and being thankful for them, I know that the hardships are disguised blessings that forge me into the person who is prepared for my purpose. Get excited to do great things that others would only fantasize about and we can change the world together.

Link up and become stronger. Individual strengths may be viewed as a weakness but, like instruments in an orchestra, when you add them all together, you get a magical masterpiece of unity.

You can have it all! I'll see you on the beaches of the world throwing rocks and creating a ripple of positive energy, so together, we can make sure that human beings all over this planet accept their greatness and shine their light so bright that we grant permission for others to do the same.

"When everything seems to be going against you, remember airplanes take off against the wind"

Have your goal in mind and make a conscious choice of "Living every moment of every day ALL IN!"

Biography

Tabetha Tuck is a mother, speaker, world traveler, and entrepreneur. She has studied personal success and personal leadership. Tabetha has challenged herself to explore, question, and discover herself, creating a life of success completely different from any other. She shares her success in her relationship with her daughter. She's taught her children and others to feel the fear and do it anyway.

Contact Information

Website: http://everydayallin.com
Facebook: https://www.facebook.com/TabethaTuckTravels
Instagram: https://www.instagram.com/tabethaltuck/

Chapter 47

KEY TO SUCCESS IS FOCUS

By Jason Reid

"Success is finding within yourself the ability to leave everyday, thing, and person better than you found them. And be happy doing it." - Jason Reid

I remember being all scrunched up over an actual non-electronic tablet, the old paper kind, with a pencil, writing the table of contents for my new "bestseller." I was probably about eleven years of age. I'm pretty sure it got thrown out a few years later, and I can't remember if I ever did get past the first chapter or not. Next was a string of businesses ranging from collecting worms in the yard to sell for bait, to making bow and arrows, to canoes, to looking for a newspaper route, to building hang gliders. None of them, including the last, ever "got off the ground." I still can't quite put my finger on exactly what it was that put such an entrepreneurial drive into me, perhaps partly being the oldest in the family, or being homeschooled, giving me a personal sense of independence.

The seed of that desire I consider a gift of "grace." It seems to me that those who have that seed know it, it might be small, but it's still there. And some of the tiniest seeds grow into the largest trees. So, for me, the question was how to cultivate that seed, so it becomes a tree of success. The answers eluded me for years, and it seemed life was against me. Everything I tried went sour. One venture to the next, from my late teens into mid-twenties, and all these great ideas (or so I thought!) would stay just out of my grasp. I, among others in my social group, was often heard saying on numerous occasions "a day late and a dollar short" of the opportunities that would seemingly slip through our fingers. "The rich get richer, and the poor get poorer" was our motto, insinuating that we were on the "poor" end of the spectrum.

In the end, I got a job, which was a good thing. I am in full agreement with Robert Kiyosaki in "Rich Dad, Poor Dad," the best reason for having a job is to gain a real-world education. There are lessons to be learned that can be best learned as an employee. First "real" job was as a carpenter building houses. From there, to a sales position at a building materials supplier. After four years, it was time to move on, and being married with two children by this time made it a serious venture, but the desire for something more won out, and we relocated. With the move came the start of yet a new business as an independent building contractor, this time, somewhat successful due to having learned a trade and determination. It wasn't easy, but we got by. Barely.

Fast forward a few years, and that brings us to the recession of 2008, a turning point in the lives of many. Work just dried up to virtually nothing, and it was a tough time in more ways than just financially. During this time, I also met a few key people who were very influential on my thinking, perhaps most importantly in helping me change my view of myself. This combined with the need to do something different to support a family, and the dream of doing more while still alive created a breakthrough for me. It wasn't a huge, radical, change-everything-in-an-instant kind, but a major deciding point that something HAD to change. And the catalyst for bringing that change about for me was FOCUS. Not in the sense of blindly seeing only one thing to the detriment of everything else, but a discipline of mind to not lose sight of the goal. In business, it can be easy to be driven, and forget the other aspects of life. Like being a husband and father, or a friend. So, the focus needs to be on the several aspects of ONE whole. My focus looks like this: Personal development, Relationships, Business. And yes, in that order. I look at this as three sides of ONE triangle.

When discussing focus, usually someone will inevitably mention the fact that you can only ride one horse at a time, a statement I fully agree with, but you do have to take care of multiple aspects of that horse to get anywhere. One must pay attention to what reins you are pulling on, watch for possible obstacles in the path, and stay on the horse all at the same time. You could concentrate only on staying on the horse and successfully do so, but you might get a surprise where you end up! And I think this way of looking at it was the key to unlocking the power of focus for me.

We all know someone who focused very well, but all they focused on was money. Focusing on that single aspect is just like staying on the horse. If that is what they truly wanted, be it far from me to state otherwise, but for most people, I think that gets them somewhere they probably didn't want to go. So as you can see, I have a definite, focused idea of what "focus" means! Though to illustrate what it has done for me, I am going to "focus" on only one side of the triangle- the business.

At the turning point, there was a decision to make. In my field of interest, there was only one way that made sense to move forward with, to make my mark. And that was the quality of craftsmanship. I focused on that product, looking for that particular, yet elusive, level of excellence I wanted. Practically speaking, this was not a pretty sight. It ended up being years of many late nights into the early hours of the morning. Thousands of dollars "wasted" in materials, listening to criticism from experts, and discovering good ideas that weren't. And yet, through it, all progress was made. Not overnight, but slowly my skill improved. I had a coach that made a tremendous difference. He couldn't do what I was doing to save his life but had the ability to help me see myself and my work from another point of view. It was a priceless experience.

Through all this was the key of focus, remaking the decision by the hour if necessary, to not take my eyes off the goal and the vision. I could see what I wanted to create in my mind, and I had to concentrate on it. Not a visualization process that brought magical results, but to not allow that image of who I wanted to be, a master in my field, fade into the background, pressured out by the noise of life. Yes, take care of what needs to be taken care of. If your mother is in the hospital, go and visit her. Maybe even if she's not. But never let the vision fade, DO something every day to bring you closer to your dream. That, to me, is focus. It's living life on purpose. Reminds me of one of Tony Robbin's great quotes,

"One reason so few of us achieve what we truly want is that we never direct our focus, we never concentrate our power. Most people dabble their way through life, never deciding to master anything in particular." - Tony Robbins.

An element of focus that was a challenge for me was to keep it positive. I remember many times, sitting there immediately after making a fatal mistake in a matter of seconds that destroyed hours of careful work. In those moments, the destiny was decided, keeping focused on the vision I wanted to achieve. And even repeating to myself over and over like a mantra, "I can do this, I can do this, I can do this." Then taking several deep breaths before starting over again. It happens by doing whatever it takes to maintain the focus like your life depends on it. Because it does. And this would be especially difficult for those whose close family members and loved ones are NOT supportive of their dream.

And it worked! People began asking for my product. The icons of my field began asking my opinions. I was offered contracts. Something was changing. I had another job to make ends meet by this time in the story. Financially, life was satisfactory. But life can be interesting sometimes, and circumstances came together to help keep me focused, pressure from behind and pull from the front you might say. It was time to make another decision and use what I had learned and move to the next level. Applying the lessons I had learned, and not stopping, has propelled me to the next level. I quit my job and went into business full-time, a daring move for anyone. The focus did not let me down, and today, I am a respected leader in my field, the business is thriving, the future looks bright, and we are just getting started.

The satisfaction of success is immense, and it would be my wish that everyone could experience it. Experiencing success is a life-changing event, once tasted, you can never live without it again. The beauty of it is that life is a journey and the opportunity to continually experience success is part of that journey, not a goal in the end. True success can actually start the first day a decision is made. I will admit it was hard to feel it then, but looking back, I can see it. I am no different than anyone else; I'm not any more special than anyone else. But the power of a decision, especially the one to live by, a different mindset than before, can separate someone from the rest of the crowd.

I am definitely not done with this success thing, and I think the ultimate success is to help other people to find it. To be the catalyst in someone's life that propels them to the next level. Now, wouldn't THAT be something satisfying to focus on?

Biography

Jason Reid is a self-made entrepreneur who has built several successful businesses. He currently owns and operates Hawkeye Falconry Supply, suppliers of *The Finest Falconry Furniture*, where all products are handcrafted to the highest specifications. He values the skills involved in his specialized field and the unique responsibilities involved in working with birds-of-prey which provides a basis for the qualities needed to be successful in any endeavor.

He has a passion for using these virtues to help others in areas of personal development, finance, and charitable work.

He has been published in American Falconry magazine and was a past columnist for "Feathers and Friends" children's magazine.

His accomplishments include a falcon breeding project that helped with the reintroduction of the once-endangered birds, and he continues to be involved in conservation projects and wild bird rehabilitation efforts.

He is a member of the North American Falconers Association, International Eagle Austringer Association, Indiana Falconers Association, and various other state and regional conservation and educational organizations. He enjoys several outdoor sports including camping and boating, as well as spending time with his family and birds. He currently resides in Fort Wayne Indiana with his wife and four children.

CONTACT INFORMATION

Facebook https://www.facebook.com/JasonReidHawkeye
LinkedIn https://www.linkedin.com/in/jason-reid-a054b7166

www.ingramcontent.com/pod-product-compliance
Lightning Source LLC
Chambersburg PA
CBHW031621210526
45464CB00004B/1695